Copyright, Congress and Technology: The Public Record

Copyright, Congress and Technology: The Public Record

Volume I:
The Formative Years, 1958-1966

Volume II:
The Political Years, 1967-1973

Volume III:
The Future of Copyright, 1973-1977

Volume IV : CONTU:
The Future of Information Technology

Volume V: CONTU'S Final
Report and Recommendations

Edited with an introduction by
Nicholas Henry.

 ORYX PRESS
1980

Operation Oryx, started more than 15 years ago at the Phoenix Zoo to save the rare white antelope—believed to have inspired the unicorn of mythology—has apparently succeeded. The operation was launched in 1962 when it became evident that the animals were facing extinction in their native habitat of the Arabian peninsula.

An original herd of nine, put together through *Operation Oryx* by five world organizations, now numbers 47 in Phoenix with another 38 at the San Diego Wild Game Farm, and four others which have recently been sent to live in their natural habitat in Jordan.

Also, in what has come to be known as "The Second Law of Return," rare biblical animals are being collected from many countries to roam freely at the Hai Bar Biblical Wildlife Nature Reserve in the Negev, in Israel, the most recent addition being a breeding herd of eight Arabian Oryx. With the addition of these Oryx, their collection of rare biblical animals is complete.

Copyright © 1980 by Nicholas Henry

Published by The Oryx Press
2214 North Central at Encanto
Phoenix, AZ 85004

Published simultaneously in Canada

Printed and Bound in the United States of America

Library of Congress Cataloging in Publication Data

Main entry under title:

Copyright, Congress, and technology.

Bibliography: v. 5, p.
Includes indexes.
CONTENTS: v. 1. The formative years, 1958-1966.
--v. 2. The political years, 1967-1973.
--v. 5. CONTU's final report and recommendations.
1. Copyright--United States--Collected works.
I. Henry, Nicholas, 1943-
KF2994.A1C57   346.7304'82   78-23747
ISBN 0-912700-13-0 (v. 1)

TO TUTU AND GRACE

Contents

Acknowledgements

I am indebted to a great many people in compiling these books, especially to Ms. Valari Elardo, my graduate assistant, who spent untold hours over a smoldering photocopying machine copying the necessary documents. Ms. Gwen Weaver has been both efficient and cheerful in putting out the necessary typing, and officials at the National Commission on New Technological Uses of Copyrighted Works have been cooperative and forthcoming in permitting me to reprint some of their important research in Volumes IV and V.

Ms. Phyllis Steckler, President of the Oryx Press, deserves recognition for her perceptiveness in seeing the need for this set, as well as her personal encouragement.

Of course, and as always, I am indebted to my understanding wife, Muriel, and my children, Miles and Adrienne, for their support in the completion of this project. This set is dedicated to them.

NH
Tempe, Arizona

Introduction to the Set

Copyright, Congress, and Technology: The Public Record is a compendium of selected public documents that were published during the remarkable effort to
revise American copyright law which occurred during the twenty-one years
between 1955 and 1976. Simply as an example of the policy-making process,
the campaign waged to change U.S. copyright law is fascinating in and of
itself; few pieces of legislation have taken as long to be enacted as a revised
copyright law. This five-volume set, however, is designed not only to trace
the development of the Copyright Act of 1976, but also is meant to set the
record straight in the areas of how the new copyright law affects the use of
new information technologies, notably photocopiers and computers, for the
benefit of librarians, educators, authors, publishers, and public officials. The
impact of copyright on these technologies is both profound and complex, and
perhaps the most simple way of conveying the thinking of policy-makers and
interest groups in their effort to resolve copyright and technology is to provide a format that allows them to speak for themselves.

These volumes also describe the actual policy-making process as it related
to the attempt to revise the United States Copyright Act of 1909 in a manner
that would accommodate the new information technologies, notably photocopying and computer-based information storage and retrieval systems. These
are the primary "neo-publishing" technologies (in the sense that they permit
the massive republishing of copyrighted works by the populace), and the
"politics of neo-publishing" was the effort to reconcile these technologies with
copyright law.

While there are other neo-publishing technologies, those that have en-
gendered the greatest concern among copyright owners and copyright users
are photocopiers and computers. Of these two, the photocopier is preeminent.
There are approximately 600,000 photocopiers in this country alone, churn-
ing out an estimated 30 billion copies every year. Most of these copies are
made in public and research libraries, and empirical studies of photocopying
use patterns in libraries indicate that as much as 60 percent of all the photocopies made each year may be of copyrighted publications. Increasingly, publishers are convinced that their sales of periodical subscriptions and books are
being undermined by popular and massive photocopying practices, and that
this is particularly the case for publications in science and technolgy.

The other major neo-publishing technology is the computer. There are
more than 100,000 computer-based information storage and retrieval systems
in the United States. While we know that these systems are reformatting and
disseminating vast quantities of the information on demand and at an incredi-
bly rapid rate, we do not know what proportion of that information may be
protected by copyright. Some material, certainly, that is processed by computers is protected by copyright, and it is highly unlikely that information

system operators and programmers are soliciting the permission of the copyright owners to use their material to any significant degree, if at all.

Both copyright owners and copyright users perceive copyright law to be virtually the only public policy that is concerned with the relationships among the new neo-publishing technologies, intellectual creativity, intellectual property, and, to quote the Constitution (Article I, Section 8), the paramount social value of promoting "the Progress of Science and useful Arts . . .". Revising copyright law to accommodate the new information technologies thus is a public policy of some consequence.

Two conclusions may be drawn from the public record about copyright law revision. One is that the process represented, and no doubt will continue to do so, a politics of technological elites. Copyright is one of the least recognized but most important public policies of our time, affecting an industry of vast magnitude. In fact, the "knowledge industry" comprises the largest single segment of the American economy, and it has been estimated by economists that the knowledge industry accounts for a third of the Gross National Product. More than 40 percent of the nation's economic growth is attributable to advances in education, and the "copyright industries" alone are the equivalent size of mining, banking, and utilities. Copyright is not merely big business, it is the biggest.

In light of the implications of the new information technologies and copyright law, it is both discomfiting and surprising to learn how small the group is that has been debating how to reconcile technology and copyright during the past three decades. The elitism of this debate is brought out in these volumes. The same names appear and reappear with frequency, but the overwhelming reality remains that public policy for new information technologies has affected and will affect far more people than those who have been talking about it. We have here a case of very small elites "representing" very limited elements of society that nonetheless are forming public policy for the new information technologies.

Why is this elitism the case? A major reason appears to be that the sheer complexity of the subject inhibits participation. Yet, complexity is a growing fact of political life in techno-bureaucratic societies, such as ours. Political decision-making in twentieth century America deals with technology, and technology is complicated. Those who understand the complex technological issues of modern political life (or who say they do) become the policymakers. Nowhere is this better illustrated than in the instance of what some have called "the politics of neo-publishing." As the reader will quickly discern, very small elites have made a public policy that affects us all.

The second conclusion that one may draw from reading these public documents, is that the politics of neo-publishing is frankly Marxist. Revising copyright law was a political brawl involving the redistribution of political and economic power between haves and have-nots. While it was not a class war in the traditional sense, the politics of neo-publishing clearly is, to use Marxian language, a fight between the owners of a means of production and the users of their products. Indeed, the formal terminology of copyright law reflects the language of Marxism: copyright "owners" and copyright "users." The neo-publishing technologies have provided an opportunity to the "exploited masses" of copyright users. By dint of these technologies, proletarian copyright users may become bourgeois copyright owners. Publishers, the historic owners of the means of intellectual production, are witnessing the undermining of their ownership through the popular use of new information technologies. As Marshall McLuhan has noted "in an age of Xerox, every man is a publisher."

Copyright is the single public policy concerned with the economics of commercial publishing. It is predicated on the idea that a would-be publisher must put up a considerable amount of capital in order to begin publishing — that is, in order to control a means of production. It follows, therefore that publishers ought to be granted certain monopolistic rights or "exclusive license" to their products. This is what copyright does, or at least did, until the neo-publishing instruments made their debuts. These technologies are redistributing a means of production and, in so doing, are undermining copyright as a standing public policy. For these reasons, the documents included in this set can be understood most satisfactorily as a Marxian class conflict — owners against users.

While such conclusions may be interesting, and perhaps even important, the major reason why this set will be useful to most readers is that an enormous amount of confusion surrounds the impact of the new copyright law on librarians, authors, educators, and publishers. Thus, these volumes are organized in such a way that they will be of optimal use to these professionals in tracing how the thinking of their colleagues has evolved just as information technologies have developed.

Volume I of *Copyright, Congress, and Technology: The Public Record* focuses on those early public documents that emerged between 1958 and 1966. The discerning reader will note that the tone of the copyright proceedings in these years is substantially different from the tone found in public documents emerging in 1967 and beyond. I have referred to this phenomenon elsewhere as "noetic politics," or the peculiar style of politics that derives from knowledge, logic, and the scientific method.[1] We see in these documents a conscious effort by the participants in copyright politics to devise legislation that will work for the benefit of all society. The normal, grubbing interest-group politics that we associate with the legislative process is relatively absent, although there are many moments of passion and greed.

It was during this period that the Register of Copyrights commissioned thirty-four scholarly studies on copyright, and issued a major report in 1961 that was hailed as a seminal work in the area. Experts, lawyers, and policy-makers of various stripes were consulted on a continuing basis during these years, and the Commission on New Technological Uses of Copyrighted Works (CONTU) was first proposed. All these instances and others represent an effort to form policy on the basis of knowledge rather than on the basis of the political power of particular interest groups.

As noted, however, this tone changes — and I think rather precipitously — in the years following. In the 1967 Congressional hearings, for example, we see spokespersons for various groups calling each other names during their testimony. The balance of power in the dispute appears to shift away from copyright owners (largely publishers and authors) and toward copyright users (largely librarians and educators), but not necessarily for reasons of wise public policy (although it may well turn out that way). Rather, the gains made by

---

1. See: Nicholas Henry, *Copyright/Information Technology/Public Policy. Part I: Copyright/Public Policies* and *Part II: Public Policies/Information Technology*. New York: Marcel Dekker, Inc., 1975 and 1976.

copyright users over the interests of copyright owners are made because the users have the votes and the owners do not. Thus, Volume II covers the years 1967 through 1973, and the tone throughout is overtly political, although there is some hard and creative analysis available in these years, which is included.

The third volume in the retrospect reprints documents emerging between 1973 and 1977, including pertinent selections from the several Congressional hearings on copyright law revision. An effort has been made to include those public documents that point the way toward the future of copyright. The entire Copyright Act of 1976 also is reproduced.

Volume IV, *CONTV: The Future of Information Technology*, reproduces the ground-breaking studies sponsored by the National Commission on New Technological Uses of Copyrighted Works, which dealt with computer soft-ware, photocopying and copyrights, public photocopying practices, library photocopying and the economics of periodical publications. The Commissions final report, the result of years of testimony by experts from across the nation, comprises Volume V.

Taken together, the five volumes are a collection that should be both convenient and authoritative in guiding copyright users and owners through the maze of copyright, technology, and public policy.

NH
Tempe, Arizona

Introduction to Volume V

Volume V of *Copyright, Congress, and Technology* is comprised entirely of the *Final Report* of the National Commission on New Technological Uses of Copyrighted Works (CONTU). The Commission, which was active from 1975 through 1978, was established by Congress as Title II of Public Law 93-573 and functioned as an arm of the Library of Congress. It was chartered "to study and compile data on: (1) the reproduction and use of copyrighted works of authorship—(a) in conjunction with automatic systems capable of storing, processing, retrieving, and transferring information, and (b) by various forms of machine reproduction, including reproduction by, or at least at the request of, instructors for use in face-to-face teaching activities; and (2) the creation of new works by the application or intervention of such automatic systems or machine reproduciton." The Commission was also authorized to "make recommendations as to such changes in copyright law or procedures that may be necessary to assure for such purposes access to copyright owners." These recommendations were to be made to the President and to Congress within a three-year period, at which time the Commission would be disbanded. To assist in compiling its report, the Commission was authorized to hold hearings, administer oaths, and subpoena witnesses.

CONTU was comprised of thirteen members, all appointed by the President. Of these members, four represented copyright owners, four represented copyright users, four represented the general public, and the thirteenth member was the Librarian of Congress. The Register of Copyrights served *ex officio*.

Representing copyright owners were the distinguished John Hersey, President of the Authors League; Herschel B. Sarbin, President of the Ziff-Davis Publishing Company; E. Gabriel Perle, Vice-President of Law for Time, Inc.; and Dan Lacy, Senior Vice-President of McGraw-Hill Publishing Company. Representing copyright users of the Commission were Elizabeth Hamer Kegan, Acting Deputy Librarian of Congress; William S. Dix, Librarian Emeritus of Princeton University; Alice E. Wilcox, Director of MINITEX, an information technology firm located in Minneapolis; and Robert Wedgeworth, Executive Director of the American Library Association. Representing the public on the Commission were George Cary, former Acting Register of Copyrights; Rhoda H. Karpatkin, Executive Director of the Consumers' Union; Arthur R. Miller, Professor of Law at Harvard University; and Melville B. Nimmer, Professor of Law at the University of California, Los Angeles, who also served as vice-chairman of the Commission. Appointed as Chairman of the Commission was the Honorable Stanley H. Fuld, a former federal judge and special counsel for the law firm of Kay, Scholer, Fierman, Hays, and Handler, in New York City.

The details of CONTU's somewhat stormy political life are detailed in the Introduction to Volume IV of this set. During its short term, CONTU commissioned analyses of 6 major facets of the copyright-and-technology issues (which are reproduced in Volume IV) and held 21 hearings on the subject. Although the verbatim transcripts of these meetings are not included in this set for reasons of space, a CONTU bibliography is reproduced in this Volume (Appendix G of the Commission's final report) which synopsizes the remarks of the witnesses called by CONTU and the topics they addressed. These transcripts are available from the National Technological Information Service for a moderate fee.

It is appropriate that Volume V is devoted exclusively to CONTU's impressive *Final Report*. This report is a compilation of the reports of four subcommittees formed by CONTU, describes the Commission and its duties, presents a lucid discussion of the complex computers-and-copyright issue, and concludes with an examination of the photocopying problem. The *Report*'s appendices are especially valuable, as they provide legislative histories of computer-related and photocopying debates; reproduce Public Law 93-573, Title II, which established the Commission; describe the background of the Commissioners, staff members, and witnesses; summarize the Commission's studies; and furnish a very useful bibliography. All 10 appendices are reproduced here.

CONTU was a remarkable experiment for a number of reasons. It was a blue-ribbon panel which accomplished not only what the normal blue-ribbon panel is supposed to accomplish, but was instrumental in expediting the copyright law revision process itself. CONTU's *Final Report* will prove useful to authors, attorneys, educators, public administrators, library managers and information specialists in virtually every nation. CONTU has made an important contribution to the world of information science.

NH
Tempe, Arizona

I. THE COMMISSION AND ITS RECOMMENDATIONS

A. Introduction

The National Commission on New Technological Uses of Copyrighted Works (CONTU) was created by the Congress as part of the effort to revise comprehensively the Copyright Laws of the United States.[1] Early in the Congressional hearings on copyright law revision it became apparent that problems raised by the use of the new technologies of photocopying and computers on the authorship, distribution and use of copyrighted works were not dealt with by the then pending revision bill. Because of the complexity of these problems, this Commission was created to provide the President and the Congress with recommendations concerning those changes in copyright law or procedure needed both to assure public access to copyrighted works used in conjunction with computer and machine duplication systems and to respect the rights of owners of copyright in such works, while considering the concerns of the general public and the consumer.

This Report presents those recommendations, based on the three years of data collection, hearings, analysis and deliberation called for in the Commission's enabling legislation. The recommendations are summarized initially and discussed subsequently in detail in the chapters of this Report dealing with computers[2] and photocopying.[3]

---

[1] . The result of this revision was P. L. No. 94-553 (1976) now codified as 17 U.S.C. § 101 et seq., selected portions of which appear in Appendix J. This law is referred to throughout this report as the "Act of 1976," "1976 Act," or "new law." The legislative history of this Act is contained in S. Rep. No. 473, 94th Cong., 1st Sess. (1975), [hereinafter cited as Senate Report]; H.R. Rep. No. 1476, 94th Cong., 2d Sess. (1976), [hereinafter cited as House Report]; and H.R. Rep. No. 1733, 94th Cong., 2d Sess. (1976), [hereinafter cited as Conference Report].

[2] See Chapter III, infra, at 21-115.

[3] See Chapter IV, infra, at 117-197.

B. Recommendations

COMPUTERS

Recommendations for Legislation

Software or Programs

The new copyright law should be amended 1) to make it explicit that computer programs, to the extent that they embody an author's original creation, are proper subject matter of copyright; 2) to apply to all computer uses of copyrighted programs by the deletion of the present Section 117; and 3) to assure that rightful possessors of copies of computer programs can use or adapt these copies for their use.

Commissioner Hersey's Dissent:
The Act of 1976 should be amended to make it explicit that copyright protection does not extend to a computer program in the form in which it is capable of being used to control computer operations.

Data Bases

The Act of 1976 should be amended to apply to all computer uses of copyrighted data bases and other copyrighted works fixed in computersensible media by the deletion of its present Section 117.

New Works

Works created by the use of computers should be afforded copyright protection if they are original works of authorship within the Act of 1976. Consequently no amendment is needed.

Recommendation for Regulations

The Register of Copyrights should adopt appropriate regulations regarding the affixation of notice to and the registration and deposit of works of authorship used in conjunction with computers.

Recommendation for Congressional Action

Any legislation enacted as a result of these recommendations should be subject to a periodic review to determine its adequacy in the light of continuing technological change. This review should especially consider the impact of such legislation on competition and consumer prices in the computer and information industries and the effect on cultural values of including computer programs within the ambit of copyright.

PHOTOCOPYING

Recommendation for Legislation

The Act of 1976 should be amended at this time only to provide specific guidance for situations in which photocopying is done by commercial organizations on demand and for profit.

Recommendation to the Copyright Office

In conducting the five-year review of photocopying practices required by section 108(i) of the Act of 1976, the Register of Copyrights should begin immediately to plan and implement a study of the overall impact of all photoduplication practices on both proprietors' rights and the public's access to published information.

Recommendation to Other Government Agencies

Publishers, libraries and government agencies should cooperate in making information about the copyright status of all published works, both current and older publications, more readily available to the public.

II. THE ESTABLISHMENT, MANDATE AND ACTIVITIES OF THE COMMISSION

The United States and other nations are facing a challenge in this last quarter of the twentieth century in the development of policies concerned with information. Forces of economic and technological development are leading to what has been called the post-industrial society; one in which the source of wealth lies not only in the production and distribution of goods but also in the creation and dissemination of information.[4] The ownership and control of information and the means of disseminating it are emerging as national and international policy issues.[5] Concerns about the impact on individual freedom posed by the control of the flow of information are at the forefront of public debate. The adequacy of the legal structure to cope with the pace and rate of technological change frequently has been called into question.[6] This Report deals with certain aspects of the ways in which the copyright law should apply to the new technological means of handling information.

4/ D. Bell, The Coming of Post-Industrial Society (1973).

5/ B. Ringer, "The Unfinished Business of Copyright Revision," 24 U.C.L.A. L. Rev. 951, 976 (1977).

6/ See, e.g., R. Saltman, Copyright in Computer-Readable Works (1977); Privacy Protection Study Commission, Personal Privacy in an Information Society (1977); National Commission on Electronic Fund Transfers, EFT in the United States (1977).

This Commission was created to assist the President and the Congress in developing a national policy for both protecting the rights of copyright owners and assuring public access to copyrighted works when they are used in computer and machine duplication systems, having in mind the public and consumer interest. Copyright in the United States is created by legislation enacted under a specific grant of power in the Constitution.[7]   The first Copyright Law was enacted in 1790 and has been amended and revised many times. During the development and growth of such diverse technologies as radio, television, phonographs and records, tape recorders, motion pictures, photoduplication machines, computers, juke boxes and community antenna systems, the copyright law, in effect, was essentially that of 1909 with a few later amendments.

For many reasons, including the impact of the technology explosion of the first two-thirds of this century, the Congress and the copyright community (authors, publishers, film makers, broadcasters, the recording industry, educators and librarians, among others) became increasingly dissatisfied with the existing copyright law. It was generally felt that a complete revision rather than piecemeal amendment was in order. To begin that revision, the Congress appropriated funds in 1955 for the Copyright Office of the Library of Congress to prepare a comprehensive study recommending changes that should be made in the law. It took twenty-one years for both Houses of Congress to agree upon a completely revised law, and that agreement may have been made possible, at least in part, by the creation of this Commission to study two of the most complex and controversial problems related to copyright revision -- photocopying and computers.

By 1967, when the Congress was considering bills to revise the 1909 Act, it was apparent that the copyright problems raised by computer uses had not been dealt with directly in the bills then before the House of

---

7 / U.S. Const., Art. I, § 8, cl. 8.

Representatives [8/] and the Senate. [9/] It was also clear that any adequate
study of this problem would seriously delay the enactment of an urgently
needed general revision bill.

To avert such a delay, in the summer of 1967, the late Senator
John L. McClellan and the Senate Subcommittee on Patents, Trademarks and
Copyrights met with representatives of authors, publishers, educators,
librarians, computer users and executive agencies. Soon after that meeting
had been held, Senator McClellan introduced a bill [10/] providing for the
establishment of the National Commission on New Technological Uses of
Copyrighted Works "to study and compile data on the reproduction and
use of copyrighted works of authorship (1) in automatic systems capable
of storing, processing, retrieving, and transferring information, and
(2) by various forms of machine reproduction." This bill passed the
Senate on October 12, 1967, during the first session, but the House
of Representatives took no action on it.

Meanwhile, various users of copyrighted materials were concerned
that the revision bill would place unwarranted restrictions on the use of
copyrighted works in the computer-based information systems then coming
into widespread use. They believed that these restrictions would retard
the creation and dissemination of materials needed for use with computer
retrieval systems and suggested a three-year moratorium on liability
for copyright infringement by uses in those systems. During that period
the new Commission, to be created by Senator McClellan's bill, could
confront and study the matter. Authors and publishers, however, were
totally opposed to such a moratorium and made it known that if it
were attached to the bill they would attempt to prevent passage of the
entire bill. The tension eased when Senator McClellan proposed to the
interested parties a middle ground, which was then embodied in a new

---

8/ H. R. 2512, 90th Cong., 1st Sess. (1967).

9/ S. 597, 90th Cong., 1st Sess. (1967).

10/ S. 2216, 90th Cong., 1st Sess. (1967).

draft of the general revision bill, <u>11/</u> introduced in the 91st Congress

on January 22, 1969. Section 117 of that bill provided that the law

on the use of copyrighted works in computer systems would be unaffected

by its enactment. The legislation included a separate title to establish

a Commission. No further action was taken, however, during the 91st

or 92nd Congress on either the general revision bill or the proposed

Commission.

During the 93rd Congress another bill was introduced which

included, among other matters, a provision establishing the Commission. <u>12/</u>

This bill was enacted on December 31, 1974, as Public Law 93-573,

which gave the Commission three years to study and compile data and

make recommendations on legislation or procedures concerning:

> (1) the reproduction and use of
> copyrighted works of authorship --
>
>> (A) in conjunction with auto-
>> matic systems capable of stor-
>> ing, processing, retrieving,
>> and transferring information,
>> and
>>
>> (B) by various forms of machine
>> reproduction, not including re-
>> production by or at the request
>> of instructors for use in face-
>> to-face teaching activities;
>> and
>
> (2) the creation of new works by
> the application or intervention of
> such automatic systems of machine
> reproduction.

On July 25, 1975, seven months after enactment of the bill,

President Ford announced appointment of the following Commissioners,

according to the criteria set out in the organic legislation:

From authors and other copyright owners:

> John Hersey, President of the Authors League of America
> Dan Lacy, Senior Vice President, McGraw Hill, Inc.
> E. Gabriel Perle, Vice President-Law, Time, Inc.
> Hershel B. Sarbin, President, Ziff-Davis Publishing Co.

<u>11/</u> S. 543, 91st Cong., 1st Sess. (1969).

<u>12/</u> S. 3976, 93d Cong., 2d Sess. (1974), enacted as Pub. L. No. 93-573,
the text of which is found in Appendix B.

From copyright users:

13/

William S. Dix, Librarian Emeritus, Princeton University
Arthur R. Miller, Professor of Law, Harvard Law School
Robert Wedgeworth, Executive Director, American Library
   Association
Alice E. Wilcox, Director, Minnesota Interlibrary Tele-
   communications Exchange

From the public:

George D. Cary, retired Register of Copyrights
Stanley H. Fuld, retired Chief Judge of the
   State of New York and the New York Court
   of Appeals
Rhoda H. Karpatkin, Executive Director, Consumers
   Union
Melville B. Nimmer, Professor of Law, UCLA Law School

The Librarian of Congress and the Register of Copyrights were designated ex

officio members of the Commission; of these two only the Librarian had a

vote in Commission matters.

Judge Fuld and Mr. Nimmer were designated Chairman and Vice Chair-
                                    14/
man of the Commission, respectively.

As previously indicated, seven months of the three-year term

allotted the Commission for the completion of its task had already passed

at the time the Commissioners were appointed. At its initial meeting on

October 8, 1975, the Commission, after appointing Arthur J. Levine as
                                                       15/
Executive Director and authorizing recruitment of a staff, proceeded

directly to outline its substantive goals. It discussed the scope of the

work entrusted to it and noted that it would study not only the issues

related to computer uses and computer-assisted creation of copyrighted

works but also the separate issue of photocopying.

The Commission, as originally conceived, was designed primarily

to assist in the resolution of issues relating to the impact of the computer

---

13/ Commissioner Dix died on February 22, 1978.

14/ Biographical statements about the Commissioners are contained in
Appendix C to this Report.

15/ Biographical statements about the Commission Staff are contained in
Appendix D to this Report.

16/

on copyrighted works,   but the organic legislation added the photocopying

issue to the Commission's mandate. The concern of copyright proprietors

with the impact of photocopying on the dissemination of their copyrighted

17/

works has grown considerably since 1967.   At the outset the Commission-

ers' first organizational task was to develop a systematic approach for

addressing the major issues in their mandate. Since the Congress was still

considering the photocopying issue, the Register of Copyrights urged the

18/

Commissioners to concentrate their initial efforts on the computer problem.

In the meantime, so that the Commission could better understand

the complexities of the photocopying issue and the views of publishers,

---

16/ S. 2216, 90th Cong., 1st Sess. (1967), in which the Commission was
initially proposed, referred to the purpose of the Commission as being

> to study and compile data on the repro-
> duction and use of copyrighted works of
> authorship (1) in automatic systems cap-
> able of storing, processing, retrieving,
> and transferring information, and (2) by
> various forms of machine reproduction.

While subsection (2) referred to machine reproduction, the drafters of
that bill had not envisioned the impact of modern reprography, and photocopying was not considered to be as significant or complex a problem as any
of those created by the computer. The Report accompanying S. 2216 does
mention photocopying as one of the problems for which a study commission
was then being proposed, see S. Rep. No. 640, 90th Cong., 1st Sess. (1967),
but testimony at hearings on bills for the general revision of the Copyright
Act indicate that the computer, rather than the photocopying machine, was
the main reason for the creation of a special study commission. See,
Hearings on S. 597, 90th Cong., 1st Sess., (1967) Parts I-IV.

17/ In Williams & Wilkins Co. v. United States, 420 U.S. 376 (1975), an
equally divided Supreme Court without a written opinion left undisturbed
the decision of the United States Court of Claims, 487 F.2d 1345 (1973),
that the photocopying of medical and scientific journals done by the National
Library of Medicine and the National Institutes of Health as part of
their medical research and education activities did not constitute
infringement of the copyrights in the journals copied.

18/ Several reasons for first considering the computer problems were evident at this time. Certain photocopying issues were addressed by Section
108 of the bill then pending in the Congress which became the 1976 Act.
Legislative proposals concerning the computer issue had not only been
omitted from that bill, but by specific statutory language (Section 117)
all rights in computer-related works were to be frozen in their pre-
revision status, presumably pending recommendations of the Commission.
The Commission believed that hearings on photocopying might impinge un-
necessarily on the provisions relating to photocopying in that bill and
that the hearings on that issue should therefore be deferred until after
the legislative effort was completed.

authors, librarians and users, it appointed an ad hoc [19] committee to report

to the full Commission on the various issues relating to photocopying.

The Commission decided that, rather than pursuing the computer-

related issues to the exclusion of photocopying, it should carry on

parallel studies. The Commission also recognized that, before it could

set any final schedule for its work, it would have to educate itself on

the actual and potential technologies and practices in the two areas of

its mandate. It had made a start on photocopying; it now directed the

staff to plan an information program on the computer issue to give the

Commission an overall view of the current state of computer science and

technology, and of the ways it might be applied in the future to the

storing, processing, retrieving and transferring of information.

In response to the Commission's request for basic information

on computer technology, representatives of companies concerned with

information and computers briefed the Commissioners on the historical

development of computers; on the current state and future potential of

computer technology; on the use and applications of data bases; and on

the way new works are created by computer use. Professional societies

assisted the Commission staff in setting up panels of experts to instruct

the Commissioners in various forms of information flow and developing

means for information access. Among the subjects covered were the impact

of technology on the processing of information; the educational functions

of computers; management of information; and the uses of micrographics

in publishing and copying technology. Representatives from consumer and

public interest organizations advised the Commission of their concerns. [20]

The Commissioners also heard presentations from representatives

of the principal trade associations in the computer and information sciences

who were conversant with the new means of transferring information and were

---

19/ Judge Fuld appointed Commissioners, Hersey, Lacy and Dix as members
of the committee.

20/ A listing of all persons appearing before the Commission including
the subject of their discussion and dates of appearance is contained in
Appendix E to this report.

concerned, in various ways, with the need to provide legal protection for the rights of the creators and publishers of works disseminated by these new means. The witnesses emphasized that new methods of storing, retrieving and printing data were changing and affecting traditional publishing practices.

After conducting these initial investigations, the Commission adopted a preliminary research plan, prepared by the staff, to guide its work through the rest of its term. The computer issues were categorized as follows: (1) computer uses of conventional works of authorship; (2) proprietary rights in data bases; (3) computer software; and (4) new works created by application of a computer. Accordingly, the Commission decided that it would hold public hearings and initiate the collection of information on computer-related issues beginning in the summer of 1976. Subcommittees dealing with the computer issues would then analyze this data and draft reports, which would be circulated for public comment and refined for a final recommendation to the Congress at the end of the Commission's term. The photocopying issue was to be the subject of hearings beginning in the winter of 1976. The Photocopy Subcommittee would then prepare its report on that issue so that it could be circulated for public comment and put in final form as recommendations to the Congress before the end of the Commission's term.

To expedite the work of the Commission, Chairman Fuld assigned the Commissioners to four Subcommittees.

Photocopying

    Vice-Chairman Nimmer
    Commissioners Hersey, Lacy, Wedgeworth, Wilcox

Computer Software

    Chairman Fuld
    Commissioners Miller, Perle

Computer Data Bases

    Commissioners Cary, Lacy, Wedgeworth

Computer-Created Works

    Commissioners Dix, Karpatkin, Miller, Sarbin

The Commission directed the staff to arrange for certain research contracts and to initiate a series of hearings to gather the views of both proprietors and users of copyrighted works. In the photo-copying area the research activities were directed primarily toward assembling data on the volume and nature of photocopying of copyrighted materials, and in the computer area toward attempting to define the impact on both users and producers of proprietary protection for computer-produced works, software and data bases. One particularly difficult problem was trying to define the impact on the ultimate consumer of changes in copyright law and procedure applicable both to photocopying and computer uses.

The results of these studies as well as the views of interested parties were presented to the Commission in a series of hearings beginning in May of 1976.[21/] Witnesses appeared representing a wide spectrum of interests concerning photocopying, computer software, data bases and new works. These witnesses appeared as individual experts in some instances but more often represented interested organizations -- publishers, authors, librarians, information companies, computer manufacturers, independent software producers, computer users and various professional associations.[22/] The information presented by these witnesses and collected by the research projects provided the foundation for the preparation of the various Sub-committee reports and the subsequent Commission deliberations.

The studies conducted for the Commission are discussed in the chapters of this Report dealing with the substantive areas to which they apply.[23/] The study that addressed the questions of impact on the general

---

21/ See Appendix G for a chronological listing of the meetings and hearings conducted by the Commission.

22/ See Appendix F for a listing of witnesses and the organizations repre-sented.

23/ A bibliography of the reports prepared for the Commission and a summary of each research project appears in Appendix H.

^{24/}
consumer, however, deserves some mention at this point since it addressed
all of the areas studied by the Commission.

Early in the Commission's deliberations, the question was raised
of the impact of any recommendations that the Commission might make on the
ultimate consumer or the public at large. The answer to the question was
not readily apparent. Consequently, the Commission directed the staff to
plan a study that would attempt to address this topic. After the staff's
development of a general plan, contracts were placed with the Public
Interest Economics Center (PIE-C) and the Public Interest Satellite Association (PISA) to prepare an economic analysis of these issues and to
convene two conferences of representatives from interested consumer and
public interest organizations to provide additional information for the
analysis.[25/] The findings of that study generally were that copyright
protection for works produced by and used in conjunction with computers
and reprographic systems was appropriate so long as it did not impede
public access to such works or otherwise extend monopoly power. The
results of that study are considered in the analysis of the Commission's
recommendations which follow.

In addition to the hearings held by the full Commission on a
regular basis, the Subcommittees met to formulate, draft and revise their
respective reports concerning their areas of inquiry. After Commission
review, these reports were offered for public comment and the full
Commission reviewed letters and took testimony from those who responded.

As work progressed, it became clear that Congress had been correct in providing three years for the Commission to complete its work.
Because there had been a seven-month delay between the legal creation of
the Commission and the appointment of its members, Representative

---

24/ M. Breslow, A. Ferguson and L. Haverkamp, An Analysis of Computer and
Photocopying Issues from the Point of View of the General Public and the
Ultimate Consumer [1978]. [Hereinafter cited as PIE-C Report.]

25/ A listing of the representatives from these organizations can be
found at page 15 of Appendix H to this Report.

Kastenmeier introduced a bill [26/] which, after it became law, [27/] granted the Commission an additional seven months to complete its work and prepare this report.

During the Commission's life, the Act of 1976 was enacted and became effective. In anticipation of the work of the Commission and of this Report, the drafters of the statute explicitly stated that it did not address or deal with computer issues. [28/] Instead, it addressed and dealt with certain photocopying issues by codifying the equitable defense of "fair use" [29/] and by expressly specifying certain additional rights of some libraries and archives. [30/] Guidelines to aid in interpreting those provisions relating to interlibrary loan photocopying were developed with the Commission's assistance and incorporated by Congress into the Conference Report. [31/] These are discussed in detail in the chapter of this Report devoted to photocopying. [32/]

The computer use issues addressed by the Commission, discussed in Chapter III, [33/] are of relatively recent vintage. In this respect they differ from certain of the photocopying issues which were the subject of concern as early as the 1930s. [34/] Under the copyright law in force during the early phases of computer development, it was unclear whether unauthorized placement of a copyrighted work into a computer amounted to the preparation of a copy in violation of the rights of the copyright owner in view of the

---

26/ H.R. 4836, 95th Cong., 1st Sess. (1977).

27/ Pub. L. No. 95-146 (1977). The text of this Act is contained in Appendix B.

28/ 17 U.S.C. § 117, and House Report, supra note 1, at 116.

29/ 17 U.S.C. § 107.

30/ 17 U.S.C. § 108.

31/ Conference Report, supra note 1, at 72.

32/ See p. 117, infra.

33/ See pp. 21-115, infra.

34/ For example, the so-called Gentlemen's Agreement on Photocopying was established in 1935 to provide guidelines for the most common types of library photographic reproduction.

Supreme Court's holding that a piano roll was not a "copy" of the music it caused to be played since it was incapable of being read by the unaided human eye. 35/

Even when an apparent work of authorship was prepared for computer use and then employed in conjunction with a computer, federal copyright could exist under the 1909 Act only if the work had been published with the requisite copyright notice. Unpublished works were protected by state law dealing with common law copyright. But if the work was published without the notice required by the federal copyright law it was in the public domain under the 1909 Act. Again, this meant that few federal copyright questions were raised.

Modern computer systems either are used, or have the capability, to transmit, store and receive information across great distances. In conjunction with telephone lines or specialized communications facilities, a computer, coupled with a cathode ray terminal or a printing device, may be used to display or copy information located either in its storage unit or in that of another computer thousands of miles away. Under the new copyright law, the information displayed or copied may often be a copyrighted work. The terms "display" and "copy" are important for the purposes of this Report, since each of those acts, unless authorized, constitutes a copyright infringement.

A brief overview of the most relevant provisions of the 1976 Act may be helpful in placing in context the discussions which follow. Federal copyright now protects original works of authorship in conventional or electronic media from the moment of their creation without the need to affix notice and publish as required under the old law. 36/   Since no action need be taken to acquire the copyright, much of the material used or stored in computer systems will be copyrighted. Copyright protection lasts for the

---

35/   White-Smith Music Publishing Co. v. Apollo Co., 209 U.S. 1 (1908).

36/   17 U.S.C. §§ 102(a) and 302.

life of the author plus fifty years [37/] or, in the case of works which are anonymous, pseudonymous, or made for hire, [38/] for seventy-five years from publication or one hundred years from creation, whichever period is shorter. [39/]

The owner of copyright in a work has the exclusive right to do or authorize the following:

    (a) prepare copies of the work;

    (b) prepare derivative works [40/] based upon it;

    (c) distribute copies of it publicly by sale, rental, lease, or lending;

    (d) perform certain works publicly; and

    (e) display certain works publicly.

When someone other than the copyright owner — or a person acting with the owner's permission — commits one of those acts it is an infringement of the copyright unless it comes within an exception provided by the law. [41/] The copyright owner possesses against such infringers such remedies as injunctions, [42/] damages and profits, [43/] costs and attorney's fees, [44/] or criminal prosecution. [45/]

37/ 17 U.S.C. § 302(a).

38/ Works made for hire include all works made by employees within the scope of their employment and certain specifically ordered or commissioned works. 17 U.S.C. § 101.

39/ 17 U.S.C. § 302(c).

40/ Derivative works include translations, abridgements, transformations and adaptations. 17 U.S.C. § 101.

41/ 17 U.S.C. § 501(a).

42/ 17 U.S.C. § 502.

43/ 17 U.S.C. § 504.

44/ 17 U.S.C. § 505.

45/ 17 U.S.C. § 506.

III.   COMPUTERS AND COPYRIGHT

A.   Introduction

The Congress, in creating the Commission, directed that it address two broad subjects concerning computers and copyright -- the creation of new works with computer assistance and the use of copyrighted works in conjunction with computers. With respect to the second subject the Commission has considered three separate issues -- the placement into computers of any copyrighted works, the use of automated data bases and copyright protection for the intellectual property in computer programs.

Because this study was to be undertaken, the Congress included a section in the new copyright law specifying that a copyright owner had the same rights with respect to computer uses of copyrighted works as were available under the copyright law prior to the effective date of the Act of 1976 -- existing state statutes, case law and the provisions of the Copyright Act of 1909. [46/]   The legislative history of the 1976 Act clearly shows that the Congress intended that the provision would be continued, eliminated or modified based upon this Commission's recommendations. [47/]

B.   Background

From the Renaissance through the Industrial Revolution to the present, technological developments have consistently extended society's power to control natural phenomena and to shape its own destiny. The rapid developments in communications and information technology of the past three decades have immeasurably expanded and extended the power of human communication.

One of the most important contributions to the communication and information revolution has been the digital computer. Animated by elements

---

46/   17 U.S.C. § 117

47/   House Report, supra note 1, at 116.

of human creative genius, these machines are opening new avenues for recording, storing and transmitting human thought. New means of communication
transcend words fixed on paper or images on film and permit authors to
communicate creatively, adaptively and dynamically with their audience.

The first commercial computers, built shortly after World War II,
were based largely on vacuum tubes and were so expensive that only the
government or the largest corporations could even consider owning them.
In order to function, the typical early computer required an environment in
which temperature and humidity were carefully monitored. It was controlled
by programs created by its manufacturer and users exclusively for that
particular computer.

Subsequent generations of computers have been characterized by
dramatic reductions in the size, energy requirements and price for a given
amount of computational power. These generations are measured by the
changes in the electronic circuitry of the computer. The four generations
now generally acknowledged have been based upon vacuum tubes, transistors,
printed circuits and integrated circuits, respectively.

C. Foundation for the Recommendations

1. Computer Programs [48/]

Computer programs are a form of writing virtually unknown twenty-
five years ago. They consist of sets of instructions which, when properly
drafted, are used in an almost limitless number of ways to release human
beings from such diverse mundane tasks as preparing payrolls, monitoring
aircraft instruments, taking data readings and making calculations for
research, setting type, operating assembly lines, and taking inventory.
They are prepared by the careful fixation of words, phrases, numbers and
other symbols in various media. The instructions that make up a program
can be read, understood, and followed by a human being. For both eco-

---

48/ Separate Opinions by Commissioners Nimmer, Hersey and Karpatkin follow
at pp. 66-93, infra.

nomic and humanitarian reasons, it is undesirable for people to carry out manually the process described in painstaking detail in a computer program. Machines, lacking human attributes, cannot object to carrying out repetitious, boring, and tedious tasks. Because machines can and do perform these tasks, people are free to do those other things which they alone can do or which they find a more rewarding expenditure of their efforts.

There have been great changes in the construction of computers and changes as well in the media in which programs are recorded. Periodic progress has seen the development, utilization and, in some cases, the passage into obsolescence of bulky plug boards, punched paper cards and tape, magnetic tapes and disks and semiconductor chips. It should be emphasized that these developments reflect differences only in the media in which programs are stored and not changes in the nature of the programs themselves.

The evolution of these media is similar to that of devices for playing recorded music. Circuit boards may be compared to music boxes, punched paper to piano rolls, while magnetic disks and tapes store music and programs in precisely the same manner. Both recorded music and computer programs are sets of information in a form which, when passed over a magnetized head, cause minute currents to flow in such a way that desired physical work gets done.

The need for protecting the form of expression chosen by the author of a computer program has grown proportionally with two related concurrent trends. Computers have become less cumbersome and expensive, so that individuals can and do own computers in their homes and offices with more power than the first commercial computers, while at the same time, programs have become less and less frequently written to comply with the requirements imposed by a single-purpose machine.

Just as there was little need to protect the ridged brass wheel in a nineteenth century music box, so too there was little reason to protect the wired circuit or plug boards of early computers. The cost of making the wheel was inseparable from the cost of producing the ridged final product. The cost of copying a reel of magnetic tape, whether it contains a Chopin Etude or a computer program, is small. Thus the following proposition seems sound: if the cost of duplicating information is small, then it is easy for a less than scrupulous person to duplicate it. This means that legal as well as physical protection for the information is a necessary incentive if such information is to be created and disseminated.

This proposition is the underlying principle of copyright, but from 1908 until early 1972 the copyright laws of the United States did not reflect acceptance of it with respect to one form of expression -- recorded sounds. Because the Supreme Court held in 1908 that since a piano roll was not readily perceptible to human eyes it was not a copy of the music it rendered on a player piano,[49] there was almost "open season," at least in terms of federal law, on the duplication of piano rolls, shellac and vinyl records and audio tape recordings. Certain states made it illegal to duplicate such works, but federal copyright remained almost powerless in this area. While this rule was often criticized, its effect was apparently not too deleterious to producers of recorded sounds as long as the cost of disk duplication made commercial piracy expensive to undertake. Records and piano rolls were doubtless duplicated and sold, but on a less than threatening scale. The development of inexpensive transistorized tape recording equipment and its use by organized pirates posed serious economic problems for either the 1908 rule or the recording industry. But the principle persevered and finally prevailed in the Sound Recording Act of 1971,[50] which provided sanctions against those who engage in the unauthorized duplication of sound recordings.

As the number of computers has increased dramatically, so has the number of programs with which they may be used. While the first computers were designed and programmed to do one or only a few specific tasks,

---

49/ White-Smith Music Pub. Co. v. Apollo Co., 209 U.S. 1 (1908).

50/ P.L. 92-140, 85 Stat. 391 (1971).

an ever increasing proportion of all computers are general-purpose machines which perform diverse tasks, depending in part upon the programs with which they are used. Early programs were designed by machine manufacturers to be used in conjunction with one model or even one individual computer. Today many programs are designed to operate on any number of machines from one or more manufacturers. In addition, and perhaps even more importantly, there is a growing proportion of programs created by persons who do not make machines. These people may be users or they may be, and increasingly are, programmers or small firms who market their wares for use by individual machine owners who are not in a position to write their own programs. Just as Victrola once made most of the first record players and records, so too did early machine manufacturers write most of the first programs. RCA, Victrola's successor, still produces sound recordings (but, interestingly enough, not phonographs), but so do hundreds of other firms. If present computer industry trends continue, it is all but certain that programs written by non-machine manufacturers will gain an increasing share of the market, not only because writing programs and building machines are two very different skills that need not necessarily co-occur, but also because program writing requires little capital investment.<u>51/</u>

The cost of developing computer programs is far greater than the cost of their duplication. Consequently, computer programs, as the previous discussion illustrates, are likely to be disseminated only if:

(1) The creator can recover all of its costs plus a fair profit on the first sale of the work, thus leaving it unconcerned about the later publication of the work; or

(2) The creator can spread its costs over multiple copies of the work with some form of protection against unauthorized duplication of the work; or

(3) The creator's costs are borne by another, as, for example, when the government or a foundation offers prizes or awards; or

(4) The creator is indifferent to cost and donates the work to the public.

51/ <u>See</u> the discussion of barriers to entry in the hardware and software markets, p. 59, <u>infra</u>.

The consequence of the first possibility would be that the price of virtually any program would be so high that there would necessarily be a drastic reduction in the number of programs marketed. In this country, possibilities three and four occur but rarely outside of academic and government-sponsored research. Computer programs are the product of great intellectual effort and their utility is unquestionable. The Commission is, therefore, satisfied that some form of protection is necessary to encourage the creation and broad distribution of computer programs in a competitive market.

The conclusion of the Commission is that the continued avail-ability of copyright protection for computer programs is desirable.[52] This availability is in keeping with nearly two centuries' development of American copyright doctrine during which the universe of works protectible by statutory copyright has expanded along with the imagination, communications media, and technical capabilities of society.

This conclusion is in accord with the recommendations of groups studying this issue for the United Kingdom[53] and the World Intellectual Property Organization.[54] Both studies recommended that computer programs be afforded protection to a degree that is virtually identical to American copyright.[55] A Canadian study[56] reached the opposite conclusion and an

---

[52] The Copyright Office presently accepts computer programs for registration. See discussion pp. 38-39 and A-4 infra.

[53] Copyright and Designs Law: Report of the Committee to consider the Law on Copyright and Designs, H.M.S.O., 1976 (frequently known as "The Whitford Report").

[54] Model Provisions on the Protection of Computer Software (1978).

[55] A recent study for the World Intellectual Property Organization (WIPO) notes that "in a number of countries it would already be possible to give such protection [to programs] on the basis of current legislation on copyright...and consequently special legislation would not be necessary. In various countries including the United States...there would seem to be no particular desire to set up special provisions to protect software." G. Kolle, "Computer Software Protection -- Present Situation and Future Prospects," 1977 Copyright 72. (1977).

[56] A. Keyes and C. Brunet, Copyright in Canada: Proposals for a Revision of the Law (1977).

Australian report $^{57/}$ considered computer issues outside its terms of reference.

The Commission also believes that the effects of the recommendations pertaining to computer programs made in the Report, as well as those pertaining to the other computer-related subjects within the Commission's jurisdiction should be periodically reviewed. This could be done on a smaller scale than that undertaken by the Commission but should be done well and often enough to prevent the copyright law from becoming as anachronistic as did the 1909 Act.

The Commission is unanimous in its belief that computer programs are entitled to legal protection. But that unanimity has not extended to the form that protection should take. $^{58/}$ The law as it exists today with respect to the protection of computer programs is not totally clear. What is clear is that today there are different and oftimes conflicting methods used by proprietors to attempt to protect their products. These include patent and copyright -- exclusively federal statutory methods; trade secret law -- derived from statutory and judicial state law; and unfair competition -- based on elements of common law and federal statute. $^{59/}$

a.   Recommendations

In order to provide reasonable protection for proprietors without unduly burdening users of programs and the general public, the following statements concerning program copyright ought to be true:

(1) Copyright should proscribe the unauthorized copying of these works.

(2) Copyright should in no way inhibit the rightful use of these works.

57/ Report of the Copyright Law Committee on Reprographic Reproduction (1976).

58/ See the separate opinions of Commissioners Nimmer, Hersey and Karpatkin beginning at pp. 66-93, infra.

59/ These methods are compared with copyright beginning at p. 40, infra.

(3) Copyright should not block the development and dissemination of these works.

(4) Copyright should not grant anyone more economic power than is necessary to achieve the incentive to create.

Relatively few changes to the Copyright Act of 1976 are required to attain these objectives, and the promulgation of regulations by the Copyright Office will ease the burden of compliance for both copyright owners and users.

Recommendations for Statutory Change

In order to make the law clear regarding both proprietors' and users' rights, the Commission suggests that the following changes to the Copyright Act of 1976 be made:

(1) That Section 117 as enacted be repealed.

(2) That Section 101 be amended to add the following definition:

> A "computer program" is a set of statements or instructions to be used directly or indirectly in a computer in order to bring about a certain result.

(3) That a new Section 117 be enacted as follows:

§117: Limitations on Exclusive Rights: Computer Programs

> Notwithstanding the provisions of § 106, it is not an infringement for the rightful possessor of a copy of a computer program to make or authorize the making of another copy or adaptation of that computer program provided:
>
> (1) that such a new copy or adaptation is created as an essential step in the utilization of the computer program in conjunction with a machine and that it is used in no other manner, or
>
> (2) that such new copy or adaptation is for archival purposes only and that all archival copies are destroyed in the event that continued possession of the computer program should cease to be rightful.
>
> Any exact copies prepared in accordance with the provisions of this section may be leased, sold, or otherwise transferred, along with the copy from which such copies were prepared, only as part of the lease, sale, or other transfer of all rights in the program. Adaptations so prepared may be transferred only with the authorization of the copyright owner.

The 1976 Act, without change, makes it clear that the placement of any copyrighted work into a computer is the preparation of a copy and,

therefore, a potential infringement of copyright. Section 117, designed
to subject computer uses of copyrighted works to treatment under the old
law, vitiates that proscription, at least insofar as machine-readable
versions are not "copies" under the 1909 Act.[60/]   Therefore, to prevent any
question about the impropriety of program piracy, and to assure that all
works of authorship are treated comparably under the new law, Section 117
should be repealed.[61/]

Because the placement of a work into a computer is the preparation
of a copy, the law should provide that persons in rightful possession of
copies of programs be able to use them freely without fear of exposure to
copyright liability. Obviously, creators, lessors, licensors and vendors
of copies of programs intend that they be used by their customers, so that
rightful users would but rarely need a legal shield against potential copyright problems. It is easy to imagine, however, a situation in which the
copyright owner might desire, for good reason or none at all, to force a
lawful owner or possessor of a copy to stop using a particular program.
One who rightfully possesses a copy of a program, therefore, should be provided with a legal right to copy it to that extent which will permit its
use by that possessor. This would include the right to load it into a
computer and to prepare archival copies of it to guard against destruction
or damage by mechanical or electrical failure. But this permission would
not extend to other copies of the program. Thus one could not, for example,
make archival copies of a program and later sell some to another while re-
taining some for use. The sale of a copy of a program by a rightful possessor to another must be of all rights in the program, thus creating a new
rightful possessor and destroying that status as regards the seller. This
is in accord with the intent of that portion of the law which provides that

---

60/ If they are not, then their unauthorized duplication would not be an
infringement, just as the unauthorized duplication of sound recordings was
largely without the scope of copyright before February 15, 1972. See
discussion at p. 25, supra.

61/ This appears consistent with Congressional intent that Section 117
should only be effective pending the Commission's report. See House
Report, supra note 1, at 116.

owners of authorized copies of a copyrighted work may sell those copies
without leave of the copyright proprietor.[62/]

Because of a lack of complete standardization among programming
languages and hardware in the computer industry, one who rightfully acquires
a copy of a program frequently cannot use it without adapting it to that
limited extent which will allow its use in the possessor's computer. The
copyright law, which grants to copyright proprietors the exclusive right to
prepare translations, transformations and adaptations[63/] of their work,
should no more prevent such use than it should prevent rightful possessors
from loading programs into their computers. Thus a right to make those
changes necessary to enable the use for which it was both sold and purchased
should be provided. The conversion of a program from one higher-level language to another to facilitate use would fall within this right, as would the
right to add features to the program that were not present at the time of
rightful acquisition. These rights would necessarily be more private in
nature than the right to load a program by copying it and could only be
exercised so long as they did not harm the interests of the copyright proprietor. Unlike the exact copies authorized as described above, this right
of adaptation could not be conveyed to others along with the licensed or
owned program without the express authorization of the owner of the copyright in the original work. Preparation of adaptations could not, of
course, deprive the original proprietor of copyright in the underlying work.[64/]
The adaptor could not vend the adapted program, under the proposed revision
of the new law,[65/] nor could it be sold as the original, without the author's
permission.[66/] Again, it is likely that many transactions involving copies

---

62/ 17 U.S.C. § 109(a).

63/ 17 U.S.C. §§ 101 and 106(2).

64/ Grove Press, Inc. v. Greenleaf Publishing Co., 247 F.Supp. 127
(E.D.N.Y. 1965).

65/ See Recommendations for new § 117, p. 30, supra.

66/ 17 U.S.C. § 106(2) and Gilliam v. American Broadcasting Co., 192
U.S.P.Q. 1 (2d Cir. 1976).

of programs are entered into with full awareness that users will modify
their copies to suit their own needs, and this should be reflected in the
law. The comparison of this practice to extensive marginal note-taking in
a book is appropriate -- that note-taking is arguably the creation of a
derivative work, but unless the note-taker tries to copy and vend that work
the copyright owner is unlikely to be very concerned. Should proprietors
feel strongly that they do not want rightful possessors of copies of their
programs to prepare such adaptations they could, of course, make such desires
a contractual matter.

Recommendation for Regulations

Regulations for notice, deposit and registration of programs
should be promulgated by the Register of Copyrights.

Copyright notice in the form prescribed in the 1976 Act should be
required on all formats in which a program is marketed. [67]   On copies of
programs in a medium capable of being read by the unaided eye, the notice
should physically appear before the list of instructions that comprise the
program. Those programs that can be read only with the aid of a machine
or device should contain notice in the medium of fixation so that the
contents of the program cannot be listed without reproducing the notice
in the position just described. Further, containers in which copies of
such machine-readable programs are sold, leased or transported should
bear notice as should such devices as (1) reels upon which magnetic
tape is wound, or (2) semiconductor chips in which programs are stored.

Regulations relating to deposit and registration requirements
should promote public access to computer programs while being flexible
enough to accommodate future changes in computer technology. In any
case, programs are frequently modified and updated to reflect improvements
or changes. The repeated deposit of each version of a program would

---

[67] Such notice must consist of the word "Copyright," the abbreviation
"Copr." or the symbol © together with the year of first publication and the
name of the copyright owner. 17 U.S.C. § 401(b).

be burdensome to both the program proprietor and the Copyright Office.

Several options appear available. A system of temporary deposit,

similar to the practice followed with respect to motion pictures, might

be appropriate. [68/] In the alternative, permanent deposit of complete copies

of original versions of programs could be required, with descriptions rather

than complete copies of amended versions being filed thereafter. In any

event, such requirements can be established best by the Copyright Office. [69/]

b. The Case for Copyright Protection for Programs

The Constitution.

Under the Constitution [70/] the Congress has the power to grant

authors exclusive rights in their writings to promote the progress of science

and the useful arts. On many occasions since 1790, the Congress has exercised

that power, first by creating a Copyright Act, and thereafter by periodically

revising it and expanding its scope. That the word "writing" in the

Constitution has broad and dynamic meaning may be seen in the nature of

works that have been found constitutionally copyrightable. Notwithstanding

the apparent distinction between them and literal writings, photographs, [71/]

commercial art, [72/] motion pictures, [73/] and sound recordings [74/] have all

been found to be writings.

68/ The Copyright Office has a long-established practice of returning
deposit copies of motion pictures to the depositor after registration.
The copies are returned subject to recall by the Library of Congress
for addition to its film collection.

69/ The Copyright Office has adopted regulations which generally comport
with these suggestions, the text of which is found in Appendix J at J-12
for notice, 37 C.F.R. § 201, and J-13 for deposit, 37 C.F.R. § 202.

70/ U. S. Const., Art. I, § 8, cl. 8.

71/ Burrow-Giles Lithographic Co. v. Sarony, 111 U.S. 53 (1884).

72/ Bleistein v. Donaldson Lithographing Co., 188 U.S. 239 (1903).

73/ Kalem Co. v. Harper Bros., 222 U.S. 55 (1911).

74/ Goldstein v. California, 412 U.S. 546 (1973).

75/

Judge Learned Hand, in an opinion   which has been characterized

as the "touchstone" for interpreting the constitutional writing require-

76/

ments,   found copyrightable a series of meaningless words coined by a

copyright claimant for use as a code for sending cables.

> If ... models or paintings are "writings,"
> I can see no reason why [the coined] words
> should not be such because they communicate
> nothing. They may have their uses for all
> that, aesthetic or practical, and they may
> be the production of high ingenuity, or
> even genius .... [O]ur Constitution [does
> not] embalm inflexibly the habits of 1789 ...
> its grants of power to Congress comprise,
> not only what was then known, but what the
> ingenuity of men should devise thereafter. 77/

As previously noted a program is created, as are most copyrighted

works, by placing symbols in a medium. In this respect it is the same

as a novel, poem, play, musical score, blueprint, advertisement or tele-

phone directory. It is not the same as a phonorecord or videotape. Those

works are created by shaping physical grooves or electromagnetic fields

so that when they are moved past sensing devices electric currents are

created which, when amplified, do physical work. Notwithstanding these

apparent differences, all these works are writings in the constitutional

sense, and eligible for copyright if the Congress so provides.

The Congress

One of the most noticeable developments in American copyright law

since 1790 has been its frequent expansion so that, after its most recent

revision, it embraces "original works of authorship ... [including] literary

works, musical works ... dramatic works ... pantomimes and choreographic

works, pictorial, graphic and sculptural works, motion pictures and sound

78/

recordings."   This is a significant change from the subject matter of

79/

Act of 1790 -- "any map, chart, book or books now printed."   Over time

---

75/   Reiss v. National Quotation Bureau, Inc., 276 Fed. 717 (S.D.N.Y. 1921).

76/   1 Nimmer on Copyright § 8.1 (1976).

77/   Reiss, supra note 75 at 719.

78/   17 U.S.C. § 102(a).

79/   1 Stat. 124.

this short list has been lengthened by the following additions:

    1802 Designs, engravings, and etchings. 80/

    1831 Musical compositions. 81/

    1856 Dramatic compositions. 82/

    1865 Photographs and negatives. 83/

    1870 Statuary and models. 84/

    1909 All the writings of an author. 85/

    1912 Motion Pictures. 86/

    1972 Sound recordings. 87/

    1976 Original works of authorship. 88/

It should be noted that neither this list nor the list in the 1976 Act is an
attempt by the Congress to delineate every specific work for which copyright
is available. Rather, the 1909 and 1976 Acts were designed to reflect the
breadth of copyright's scope while the specific emendations of other years
were attempts to accommodate new technologies or to rectify restrictive judicial constructions. On no occasion in American history has copyright protection been withdrawn from a class of works for which it has been available.

The Statutory Copyrightability of Programs.

    This expansion of American copyright unquestionably has already
encompassed computer programs. In 1964 the Register of Copyrights announced
that computer programs would be accepted for registration provided that
(1) they contained sufficient original authorship, (2) they had been published

---

80/ 2 Stat. 171.

81/ 4 Stat. 436.

82/ 11 Stat. 139.

83/ 13 Stat. 540.

84/ 16 Stat. 212.

85/ 35 Stat. 1076.

86/ 37 Stat. 488.

87/ 85 Stat. 391.

88/ 17 U.S.C. § 102(a).

and (3) copies submitted for registration were in human-readable form.[89/]
The Register acknowledged that there might be two grounds for doubt about
the registrability of programs -- they might not be within the concept of
"writings of an author" and machine-readable versions might not be "copies"
of the program. Registration, therefore, was made contingent upon the
presence of authorship and the deposit of human-readable copies. Because
publication was a prerequisite for federal copyright under the 1909 Act
and because few programs until recently have been mass-marketed, only some
2,000 programs were registered under the statute.[90/] The new law, under which
publication, registration and direct human readability are not prerequisites
to copyright, provides that federal copyright exists in any literary work
from the moment it is fixed.[91/] That dramatic change in the law and the
growing trend toward mass-marketed programs mean that copyright is likely
to be increasingly important in protecting computer programs, particularly
those of small entrepreneurs who create their works for individual consumers
and who can neither afford nor properly use other forms of protection.[92/]

The Register's 1964 determination has never been challenged.
Although this hardly is dispositive, it was clearly the Congress' intent
to include computer programs within the scope of copyrightable subject
matter in the Act of 1976. Certain proponents of program copyrights
have suggested amending the law to include programs in the list of copyrightable works.[93/] In discussing the expansive history of American
copyright, the House and Senate, in identical language, state why that
is unnecessary.

89/ Copyright Office Circular 31D (January 1965).

90/ The number of programs in which copyright was asserted was likely much
larger. Inasmuch as registration neither was nor is a prerequisite to copyright, there is no way ever to know the number of copyrighted programs in
existence.

91/ 17 U.S.C. § 102(a).

92/ See discussion of these forms, p. 40, et seq., infra.

93/ Transcript, CONTU Meeting No. 6 at 13.

The history of copyright law has been one
of gradual expansion in the types of works
accorded protection, and the subject
matter affected by this expansion has
fallen into two general categories. In
the first, scientific discoveries and
technological developments have made
possible new forms of creative expression that never existed before. In some
of these cases the new expressive forms --
electronic music, filmstrips, and computer
programs, for example -- could be regarded
as an extension of copyrightable subject
matter Congress had already intended to
protect, and were thus considered copyrightable from the outset without the
need of new legislation. In other cases,
such as photographs, sound recordings, and
motion pictures, statutory enactment was
deemed necessary to give them full recognition as copyrightable works. [Emphasis
added]. 94/

Thus the Congress is on record regarding not merely the issue of program

copyrightability but also the ease with which programs fit into copyright.

Unlike the cases of such apparent non-writings as photographs, sound

recordings, and motion pictures, no changes in the law, according to the

Congress, were necessary to afford copyright protection to programs. As

to the location of programs within the classes of copyrightable works set

out in Section 102(a), the House Report makes it clear that the Congress

perceived programs to be "literary works." This is what the Report states:

The term "literary works" does not connote
any criterion of literary merit or qualitative value: it includes catalogs, directories, and similar factual, reference, or
instructional works and compilations of
data. It also includes computer data bases,
and computer programs to the extent that
they incorporate authorship in the programmer's expression of original ideas, as
distinguished from the ideas themselves. 95/
[Emphasis added].

Thus it is clear that those who wrote the Copyright Act of 1976

and those who have administered portions of the 1909 Act concur in the posi-

tion that programs are copyrightable. Action by either the Congress or the

---

94/ Senate Report, supra note 1, at 50-51 and House Report, supra note 1,
at 51.

95/ House Report, supra note 1, at 54.

courts would be necessary to change this. [96/]   The Commission, of course, has

not felt itself bound by these prior legislative or administrative determina-

tions of program copyrightability.

C. Copyright and Other Methods Compared

The purpose of copyright is to grant authors a limited property

right in the form of expression of their ideas. The other methods

used to protect property interests in computer programs have different

conceptual bases and, not surprisingly, work in different ways. An appre-

ciation of those differences has contributed to this Commission's re-

commendation that copyright protection not be withdrawn from programs.

Patents are designed to give inventors a short-term, powerful monopoly in

devices, processes, compositions of matter and designs which embody their

ideas. The doctrine of trade secrecy is intended to protect proprietors

who use a "formula, pattern, device or compilation of information" in

their business "which gives [them] an opportunity to obtain an advantage

over competitors who do not know or use it." [97/]   Unfair competition is a

legal theory which, among other things, proscribes misrepresentation about

the nature and origin of products in commerce. Each of these forms of

protection may inhibit the dissemination of information and restrict

competition to a greater extent than copyright.

In certain circumstances, proprietors may find patent protection

more attractive than copyright, since it gives them the right not only

to license and control the use of their patented devices or processes,

but also to prevent the use of such devices or processes when they are

independently developed by third parties. Such rights last for seventeen

---

96/ In deciding whether a class of works is copyrightable courts have displayed a certain willingness to accept the practices of the Copyright Office.
See, e.g., Goldstein v. California, 412 U.S. 546, 568-69 (1973), in which
the Supreme Court discussed the Register's position on copyright in sound
recordings; and Eltra v. Ringer, 194 U.S.P.Q. 198 (E.D. Va. 1976), aff'd
385 P.T.C.J. A-14, (4th Cir. 1978), in which copyright for type faces was
rejected in large part due to the Copyright Office practice.

97/ Restatement, Torts, § 757, comment b (1939).

years. The acquisition of a patent, however, is time-consuming and expensive, in large part, because a patentee's rights are great and the legal hurdles an applicant must overcome are high. A work must be useful, novel and non-obvious to those familiar with the state of the art in which the patent is sought.[98/] The applicant must prove these conditions to the satisfaction of the Patent and Trademark Office or, failing that, to the Court of Customs and Patent Appeals or the Supreme Court.

It is still unclear whether a patent may ever be obtained for a computer program. On three occasions the Supreme Court has considered cases involving program patents.[99/] In each it has found the programs before it to be ineligible for such protection. However, it has never addressed the broader question whether programs are patentable subject matter. The holdings of these three cases, although carefully limited in scope, make it appear that it would be difficult for any applicant to secure a patent in a program, since novel and useful mathematical formulas may not be patented[100/] and since useful "post-solution applications" of them meet the same fate.[101/] In most countries where the patent question has been answered it has been held that programs are ineligible for patent protection.[102/] Even if patents prove available in the United States, only the very few programs which survive the rigorous application and appeals procedure could be patented. Once such protection attached, of course, all others would be barred from using the patented process, even if independently developed.

Trade secrecy is a doctrine known in every American jurisdiction. As a creature of state statute or common law it differs somewhat from state

---

98/   35 U.S.C. §§ 101, 102 and 103.

99/   Gottschalk v. Benson, 409 U.S. 63 (1972); Dann v. Johnston, 425 U.S. 219 (1976); and Parker v. Flook, ___ U.S. ___, 46 U.S.L.W. 4791 (1978).

100/   Benson, supra note 99.

101/   Flook, supra note 99.

102/   See, e.g., the decision of the Supreme Court of the Federal Republic of Germany in Siemens AG v. AEG Telefunken, June 22, 1976; the discussion in Pagenberg, "Patentability of Computer Programs on the National and International Level," 5 Int'l Rev. of Indust. Prop. & Copyright Law 1 (1974); and the new patent convention adopted by the European Economic Community which explicitly excludes computer programs from patent protection.

to state.<u>103/</u>   The premise on which it is based is this: if a business
maintains confidentiality concerning either the way in which it does something or some information that it has, then courts should protect the
business against the misappropriation of that secret. Although many proprietors feel secure when using trade secrecy, there are several problems
they must face with respect to its use in protecting programs. Because
secrecy is paramount, it is inappropriate for protecting works that contain
the secret and are designed to be widely distributed.<u>104/</u>   Although this
matters little in the case of unique programs prepared for large commercial
customers, it substantially precludes the use of trade secrecy with respect
to programs sold in multiple copies over the counter to small businesses,
schools, consumers and hobbyists. Protection is lost when the secret is
disclosed, without regard to the circumstances surrounding the disclosure.
The lack of uniform national law in this area may also be perceived by
proprietors as reducing the utility of this method of protection.

From the user's standpoint, there are additional drawbacks.
Users must cover the seller's expenses associated with maintaining a secure
system through increased prices. Their freedom to do business in an unencum-
bered way is reduced, since they may need to enter into elaborate nondisclosure
contracts with employees and third parties who have access to the secrets
and to limit that access to a very small number of people. Since secrets
are by definition known to only a few people, there is necessarily a reduced
flow of information in the marketplace, which hinders the ability of
potential buyers to make comparisons and hence leads to higher prices.<u>105/</u>

Experts in the computer industry state that a further problem
with respect to trade secrecy is that there is much human effort wasted

---

103/ See, D. Bender, "Trade Secret Software Protection," 3 <u>Computer L. Svc.</u>
§ 4-4, art. 2 (1977), and S. Nycum, <u>The Criminal Aspects of Computer Abuse</u>,
Stanford Research Inst. (1976).

104/ See, R. Milgrim, <u>Trade Secrets</u>, § 2.05[2] (1976).

105/ P. Samuelson, <u>Economics</u>, 10th ed., (1976) 48; Y. Braunstein, <u>et al.</u>
<u>Economics of Property Rights as Applied to Computer Software and Data</u>
<u>Bases</u> (1977).

when people do for themselves that which others have already done but are keeping secret. This was emphasized in the reports to the Commission prepared by the Public Interest Economics Center and the New York University economists.[106/]

The availability of copyright for computer programs does not, of course, affect the availability of trade secrecy protection. Under the Act of 1976 only those state rights that are equivalent to the exclusive rights granted therein (generally, common law copyright) are preempted.[107/] Any decline in use of trade secrecy might be based not upon preemption but on the rapid increase in the number of widely distributed programs in which trade secret protection could not be successfully asserted.

The common law doctrine of unfair competition of the misappropriation variety is based upon the principle that one may not appropriate a competitor's skill, expenditure and labor. It prohibits false advertising and the "passing off" of another's work as one's own. While there is a small body of federal unfair competition law,[108/] it is largely a state doctrine with the same lack of national uniformity that besets trade secrecy. Although unfair competition may provide relief ancillary to copyright in certain situations, its scope is not as broad and it seems unlikely that it, alone, could provide sufficient protection against the misappropriation of programs. For example, the unauthorized copying of any work for any purpose could be a copyright infringement without amounting to unfair competition.

The following table presents some of the considerations weighed by the Commission in reaching its conclusion. Comments are included to those items which are starred (*). The answers to such economic questions as the effect of protection on the market and the opportunity it creates for an uncompetitive rate of return tend to show that, of the various

---

106/ See Appendix H for a description of these reports.

107/ 17 U.S.C. § 301(a).

108/ See, e.g., 15 U.S.C. § 1125(a) and Allison, J.R., "Private Cause of Action for Unfair Competition Under the Lanham Act," 14 Am. Bus. L.J. 1 (1976).

potential modes of protection, copyright has the smallest negative impact.

Characteristics of Protective Mechanisms

		Copyright	Patent	Trade Secrecy
General Considerations				
1.	National Uniformity	yes	yes	no
2.	Protection Effective Upon	creation of work	successful prosecution of application	entrance into contractual relationship
3.	Cost of Obtaining Protection	nil	moderate	moderate
4.	Term of Protection	life plus 50 years or 75 years	17 years	possibility of both perpetual protection and termination at any time
* 5.	Cost of Maintaining Protection	nil	nil	significant

		Copyright	Patent	Trade Secrecy
General Considerations (cont'd)				
* 6.	Cost of Enforcing Rights Against Violators	moderate	moderate	higher
7.	Availability of (a) Statutory Damages (b) Attorney's Fees from Infringers	a. yes b. yes	a. no b. yes	a. no b. no
8.	Protection Lost by	gross neglect	unsuccessful litigation	disclosure
Software Considerations, Including Effects of Subcommittee Proposals				
9.	Consistency with other copyright areas	yes	no	no
*10.	Availability of protective mechanism for some programs	yes	unclear	yes
*11.	Universal Availability of protective mechanism for all programs	yes	no	no
12.	"Process" protectable	no	yes	yes
13.	Suited to Mass Distribution	yes	yes	no

COMMENTS WITH RESPECT TO STARRED ITEMS IN THE TABLE

Item No.

5.   Once copyright or patent is secured, it costs little or nothing
to keep it in force; on the other hand, expensive security measures
must be taken to avoid losing a trade secret. At least part of the
cost of this security is passed on to the user.

6.   Copyright and patent infringers in some instances can be persuaded to comply without the institution of a lawsuit. If litigation
is necessary, it may be expensive, but in copyright and patent
cases attorney's fees may be awarded to successful plaintiffs.
At trial the proprietor bears the burden of proving that the
trade secret is valid; in patent cases there is a presumption
of valididty and in copyright actions a registration certificate is
prima facie evidence of the copyright's validity. The proof of the
validity of a trade secret may be expensive and difficult, as it
almost necessarily involves the retention of expert witnesses.
Although witnesses may be needed in copyright and patent suits
in those cases there will have been at least some compliance with
federal law regarding public notice of claimed rights before the
lawsuit is initiated. A suit to enforce a trade secret, even
though successful, may destroy the secret if it is offered into
evidence and becomes part of the public record of the trial.

10.   As of the present, serious doubt exists whether programs are
proper subjects for patent protection. (See p. 41, supra).

11.   Even if programs are patentable, only those that are truly
novel and nonobvious will be protected. Trade secrecy is, of
course, unavailable when the contents of a program have been disclosed.

d. The Scope of Copyright in Programs

This section of the Report will explain the extent and limitations

of a copyright for a computer program. The discussion of what rights copy-

right proprietors have and how those rights are limited does not depend upon

the Commission's proposal but is based upon various currently existing copy-

right doctrines.

The rights of any copyright owner are set out in Section 106 of

the Act of 1976. Many of the other sections of Chapter One of that Act

place limitations on those rights. Cases construing previous copyright

acts also serve to define the bounds of copyright under the new law, at

least when the new law does not end the vitality of those cases. Before

examining the specific rights found in Section 106 it is necessary to

determine whether a work is copyrighted. If it is not, then the rights

of a copyright owner are of no consequence. Section 102(a) provides the basis for determining whether a work is copyrightable. [109]

The rule is simple -- a copyrightable work is an original work of authorship
fixed in a tangible medium of expression. [110]   There is a wealth of judicial
interpretation behind the word "original." Suffice to say that a work is
original if it "[o]wes its origin to the author, i.e. is independently
created, and not copied from other works." [111]

A description of what may not be copyrighted is found in the same
section of the copyright law -- ideas, procedures, processes, systems,
methods of operation, concepts, principles or discoveries. [112]   Because
the distinction between copyrightable computer programs and uncopyrightable
processes or methods of operation does not always seem to "shimmer
with clarity" [113] it is important that the distinction between programs
and processes be made clear. There is a venerable copyright case
and recent Congressional language which make the distinction in the
copyright sense relatively easy to articulate. In Baker v. Selden [114] the
Supreme Court held that a valid copyright in a book describing a system
of accounting, based upon the now-universal T-accounts, did not bar others
from using that accounting system. This holding is often misconstrued
as imposing a limit on the copyrightability of works which express ideas,
systems or processes. As Professor Nimmer observes, "the rationale
for the doctrine of Baker v. Selden in no event justifies the denial
of copyrightability to any work." [115]   The case properly stands for the

---

109/ The term "copyrightable" is less accurate under the new law than the old,
but the concept may be useful. Since copyright now exists from the instant a
work is fixed, all "copyrightable" works are perforce copyrighted.

110/ 17 U.S.C. § 102(a).

111/ 1 Nimmer on Copyright, § 10.1 (1976), citing Alfred Bell & Co., Ltd.
v. Catalda Fine Arts, Inc., 191 F.2d 99 (2d Cir. 1951) and Wihtol v. Wells,
231 F.2d 550 (7th Cir. 1956).

112/ 17 U.S.C. § 102(b).

113/ Parker v. Flook, __ U.S. __, __ ; 46 U.S.L.W. 4791, 4792 (1978).

114/ 101 U.S. 99 (1879).

115/ 1 Nimmer on Copyright, § 37.31 (1976).

proposition that using the system does not infringe the copyright

in the description. This rule is found in Section 102(b) of the

new law. Both houses of the Congress agreed as to its application

to computer programs:

> Section 102(b) is intended, among other
> things, to make clear that the expres-
> sion adopted by the programmer is the
> copyrightable element in a computer
> program, and that the actual processes
> or methods embodied in the program are
> not within the scope of the copyright
> law. 116/ [Emphasis added].

Copyright, therefore, protects the program as long as it remains fixed

in a tangible medium of expression but not the electro-mechanical func-

tioning of a machine. The way copyright affects games and game-playing

is closely analogous -- one may not adopt and republish or redistribute

copyrighted game rules, but the copyright owner has no power to prevent

others from playing the game. 117/

Thus one is always free to make a machine perform any conceivable

process (in the absence of a patent), but one is not free to take another's

program. This general rule is subject to exceptions which restrict the

power of copyright owners. These exceptions might be thought of as the

"insufficient intellectual labor" exception and the "idea-expression

identity" exception. Although they lead to similar results, they are

really slightly different.

Apparent works of authorship may not qualify for copyright if they

are not "the fruits of intellectual labor." 118/ This reasoning has barred

copyright for blank forms for recording data 119/ and for instructions of the

rankest obviousness and simplicity, such as "apply hook to wall." 120/ This

exception would mean that a "program" consisting of a very few obvious steps

could not be a subject of copyright.

116/ Senate Report, supra note 1, at 54; House Report, supra note 1, at 57.

117/ 1 Nimmer on Copyright, §37.83 (1976).

118/ Trade-Mark Cases, 100 U.S. 82 (1879).

119/ Brown Instrument Co. v. Warner, 161 F.2d 910 (D.C. Cir. 1947).

120/ E. H. Tate Co. v. Jiffy Enterprises, Inc., 16 F.R.D. 571 (E.D. Pa. 1954).

The "idea-expression identity" exception provides that copyrighted
language may be copied without infringing when there is but a limited number
of ways to express a given idea. This rule is the logical extension of the
fundamental principle that copyright cannot protect ideas.^{121/}   In the computer
context this means that when specific instructions, even though previously
copyrighted, are the only and essential means of accomplishing a given task,
their later use by another will not amount to an infringement. In discussing
an insurance company's use of a lawyer's copyrighted forms, a federal court of
appeals stated in Continental Casualty Co. v. Beardsley:

> [T]he use of specific language ... may be so essential
> to accomplish a desired result and so integrated with
> the use of a ... conception that the proper standard of
> infringement is one which will protect as far as pos-
> sible the copyrighted language and yet allow the free
> use of the thought beneath the language. The evidence
> here shows that [the company] insofar as it has used
> the language of [the lawyer's] forms has done so only
> as incidental to its use of the underlying idea.... In
> so doing it has not infringed. 122/ [Emphasis added].

The underscored language from the Beardsley decision indicates
that copyright protection for programs does not threaten to block the use
of ideas or of program language previously developed by others when that
use is necessary to achieve a certain result. When other language is
available, programmers are free to read copyrighted programs and use the

---

121/   See 2 Nimmer on Copyright, § 166 (1976) and 17 U.S.C. § 102(b).

122/   253 F.2d 702, 706 (2nd Cir. 1958). See also, Harcourt, Brace & World, Inc.
v. Graphic Controls Corp., 329 F.Supp. 517 (S.D.N.Y. 1971).

[123/]

ideas embodied in them in preparing their own works.   This practice, of

course, is impossible under a patent system, where the process itself is

protected, and difficult under trade secrecy, where the text of a program

is designed not to be revealed.

Programs are a relatively new type of writing and the way in

which copyright protects them is not universally understood. Because they

are used in conjunction with machines there has not been universal agreement

about the propriety of copyright protection. Programs should no more be con-

sidered machine parts than videotapes should be considered parts of

projectors or phonorecords parts of sound reproduction equipment. All

three types of works are capable of communicating with humans to a far

greater extent than the coined code words discussed by Judge Hand in

[124/]

Reiss v. National Quotation Bureau.   In all three instances the medium in

which copyrighted material is stored is moved past a sensing device at a

---

123/ The availability of alternative non-infringing language is the rule
rather than the exception. The following colloquy to that effect took place
at the tenth Commission meeting. Transcript CONTU Meeting No. 10 at 44-45.

Commissioner Miller: How many different ways are there to produce a
                      program...?

Dan McCracken:* An infinite number in principle, and in practice dozens,
                 hundreds.

Miller: So it is comparable to the theoretically infinite number of ways of
         writing Hamlet?

McCracken: I believe so. It is not really true that there is a very re-
            strictive way to write a program [which might make it] not copy-
            rightable. I don't believe that at all.

Miller: When you say "infinite," I assume that along that scale there are
         increases and decreases in the efficiency with which the machine
         will operate?

McCracken: Perhaps.

Miller: In all of the programs that we have been talking about this morning,
         with particular reference to...compiler programs, does it continue
         to be true that there are an infinite number of ways of writing
         particular programs to do particular jobs?

McCracken: Yes.... There are hundreds of [different] compiler [programs
            for] going from FORTRAN to some machines....

*Vice President of the Association for Computing Machinery

124/ 276 Fed. 717 (S.D.N.Y. 1921), discussed p. 35, supra.

set speed, causing electric current to flow, and ultimately resulting in
the movement of machine parts to print words, display pictures, or create
sounds. All of these events may occur through the use of machines without
placing copyrighted works in them. A typist may create a printed document
that is indistinguishable from computer output; a television system may
produce pictures without the use of a fixed work; and instruments may be
used to create the sounds which are found on phonorecords. All that copyright protection for programs, videotapes and phonorecords means is that
users may not take the writings of others to operate their machines. In
each instance, one is always free to make the machine do the same thing as
it would if it had the copyrighted work placed in it, but only by one's own
creative effort rather than by piracy.

It has been suggested by Vice-Chairman Nimmer in his separate
opinion 125/ that programs be copyrighted only when their use leads to copyrighted output. If this approach were adopted, it would make a program for
text editing or the production of graphics copyrightable. It would, however,
exclude a program which might be used to assist traffic flow in rush hours
or to monitor the vital signs of patients under intensive care. This
distinction is not consistent with the design of the Act of 1976, which
was clearly to protect all works of authorship from the moment of their
fixation in any tangible medium of expression. Further, it does not square
with copyright practice past and present which recognizes copyright protection for a work of authorship regardless of the uses to which it may be put.
The copyright status of the written rules for a game or a system for the
operation of a machine is unaffected by the fact that those rules direct
the actions of those who play the game or carry out the process. Nor has
copyright been denied to works simply because of their utilitarian aspects.
It follows, therefore, that there should likewise be no distinction made
between programs which are used in the production of further copyrighted
works and those which are not. Should such a distinction be made, the likeli-

---

125/ See pp. 66-69, infra.

hood is that entrepreneurs would simply require that programs produce a
written and, by that token, an unquestionably copyrightable version of
their output in order to obtain copyright in the programs themselves.
Although the distinction tries to achieve the separation of idea from
form of expression, that objective is better achieved through the courts
exercising their judgment in particular cases.

The Commission has considered at length the various forms in
which programs may be fixed. Flowcharts,[126/] source codes[127/] and object
codes[128/] are works of authorship in which copyright subsists, provided they
are the product of sufficient intellectual labor to surpass the "insufficient intellectual labor" hurdle, which the instructions "apply hook to
wall" fails to do.[129/] They may not be copied unless such copying is
authorized by the proprietor of the copyright therein or by law. That
protection continues as long as the program remains fixed in a tangible
medium, up to the period provided in the Act of 1976.[130/]

That the words of a program are used ultimately in the implementation of a process should in no way affect their copyrightability. Traditional works have led to processes both more rigid and more flexible
than those to which computer programs lead. When a phonorecord or
motion picture is used in conjunction with a properly working machine
the same result will occur on the first, the second, or the thousandth
running. The chorus will remain silent until the fourth movement
of Beethoven's Ninth Symphony and Bogart will stay in Casablanca forever.

126/ A flowchart is a graphic representation for the definition, analysis
or solution of a problem in which symbols are used to represent operations,
data flow, or equipment.

127/ A source code is a computer program written in any of several
programming languages employed by computer programmers.

128/ An object code is the version of a program in which the source code
language is converted or translated into the machine language of the computer with which it is to be used.

129/ See note 120, supra.

130/ For the works of individuals, life plus 50 years. For the works of
employed, pseudonymous or anonymous authors, 75 years. 17 U.S.C. § 302.

A similar rigidity is found when one uses a copyrighted chart to determine
the sine of a fifty degree angle. The process is virtually immutable.
That is less true when a program is used, since it contains alternative
branches selected only after use has begun, meaning that the process may
be different with every use.

The text of the new copyright law makes it clear that the placement
of a copyrighted work into a computer -- or, in the jargon of the trade, the
"inputting" of it -- is the preparation of a copy. This may be ascertained
by reading together the definitions of "copies" and "fixed" found in Section
101. In pertinent part, they read as follows:

> "Copies" are material objects ... in which a
> work is fixed ....
>
> A work is "fixed" ... when its embodiment in
> a copy ... is sufficiently permanent or stable
> to permit it to be perceived, reproduced, or
> otherwise communicated for a period of more
> than transitory duration.

Because works in computer storage may be repeatedly reproduced they are
fixed, and thus are copies.[131]

It is difficult, either as a matter of legal interpretation or
technological determination, to draw the line between the copyrightable element of style and expression in a computer program and the process which
underlies it. Some examples of the ways in which copies of programs can
be made may help to explain the nature of this problem and to place it
in its proper perspective.

A computer program may be misappropriated in a variety of ways.
In the first and most straightforward instance the program listing or the
programmer's original coding sheets could be photocopied, which would clearly
be an infringement. The unarguably copyrightable writing has been taken. But
what if the program, rather than being recorded on paper, is recorded on magnetic tape or disk? If the tape is used, without authorization, to produce a

---

131/ Insofar as a contrary conclusion is suggested in one report accompanying the
new law, this should be regarded as incorrect and should not be followed, since
legislative history need not be perused in the construction of an unambiguous
statute. Cf. House Report, supra note 1 at 53, with the plain language in the
statute defining "fixed."

printed human-readable, version of the program, again an infringement has
occurred. Should the result be different if the tape is copied? That copy
can still be used to prepare a printed version at will. There is a one-to-
one correspondence between the printed characters on paper and the magnetized areas of the tape. The tape is simply a version of the program from
which a human-readable copy can be produced with the aid of a machine
or device.

When a program is copied into the memory of a computer it still
exists in a form from which a human-readable version may be produced.
That is, the copy in the computer's memory may be duplicated, just as a
version listed on paper or coded on magnetic tape may be. Only when the
program is inserted, instruction by instruction, into the processing element of the computer and electrical impulses are sent through the circuitry
of the processor to initiate work is the ability to copy lost. This is
true at least under the present state of technology. If it should prove
possible to tap off these impulses then, perhaps, the process would be
all that was appropriated, and no infringement of the copyright would occur.

The movement of electrons through the wires and components of a
computer is precisely that process over which copyright has no control.
Thus, copyright leads to the result that anyone is free to make a computer
carry out any unpatented process, but not to misappropriate another's
writing to do so.

Drawing the line between the copyrightable form of a program and
the uncopyrightable process which it implements is simple in the first instance described above. But the many ways in which programs are now used
and the new applications which advancing technology will supply may make
drawing the line of demarcation more and more difficult. To attempt to
establish such a line in this Report written in 1978 would be futile.
Most infringements, at least in the immediate future, are likely to involve
simple copying. In the event that future technology permits programs
to be stated orally for direct input to a computer through auditory
sensing devices or permits future infringers to use an author's program

without copying, difficult questions will arise. Should a line need
to be drawn to exclude certain manifestations of programs from copyright,
that line should be drawn on a case by case basis by the institution
designed to make fine distinctions, the federal judiciary.

e. The Economic Effects of Program Copyright

That copyright gives authors exclusive rights in their
writings seems to cause some to equate it with all monopolies. This has
led to the fear that protection for programs may give the copyright owner
the power to dominate the program market, the machine market, or both.

To begin with, it is necessary to distinguish between those lawful
monopolies whose existence is permitted or even encouraged on policy grounds
and unlawful monopolies which are declared to be inimical to the public
good. Permitted monopolies generally are found in regulated industries,
such as public utilities, in which economies of scale are so great that
the existence of more than one firm makes little sense and in which
regulation, when properly accomplished, prevents such abuses as monopoly
pricing or refusals to deal. Limited monopolies such as patents and
copyrights are encouraged, while the public interest is protected
in various ways. Protection of the general good is found in the limited
term and stringent standards associated with patents, the proscription
of the protection of ideas under copyright, and the refusal to allow the
extension of patents or copyrights beyond their limited scopes. This last
matter may be the heart of the concern about the economic effects of program
copyright.

The utilization of lawful patents to attempt to monopolize
unpatented processes has been consistently found unlawful.[132] Because copyright grants no monopoly over ideas, a parallel line of cases does not
really exist, but in certain instances courts have reached similar results.
In a leading copyright-antitrust case Judge Frank outlined how competing

---

132/ Morton Salt Co. v. G. S. Suppiger Co., 314 U.S. 488 (1942); Mercoid
Corp. v. Mid-Continent Investment Co., 320 U.S. 661 (1944).

public interests could be balanced:

> We have here a conflict of policies: (a) that
> of preventing piracy of copyrighted matter and
> (b) that of enforcing the anti-trust laws. We
> must balance the two, taking into account the
> comparative innocence or guilt of the parties,
> the moral character of their respective acts,
> the extent of the harm to the public interest,
> the penalty inflicted on the [copyright owner]
> if we deny it relief. As the defendants' piracy
> is unmistakably clear, while the [owners'] in-
> fraction of the anti-trust laws is doubtful and
> at most marginal, we think the enforcement of
> the first policy should outweigh the enforce-
> ment of the second. 133/

Thus it is not the fact of a constitutional and statutory monopoly which is
disfavored, but only abuses of the lawful monopoly. 134/

One of the hallmarks of a competitive industry is the ease with
which entrepreneurs may enter into competition with firms already doing
business. The absence of significant barriers to entering the program-
writing market is striking. There are several hundred independent firms
whose stock in trade is computer programs. 135/ New software firms can be
formed with few people and little money; entry into the market has thus
far been fairly easy. 136/ None of the evidence received by the Commission
suggests that affording copyright to programs would in any way permit program authors to monopolize the market for their products. Nor is there
any indication that any firm is even remotely close to dominating the
programming industry.

The effect of program copyright on the retail prices of consumer
goods and services is so small as to be undetectable. Across a wide variety
of industries, packaged software amounts to between one and two percent of

---

133/ <u>Alfred Bell & Co. v. Catalda Fine Arts, Inc.</u>, 191 F.2d 99, 106 (2d Cir.
1951).

134/ For another case in which the same court refused to permit a copyright
owner to use his lawful monopoly to the detriment of the public, <u>see</u>
<u>Rosemont Enterprises, Inc. v. Random House, Inc.</u>, 366 F.2d 303 (2d
Cir. 1966).

135/ Harvey, "The Developing Software Industry," <u>Infosystems</u> 34 (July 1976).

136/ Computer Sciences Corporation, which has over $100 million in annual
sales, is said to have been founded on capital investment of less than
$1,000.

data processing expenses which themselves comprise a like percentage of a firm's gross income.[137/]   This has led one commentator to describe data processing costs as a whole as "a noise-level expense, probably less than the phone bill of an average company."[138/]   Thus from each one hundred dollars of income a firm is likely to spend between one and two dollars on data processing, of which from one to four cents are spent on packaged software. There is no easy way to separate the costs of protection out from that figure, but it is clear that such costs are miniscule when compared to a firm's total operating expenses.

The market for computer hardware has been characterized by severe but not insurmountable barriers to entry. Economies of scale are very great; a firm must be prepared to invest tremendous amounts of money in creating, building and marketing machines.[139/]   Natural barriers to entry, such as economies of scale, should not receive the opprobrium properly reserved for anticompetitive conspiracies. Barriers erected by present members of an industry may well be, and frequently are, antitrust violations.

The inability of hardware firms to dominate the software market was recognized by the Public Interest Economics Center, when it stated:

> [W]hatever their historical dominance, the hardware
> corporations lack the ability to control entry into the
> software market, and ... their market shares are being
> steadily eroded by the independents. Thus, we can ten-
> tatively conclude that protection of software ... serves
> to benefit consumers by enhancing competition and
> increasing long-run supply. 140/

In the market for computers monopolistic practices have been attacked by the Department of Justice on numerous occasions. As the result of an early consent decree, IBM, the largest firm in the industry, has agreed to sell its equipment instead of only leasing it. In 1969,

---

137/ McLaughlin, "1976 DP Budgets," Datamation 52 (February 1976).

138/ Id.

139/ Amdahl Corporation, a newcomer to the market for large computers, spent five years and $45 million before shipping its first order. "Can Amdahl Live with IBM's New Strategy?," Business Week 56B (August 5, 1977).

140/ PIE-C Report, supra note 24, at IV-13.

immediately after the Justice Department filed its antitrust suit, IBM stopped selling its machines and programs as a package, thus ending a tying arrangement the legality of which had been questioned. The government is currently prosecuting that action against IBM through which it seeks the division of IBM into several firms, much as resulted in the Standard Oil case.[141/] This relief, as is typically the case in an antitrust action, is directed toward the sources of a firm's alleged dominance of an industry. It is interesting to note that neither the government nor any private antitrust plaintiffs has ever argued that IBM's assertion of copyright in its programs is even remotely related to its alleged anticompetitive behavior.

      Successful antitrust attacks where copyright was important to the cause of action apparently have occurred only with respect to performing rights organizations. Both ASCAP and BMI operate under consent decrees which resulted from Justice Department actions directed toward the monopoly created when performance rights were not only pooled but were available exclusively from the pool. The resulting settlements permitted the pooling to continue upon the provision that customers could go to individual proprietors as well as to the defendants to obtain performance rights. Another attack on ASCAP showed again that it is not the copyright monopoly which is disfavored, but rather attempts to extend that right to acquire monopoly power in the market. When a music publisher who belonged to ASCAP sought damages for infringement from film exhibitors who had without license shown films containing plaintiff's music on the soundtrack, in denying the relief sought, the court ruled:

> Refuge cannot be sought in the copyright monopoly which was not granted to enable plaintiffs to set up another monopoly, nor to enable the copyright owners to tie a lawful monopoly with an unlawful monopoly and thus reap the benefits of both. [142/]

141/ Standard Oil Co. v. United States, 221 U.S. 1 (1911).

142/ M. Witmark & Sons v. Jensen, 80 F. Supp. 843, 848-49 (D. Minn. 1948).

The policy implications of such cases seem clear and correct --
the lawful copyright monopoly may not be used other than as intended. A
copyright owner may monopolize his expression but not the market in which
it is purveyed. To suggest, as does the Public Interest Economics Center
(PIE-C), that no "large" hardware manufacturers be permitted to assert
copyright in programs they write is to propose an instrument of dubious
legality and effectiveness. 143/   Certainly any large firm could create a
separate entity to do its program-writing to avoid any proscription of its
ownership of program copyrights. The PIE-C proposal may be less than
relevant to the extent that it might lull its advocates into a false sense
of having dealt with the problem of industrial concentration when they have
not. Being against bigness at all costs should not be a substitute for
analytical action on behalf of the general public and consumers.

On the whole, the direct approach against alleged monopolists
seems far superior to fighting perceived economic evils on copyright
grounds. The enforcement and, where necessary, emendation of present antitrust laws is more appropriate to the problem, if any, than the invention
of a class of works which are generally copyrightable but not when their
authors are disfavored, for whatever well-intentioned reasons. In the
patent and copyright antitrust cases there is no language suggesting
that statutory protection should be unavailable to the defendants, notwithstanding the proof that they had abused their lawful monopolies. To create
such a remedy on bald suspicion would indeed be unjust.

f.   The Cultural Effects of Program Copyright

The introduction of new means of communication with their atten-
dant new modes of expression often raises questions regarding the intrinsic
values of such works. The works of Beethoven, Chopin, Stravinsky and
Hindemith all enjoyed less than immediate success. Early works of all of
these innovative composers were condemned for being outside what was then

---

143/   PIE-C Report, supra note 24, at IV 13.

felt to be the cultural mainstream. But, as perceptions have changed, the contributions these composers made to breaking with tradition and enriching the breadth of expression in our musical heritage have overcome the barriers to new ideas which traditionalists would have imposed.

The history of copyright legislation and the interpretations courts have given to the Copyright Clause all demonstrate that there is no basis, as some would suggest, for the imposition of a standard of literary or artistic merit for determining copyrightability. The perils of such an approach have long been recognized. Mr. Justice Holmes, in upholding copyright in a chromolithographed circus poster, said that:

> It would be a dangerous undertaking for persons trained only in the law to constitute themselves final judges of the worth of pictorial illustrations, outside of the narrowest and most obvious limits. At the one extreme some works of genius would be sure to miss appreciation. Their very novelty would make them repulsive until the public had learned the new language in which their author spoke. It may be more than doubted, for instance, whether the etchings of Goya or the paintings of Manet would have been sure of protection when seen for the first time. At the other end, copyright would be denied to pictures which appealed to a public less educated than the judge. Yet if they command the interest of any public, they have a commercial value -- it would be bold to say that they have not an aesthetic and educational value -- and the taste of any public is not to be treated with contempt. 144/

This principle has been consistently followed in cases emphasizing that "[a]ll that is needed to satisfy both the Constitution and the statute is that the 'author' contributed something more than a 'merely trivial' variation, something recognizably 'his own'." [footnote omitted] 145/ These judicial opinions clearly illustrate that courts have assiduously avoided adopting the critic's role in evaluating the aesthetic merits of works of authorship. To attempt to deny copyrightability to a writing because it is capable of use in conjunction with a computer would contra-

---

144/ Bleistein v. Donaldson Lithographing Co., 188 U.S. 239, 251-52 (1903).

145/ Alfred Bell and Co. v. Catalda Fine Arts, Inc. 191 F.2d 99, 102-03. (2d Cir. 1951); see also Esquire Inc. v. Ringer, 194 U.S.P.Q. 30 (D.D.C. 1976).

vene this sound policy. Where could a meaningful line of demarcation be
drawn? Between flow-chart and source code? Between source code and object
code? At the moment of input into a computer or microprocessor? The
Commission believes that none of these is appropriate. The line which
must be drawn is between the expression and the idea; between the writing
and the process which is described. This proposal acknowledges the propriety of keeping cultural value judgments out of copyright. The only
legitimate question regarding copyrightability is: "Is the object an
original work of authorship?"

The Copyright Clause of the Constitution empowers the Congress to
establish a patent and a copyright system to improve the general public
welfare, by "[p]romoting...the progress of Science and Useful Arts."
Patent protects inventions and copyright protects the writings of authors.
As previously discussed the term "writing" has been liberally construed to
embrace the fruits of intellectual and aesthetic labor embodying any
modicum of original effort. Copyright protects a wide range of works;
some with great cultural value such as the novels of Pulitzer Prize
winners and Nobel Laureates, original paintings, award winning movies
and masterful musical compositions. It likewise shields works of little
or no aesthetic merit: advertising copy, picture post cards, videotaped
wrestling matches, violent and sexually explicit films and the most banal
popular music. The contribution of these latter works to our culture is
at best questionable. Neither the Supreme Court nor any governmental or
private body has been able to assess the social or cultural impact of
sexually explicit materials, let alone the cultural impact of the protection of such works by copyright. Their contribution to the "quality of
life" is not quantifiable; its impact may not even be qualitatively
identifiable. The kinds of qualitative impacts which computer software
may have on the "quality of life" may at least be described.

Declining costs and improved performance of electronic hardware
are bringing powerful miniature computer systems into small businesses and
the home. These computers and the more powerful and cheaper generations

of similar systems which will follow have the potential to enrich our lives and aid in communication among humans in ways as yet inconceivable. Personalized high quality education, at present available only to the wealthy, will be within the reach of the small school system and the average consumer in the home. Health care in public clinics will be provided on a more individualized, personal basis by using computers to aid the physician in communicating with his patient through complete and accurately maintained medical records. Leisure time can be enriched both by studying and by gameplaying on home computer systems. The possibilities provided by the technology are virtually limitless. They are dependent only on the ingenuity employed in developing the programs that enable humans to communicate their ideas to one another through the intermediation of the machine and on the willingness of creators of such works to disseminate them at reasonable prices. In considering the "quality of life" in this country, failing to consider the positive contributions of computers and the programs with which they are used would indeed be a mistake.

At the same time, any dehumanizing effects which might be attributable to the increasing impact of computer uses upon society are utterly unrelated to the mode of protection employed to protect program language. It is clear that the uses to which computers are put depend entirely upon the intent of their users and not at all on the mechanisms designed to protect programs. To say that copyright for programs somehow is responsible for social problems ostensibly caused by computer uses is akin to arguing against copyrights for the worst of television shows or against patent protection for components of gas-guzzling cars on the grounds that such works are detrimental to American culture.

g. Concurring Opinion of Commissioner Nimmer

I concur in the Commission's opinion and in its recommendations regarding software. I do, however, share in a number of the doubts and concerns expressed in Commissioner Hersey's thoughtful dissenting

146/
opinion. What is most troubling about the Commission's recommendation
of open-ended copyright protection for all computer software is its
failure to articulate any rationale which would not equally justify
copyright protection for the tangible expression of any and all original
ideas (whether or not computer technology, business, or otherwise). If
"literary works" are to be so broadly construed, the Copyright Act becomes
a general misappropriation law, applicable as well in what has traditionally
been regarded as the patent arena, and, indeed, also in other areas to which
neither copyright nor patent law has previously extended. This poses a serious constitutional issue in that it is arguable that such an approach
stretches the meaning of "authors" and "writings" as used in the Copyright
Clause of the Constitution beyond the breaking point. Apart from the constitutional issue, it raises policy questions, the full implications of
which remain murky at best. Still, at this time, knowing what we now know
about the nature of the computer industry, its needs, and its potential for
great contributions to the public welfare, I am prepared, on balance,
to support the Commission's conclusions and recommendations.

At the same time I should like to suggest a possible line of
demarcation which would distinguish between protectible and nonprotectible
software in a manner more consistent with limiting such protection to the
conventional copyright arena. This suggestion is made not because I recommend its immediate implementation, but rather because it may prove useful
in the years to come if the Commission's recommendation for protection of
all software should prove unduly restrictive. In such circumstances it may
prove desirable to limit copyright protection for software to those computer
programs which produce works which themselves qualify for copyright protection. A program designed for use with a data base, for example, would
clearly be copyrightable since the resulting selection and arrangement
of items from such data base would itself be copyrightable as a compilation.
Thus, a program designed for use in conjunction with a legal information

---

146/ See p. 69, infra.

retrieval system would be copyrightable since the resulting enumeration
of cases on a given topic could claim copyright. A program designed
for a computer game would be copyrightable because the output would
itself constitute an audiovisual work. (For this purpose the fact that
such audiovisual work is not fixed in a tangible medium of expression,
and for that reason is ineligible for copyright protection should not
invalidate the copyright in the computer program as long as the program
itself is fixed in a tangible medium of expression.) On the other hand,
programs which control the heating and air-conditioning in a building,
or which determine the flow of fuel in an engine, or which control traffic
signals would not be eligible for copyright because their operations do not
result in copyrightable works. The fact that such a program might also provide for a printout of written instructions (which would be copyrightable)
would only render protectible that particular aspect of such a program.

The distinction here suggested appears to me to be consistent with
the recognized copyrightability of sound recordings. It sometimes has
been argued that while printed instructions tell <u>how</u> to do work, computer
programs actually <u>do</u> the work. But this is also true of sound recordings,
which in a sense constitute a machine (the phonorecord) communicating with
another machine (the record player). A sound recording contained in a phonorecord does not tell a record player <u>how</u> to make sounds which constitute
a Cole Porter melody. Rather, it activates the record player in such manner
as actually to create such a melody. But Commissioner Hersey has made another
and most important distinction. "The direct product of a sound recording,
when it is put in a record player, is the sound of music -- the writing of
the author in its audible form."^{147/} The point is that the operation of the
sound recording produces a musical work which itself is copyrightable. That
is sufficient to render the sound recording itself copyrightable quite apart
from the separate copyright in the musical work. This principle is directly
analogical to the distinction suggested above with respect to computer
programs.

147/ <u>Infra</u>, p. 73.

h. Dissent of Commissioner Hersey

This dissent from the Commission Report on computer programs takes the view that copyright is an inappropriate, as well as unnecessary, way of protecting the usable forms of computer programs.

Its main argument, briefly summarized, is this:

In the early stages of its development, the basic ideas and methods to be contained in a computer program are set down in written forms, and these will presumably be copyrightable with no change in the 1976 Act. But the program itself, in its mature and usable form, is a machine control element, a mechanical device, which on Constitutional grounds and for reasons of social policy ought not to be copyrighted.

The view here is that the investment of creative effort in the devising of computer programs does warrant certain modes of protection for the resulting devices, but that these modes already exist, or are about to be brought into being, under other laws besides copyright; that the need for copyright protection of the machine phase of computer programs, quite apart from whether it is fitting, has not been demonstrated to this Commission; and that the social and economic effects of permitting copyright to stand alongside these other forms of protection would be, on balance, negative.

The heart of the argument lies in what flows from the distinction raised above, between the written and mechanical forms of computer programs: Admitting these devices to copyright would mark the first time copyright had ever covered a means of communication, not with the human mind and senses, but with machines.

ARE MATURE PROGRAMS "WRITINGS"?

Programs are profoundly different from the various forms of "works of authorship" secured under the Constitution by copyright. Works of authorship have always been intended to be circulated to human beings and to be used by them -- to be read, heard, or seen, for either pleasurable or practical ends. Computer programs, in their mature phase, are addressed to machines.

All computer programs go through various stages of development. In the stages of the planning and preparation of software, its creators set down their ideas in written forms, which quite obviously do communicate to human beings and may be protected by copyright with no change in the present law.

But the program itself, in its mature and usable form, is a machine control element, a mechanical device, having no purpose beyond being engaged in a computer to perform mechanical work.

The stages of development of a program usually are: a definition, in eye-legible form, of the program's task or function; a description; a listing of the program's steps and/or their expression in flow charts; the translation of these steps into a "source code," often written in a high-level programming language such as FORTRAN or COBOL; the transformation of this source code within the computer, through intervention of a so-called compiler or assembler program, into an "object code." This last is most often physically embodied, in the present state of technology, in punched cards, magnetic disks, magnetic tape, or silicon chips -- its mechanical phase.

Every program comes to fruition in its mechanical phase. Every program has but one purpose and use -- one object: to control the electrical impulses of a computer in such a particular way as to carry out a prescribed task or operation. In its machine-control form it does not describe or give directions for mechanical work. When activated it does the work.

An argument commonly made in support of the copyrightability of computer programs is that they are just like ordinary printed (and obviously copyrightable) lists of instructions for mechanical work. The Computer Report calls programs (above, p. 23) "a form of writing [which] consists of sets of instructions." But this metaphor does not hold up beyond a certain point. Descriptions and printed instructions tell human beings how to use materials or machinery to produce desired results. In the case of computer programs, the instructions themselves eventually become an essential part

of the machinery that produces the results. They may become (in chip or
hardwire form) a permanent part of the actual machinery; or they may become
interchangeable parts, or tools, insertable and removable from the machine.
In whatever material form, the machine-control phase of the program, when
activated, enters into the computer's mechanical process. This is a device
capable of commanding a series of impulses which open and close the electronic gates of the computer in such order as to produce the desired result.

Printed instructions tell how to do; programs are able to do. The
language used to describe and discuss computer programs commonly expresses
this latter, active, functional capability, not the preparatory "writing"
phases. For example, this Commission's report on New Works (below, p. 84)
uses the following verbs to characterize the doings of various programs
in computers: "select," "arrange," "simulate," "play," "manipulate,"
"extract," "reproduce," and so on. It is not said that the programs
"describe" or "give instructions for" the functions of the computer. They
control them. This is the mechanical fact.

The Issue of Communication

The Commission report on Computer Programs suggests that musical
recordings also do work, analogous to what we have been describing. "Both
recorded music and computer programs are sets of information in a form
which, when passed over a magnetized head, cause minute currents to flow
in such a way that desired physical work gets done." (above, p. 24)

But these are radically different orders of work. And the difference touches on the very essence of copyright.

We take it as a basic principle that copyright should subsist in
any original work of authorship that is fixed in any way (including books,
records, film, piano rolls, video tapes, etc.) which communicate the work's
means of expression.

But a program, once it enters a computer and is activated there,
does not communicate information of its own, intelligible to a human being.
It utters work. Work is its only utterance and its only purpose. So far

as the mode of expression of the original writing is concerned, the matter ends there; it has indeed become irrelevant even before that point. The mature program is purely and simply a mechanical substitute for human labor.

The functions of computer programs are fundamentally and absolutely different in nature from those of sound recordings, motion pictures, or videotapes. Recordings, films, and videotape produce for the human ear and/or eye the sounds and images that were fed into them and so are simply media for transmitting the means of expression of the writings of their authors. The direct product of a sound recording, when it is put in a record player, is the sound of music -- the writing of the author in its audible form. Of film, it is a combination of picture and sound -- the writing of the author in its visible and audible forms. Of videotape, the same. But the direct product of a computer program is a series of electronic impulses which operate a computer; the "writing" of the author is spent in the labor of the machine. The first three communicate with human beings. The computer program communicates, if at all, only with a machine.

And the nature of the machine that plays the sound recording is fundamentally and absolutely different from that of the machine that uses software. The record player has as its sole purpose the performance of the writing of the author in its audible form. The computer may in some instances serve as a storage and transmission medium for writings (but different writings from those of the computer programmer -- i.e., data bases) in their original and entire text, in which cases these writings can be adequately secured at both ends of the transaction by the present copyright law; but in the overwhelming majority of cases its purposes are precisely to use programs to transform, to manipulate, to select, to edit, to search and find, to compile, to control and operate computers and a vast array of other machines and systems -- with a result that the preparatory writings of the computer programmer are nowhere to be found in recognizable form, because the program has been fabricated as a machine control element that does these sorts of work. It is obvious that the means of expression of the preparatory writing -- that which copyright is supposed to protect --

is not to be found in the computer program's mechanical phase.

An appropriate analogy to computer programs, in their capacity to do work when passed over a magnetized head, would be such mechanical devices as the code-magnetized cards which open and close locks or give access to automated bank tellers. These are not copyrightable.

But a more telling analogy, since it speaks to the supposed instructional nature of programs, is afforded by that relatively primitive mechanical device, the cam. A cam, like a mature computer program, is the objectification of a series of instructions: "Up, down, up, down ...," or, "In, out, in, out ...." A cam may be the mechanical fixation of rather intricate and elegant instructions. A cam controlling a drill may embody such instructions as, "Advance rapidly while the hole is shallow, pause and retract for a short distance to clear chips, advance more slowly as the hole goes deeper, stop at a percise point to control the depth of the hole, retract clear of the hole, dwell without motion while the work piece is ejected and another loaded; repeat procedure." (Computer programs can and do embody precisely similar instructions.) But although such a cam was originally conceptualized, described, and written out as this series of instructions for desired work and is, in its mature form, the material embodiment of the instructions, capable of executing them one by one, no one would say (as the Commission now says of another form of "instructions," the mature computer program) that it is a literary work and should be copyrighted.

To support the proposition that programs are works of authorship the Report says (above, p. 23) that "the instructions that make up a program can be read, understood, and followed by a human being," and (above, p. 52) that programs "are capable [emphasis theirs] of communicating with humans ...." Programmers can and sometimes do read each other's copyrightable preparatory writings, the early phases of software, but the implication of these statements is that programs in their machine form also communicate with human "readers" -- an implication that is necessarily hedged by the careful choices of the verbs "could be" and "are capable of"; for if a skilled programmer can "read" a program in its mature, machine-readable form, it is only in the sense that a skilled home-appliance technician can "read" the equally mechanical printed circuits of a television receiver.

It is clear that the machine control phase of a computer program is not designed to be read by anyone; it is designed to do electronic work that substitutes for the very much greater human labor that would be required to get the desired mechanical result. In the revealing words of the Report (above, p. 23) programs "are used in an almost limitless number of ways to release human beings from ... diverse mundane tasks ...."

The Commission Report thus recommends affording copyright protection to a labor-saving mechanical device.

IS COPYRIGHT PROTECTION NEEDED?

We can agree with a memorandum of the Commission's Software Subcommittee that computer programs "are the result of intellectual endeavors involving at least as much human creativity as the preparation of telephone books or tables of compound interest" -- or, we might add (thinking of the mechanical phases of programs), as the design of high-pressure valves for interplanetary rockets or of special parts for racing cars for the Indianapolis 500. The investment in these endeavors, often dazzling in their intricacy and power, does indeed warrant legal protection of the resulting devices.

But is copyright a necessary form of protection? According to the evidence placed before the Commission it is not.

In all the months of its hearings and inquiries, this Commission has not been given a single explicit case of a computer "rip-off" that was not amenable to correction by laws other than copyright. Interestingly, this exactly parallels the experience of the World Intellectual Property Organization (WIPO) in its search for a model form of protection for computer programs. (see above, p. 27-28) Alistair J. Hirst, attending the WIPO discussions as representative of the International Confederation of Societies of Authors and Composers, noted in an article of June, 1978, [148/]

148/ CISAC document no. CJL/78/45.266, p. 2.

> At no stage in the meetings of the Group was any
> convincing case ever made out for the proposition
> that computer software did actually need any
> additional legal protection; the most the repre-
> sentatives of the computer industry could say was
> that they "would like some further form of legal
> protection." No documented instances of piracy
> were adduced; and there was no serious suggestion
> that technological progress in the software field
> had been inhibited by any shortcomings there might
> be in the legal protection presently available.

CONTU has had precisely the same lack of evidence on this score. A book recently published,[149/] describing a large number of computer crimes committed

in this country, cites no single piracy or other misappropriation that would

have fallen under copyright law. A study of 168 computer crimes by the Stanford Research Institute,[150/] made available to the Commission, also failed to

turn up any single such case.

It appears that the existing network of technological, contractual,

non-disclosure, trade-secret, common-law misappropriation, and (in a few in-

stances) patent forms of protection, possibly to be joined soon by Senator

Abraham Ribicoff's Computer System Protection Act[151/] -- to say nothing of laws

on fraud, larceny, breaking and entering, and so on -- will be wholly ade-

quate, as they apparently have been up to now, to the needs of developers.

We will discuss below (p. 84) the ways the various forms of

protection will likely affect the issue of access versus secrecy.

LEGISLATIVE INTENT AND THE CONSTITUTIONAL BARRIER

"It was clearly the Congress' intent," the Report says (above,

p. 38) "to include computer programs within the scope of copyrightable sub-

ject matter in the Act of 1976." This intent was by no means clear. It is

true that in several places in the legislative reports there are passing

references to computer programs which seem to assume their copyrightability

under the 1909 Act and, by extension, the 1976 Act. Prior to these reports,

---

149/ T. Whiteside. Computer Capers: tales of electronic thievery, embezzle-
ment and fraud (1978).

150/ D. Parker. Computer Abuse, Stanford Research Institute, (1973).

151/ S. 1766, 95th Cong., 1st Sess. (1977).

the only authority for considering them potentially copyrightable was the
Register of Copyright's letter of May 19, 1964 -- itself hedged with doubt
whether programs were within the category of "writings of an author" in the
Constitutional sense. (On this, see more below, p. 78). And even these
legislative reports contain cautionary language on computer programs, to
the effect that they would be copyrightable only "to the extent that they
incorporate authorship in the programmer's expression of original ideas,
as distinguished from the ideas themselves."[152/] Section 117 of the new copyright law provided for a moratorium precisely awaiting the conclusions of
this Commission, and it indicates beyond a doubt that Congress has not
reached the point of clear intention at least with respect to the use
of copyrighted works.

The legislative history of the new law can give little comfort
to any who would suggest that a thoughtful legislative judgment had been
made about the propriety of copyright protection for computer programs.
Where the Commission Report finds the legislative history disconcerting,
it simply avers, on its own authority, that the House Report "should be
regarded as incorrect and should not be followed." (note 131, p. 55 above),

Even if the legislative intent were unmistakable, there would remain the distinct possibility of a Constitutional barrier to the copyrighting of computer programs. It is an underlying principle of copyright
law, expressed in Section 102(b) of the 1976 Act, that copyright does not
extend to "any idea, procedure, process, system, method of operation ...
regardless of the form in which it is described, explained ... or embodied
in such work." This section of the statute is intended to recognize the
distinction between works conveying descriptions of processes and works
which are themselves the embodiment of a system or process. In Baker v.
Selden (101 U.S. 99 (1879)), the Supreme Court found that, as a matter of
Constitutional law, the latter are not protected by copyright.

That decision has been consistently applied to deny copyright to
utilitarian works -- not those, like phonorecords, which contain expression

---

152/ House Report, supra note 1, at 54.

made perceptible by the use of a machine, but rather those which exist

solely to assist a machine to perform its mechanical function. Professor

Nimmer, while criticizing some interpretations of the <u>Baker v. Selden</u>

decision, recognized that it properly bars copyright protection for a work

embodying a method of operation when duplicated of necessity in the course

of its use. <u>153/</u> This dissent urges the view (to which Commissioner Nimmer's

Concurrence, (pp. 66-69 above), seems to lend further weight) that

computer programs are exactly the type of work barred from copyright by

these considerations.

DISTORTION BY SHOEHORN

We now come to two technical points that arise in the Commission's

position on computer programs, matters that we stress here at some length

as two examples of the forcible wrenching that is involved in fitting the

mature computer program into copyright law -- and consequent distortions of

traditional copyright usages. It is urged that such distortions, with the

formidable power of the computer industry behind them, must in the long run

tend to corrupt and erode the essential purposes of copyright.

<u>Copies?</u>

In its attempts to justify the copyrighting of mechanical

devices -- the mature phases of computer programs -- the Commission's

Software Subcommittee was obliged, at successive stages, to resort to

certain euphemisms.

The first draft of its report described the usable, mechanical

phases of computer programs as "derivative works" -- a term traditionally

used, with respect to the printed word, for condensations, dramatizations,

translations, and so on (each of which has always had to be copyrighted

separately from the parental work). When the invalidity of this suggestion

became evident, the second draft of the Report characterized the programs

in their usable machine forms, equally with their written forms, as "literary

works." When the difficulty in maintaining that the mechanical commands

---

153/ 1 <u>Nimmer on Copyright</u>, § 37.2 (1976).

on punched cards, magnetic tapes, disks, and printed circuits in chips were
identical with programs' preparatory writings had been considered, the
third draft of the Report brought yet another shift of terms. The mechanical
phases of programs were now described as "copies."

On several grounds this euphemism proves as unserviceable as the
previous ones. (And so, in this view, will every euphemism that attempts
to justify the copyrighting of a machine control element.)

"Copies," for the control of which the rights vested in copyright
were devised, are defined in the 1976 Act as

> material objects, other than phonorecords, in which
> a work is fixed by any method now known or later
> developed, and from which the work can be perceived,
> reproduced, or otherwise communicated, either directly
> or with the aid of a machine or device. 154/

This definition has always referred to one form or another of reproduction
of an original work, for the purpose of dissemination to, and perception by,
human beings. In plain language: books, monographs, films, prints, and
other such replications we all recognize as copies in the true copyright
sense. Their uses always involved perception by one human sense or another
of the linguistic intentions, the images, or the sounds of the original
works. A data base, when keyed or run into a computer, is being copied in
this sense, for the data are maintained in the copy as data, and they issue
as data for human use in the end product. But a program, when keyed or run
into a computer, is transformed by a compiler program into a purely machine
state. The term "copy" is meaningless for the reason that in this transformation the means of expression of the original work becomes totally
irrelevant. All that matters is the program's functional use.

Furthermore, many programs (in fact, a greater and greater proportion of commercial programs) never are "input" into computers in the
conventional sense. They are distributed already transformed into their
purely mechanical form, as printed circuits on chips in microprocessors.
They are, in all but name, hardware. They are no more copies in the copy-

---

154/ 17 U.S.C. § 101.

right sense than are repeatedly stamped-out solid-state circuits of television sets. These programs in microprocessors are built into, or can
be clipped into, automobiles, airplanes, telephone and television sets,
microwave ovens, games, and an ever-growing number of industrial and home
gadgets. How can this vast class of machine control elements ever be considered "copies" of "literary works"?

We are dealing here with an entirely new technology, one with a
highly intricate multiplicity of means of fixation, of transformation, of
movement from one medium (of communication) to another (of mechanical
function) and back again. The fact that some of these many intricate
fixations and changes enable a human-readable version of a program to be
stored in a computer parallel to its mechanical variant, or to be reconverted
to eye-readable form from its mechanical variant, does not mend at all the
basic distortion that arises from this abuse of the term "copies."

In discussing "copies," the Commission Report (pp. 56-57 above)
admits the central difficulty to which this dissent addresses itself:

> [T]he many ways in which programs are now used and the new
> applications which advancing technology will supply may
> make drawing the line of demarcation [between the copy-
> rightable form of a program and the uncopyrightable pro-
> cess which it implements] more and more difficult. To
> attempt to establish such a line in this Report written
> in 1978 would be futile. Most infringements, at least
> in the immediate future, are likely to involve simple
> copying. In the event that future technology permits
> programs to be stated orally for direct input to a
> computer through auditory sensing devices or permits
> future infringers to use an author's program without
> copying, difficult questions will arise.

It is the thesis of this dissent that all such difficulties, present and future, disappear if the euphemism in the word "copies" is recognized for what it is, and if a clear line is drawn forthwith. The line can
and should be drawn in 1978. The line should be drawn at the moment of the
program's transformation, by whatever present or future technique, to a
mechanical capability. This is the moment at which the program ceases to
communicate with human beings and is made capable of communicating with
machines.

Here is dramatized, in our view, the central flaw -- and the subtle dehumanizing danger -- of the Commission's position on programs. To call a machine control element a copy of a literary work flies in the face of common sense. Ask any citizen in the street whether a printed circuit in a microprocessor in the emission control of his or her car is a copy of a literary work, and see what answer you get. But if our government tells the citizens in the street that this is so, and makes it law, what then happens to the citizen's sense of distinction between works that speak to the minds and senses of men and women and works that run machines -- or, ultimately, the citizen's sense of the saving distinction between human beings themselves and machines themselves?

Adaptations

A particularly serious blurring of valid traditional distinctions lies in the Report's extension of copyright protection to adaptations of programs (p. 30 above). There is not merely a question here of unfairness to all other sorts of adaptations, which must be re-copyrighted (as in the case, for example, of a telephone directory, which is annually adapted -- and must be re-copyrighted each year). What is shocking, in its transparency, is the reason given by the Report for authorizing these adaptations -- "to facilitate use." (p. 32 above)

The transparency lies in the fact that the means of expression of the original program -- the only thing in which copyright is reposed -- is here again totally irrelevant. The only test the user is required to meet is whether the machine phase of the program, having been adapted, will then work. And what will make it work is certainly not its means of expression but its mechanical idea, which remains constant however expressed.

In his testimony before CONTU in Cambridge, Mass., on November 17, 1977, Professor J.C.R. Licklider of M.I.T. raised as one of his concerns about the idea of copyrighting the mechanical phases of programs precisely this matter of adaptation.[155] He gave the example in which a protracted program may be taken from "machine language, or FORTRAN, or whatever level ...

155/ See Transcript CONTU Meeting No. 18 at 130-132.

to a higher level and back to a lower level," and stressed that all that sur-
vives from one version to the other is "the essential underlying idea, not
the mode, not the form of expression."

In the present reality of computer usage, particularly in sophisticated operations, a great deal of programming ingenuity goes precisely into
various kinds of adaptation, commonly called "program maintenance": new
mechanical functions may be added to an existing program; a program may be
modified, possibly extensively, to make it workable in a different or more
up-to-date computer; or a program may be changed to mesh with other programs
in a complex multi-processor. Under these and many other circumstances, the
protection would remain in effect for an underlying idea that was itself
being adapted, or perhaps even being transformed into something quite
different from the original idea. The mode of expression of the original
writing would be long, long gone. As Professor Licklider pointed out, only
the "effect of the action of the program" is of consequence in a series of
such changes; programmers, he said, "don't care a thing for the particulars
of the expression."156/

The limitations on adaptations suggested in the Commission Report
will, in the real world of program maintenance, be unthinkably difficult to
police.

By the admission of this word, "adaptation," in this new sense,
with no means test except workability, the Commission has bypassed a fundamental distinction of copyright from other forms of protection, and may
well have opened the way for covert protection, in the name of copyright,
of the underlying mechanical idea or ideas of a program, rather than of its
original means of expression.

SOCIAL EFFECTS

Access

The Commission Report has based much of its case on its conclusion
that copyright would assure greater public access to innovative programs

---

156/ Id. at 131.

than would continued reliance on trade-secrecy law.

The evidence the Commission has received casts considerable doubt on this argument.

In the first place, the testimony CONTU has heard makes it quite clear that the industry would have no intention of giving up trade-secrecy protection in favor of copyright; to the contrary, every indication is that it would fight hard to assert its undeniable continuing right to the former.

It is obvious that the industry, faced with a choice between secrecy and dissemination, as represented in the choice between trade-secrecy laws and copyright, has overwhelmingly opted for the former. From 1964, when the Register first received programs for registration, to January 1, 1977, only 1205 programs have been registered (and two companies, IBM and Burroughs, accounted for 971 of them). According to International Computer Programs, Inc., which publishes a newsletter on the programming industry, something in the order of 1,000,000 programs are developed each year (taking into account adaptations of existing programs so radical as to make them new programs). There are roughly 300,000 programmers in the United States who spend at least part of their time developing new programs. These figures show how miniscule has been the industry's interest in copyright, and they strongly suggest that such registration as has taken place has been in the nature of bet-hedging, reflecting efforts of major hardware manufacturers to assert any possible colorable claim to protection, regardless of its real legal merits.

The Commission Report (p. 44 above) recognizes that "the availability of copyright for computer programs does not, of course, affect the availability of trade secrecy protection." It suggests leaving all future "difficult questions" for settlement by the courts on a case-by-case basis. (p. 57 above)

The uncertainty resulting from this situation, as Robert O. Nimtz of the Bell Laboratories has pointed out in a response to the Commission's Draft Report, "would have the unfortunate consequence of driving computer program owners into even deeper secrecy" -- by encryption, physical barriers to access, contractual restraints, nondisclosure agreements, and further innovative technical tricks for locking out pirates, thieves, and competitors. "Secrecy will be seen as the only effective protection for their crea-tions."[156] Such being the case, public access to innovative programs would likely be inhibited rather than eased by the addition of the copyright solution to those that already exist and that would continue to exist.

Indeed, it is evident that, with eased requirements for deposit and disclosure, copyright itself would be used as one more device to prevent, rather than enable, access to innovative programs -- one more device of industrial security. The entitlement of copyright protection to "adaptations" of programs might, under these circumstances, even further inhibit access, insofar as it provided owners with a covert means of protecting the underlying ideas of their program. And the lengthy term of 75 years for corporate owner-ship of copyright would be a negative balance, at the very least, against the presumed "thinness" of the protection.

Economic Costs

All of this, rather than reducing the transaction costs of using and protecting programs, as the Commission argues, would in fact raise the costs -- for producers, transacting copyright while spending more and more money looking harder than ever for new and surer forms of secrecy; for users, to whom the added costs of this search and its found devices would be passed along in higher prices; and for the tax-paying public, which would have to bear the costs of the added burdens on the Copyright Office and the courts.

A more likely prospect for the reduction of money costs would lie in the exclusion of usable computer programs from copyright. This would elimi-nate or diminish the uncertainty as to legal protection available for computer programs. All questions of the Constitutionality of such protection would become moot; some of the guesswork which would otherwise have colored all business planning for securing software would be voided.

156/   Nimtz Comment, letter to CONTU, August 30, 1977, at 9.

An additional consideration would be the easing of the administrative burden on the Copyright Office. The Office, already monstrously overloaded by administration and regulation of the new law, is presently unsuited for making evaluations of computer programs which might be registered for copyright. Eliminating this responsibility would save a public expenditure and place the costs of commercial protection on those enterprises seeking its benefits.

Concentration of Economic Power

While it has always been the case that corporate entities could be copyright proprietors, the picture CONTU has been given, when rights in computer programs are concerned, is that the proprietor is almost invariably corporate. If there is an individual "author," it will be an author for hire, whose creativity is in strict harness and whose property rights are nonexistent.

The sheer bigness of the corporate enterprise in computers is staggering. According to testimony by Peter McCloskey, President of Computer and Business Equipment Manufacturers' Association (CBEMA), the combined revenues of the 42 members of that association of manufacturers of computers and related business equipment rose in 1976 to 32.7 billion dollars; as to software, we heard at one point an estimate of 17 billion dollars of production in the next three years.[158] The art is growing and changing with blinding speed. In his testimony Ralph Gommery of IBM suggested, with perhaps a pinch of hyperbole, that if the automobile industry had progressed on the same curve as computers in the last 15 years, we would now have been able to buy for $20 a self-steering car that would attain speeds up to 400 m.p.h. and be able to drive the length of California on one gallon of gasoline.

In a study funded by this Commission, Harbridge House concluded that the availability of copyright protection for computer software is "of monumental insignificance to the industry."[159] It is important for us to

---

158/ Transcript CONTU Meeting No. 6 at 11.

159/ Legal Protection of Computer Software: An Industrial Survey, Harbridge House (1977) iii.

bear in mind that the universe of this study consisted almost entirely of smallish, independent corporate producers. The two trade associations that were most active in pressing their views on this Commission, the above-mentioned CBEMA and the Information Industry Association, represent primarily major industrial corporations. The Association of Data Processing Service Organizations, which more than any other trade association represents independent computer program producers, was conspicuously absent from Commission appearances and limited its participation to a written response in support of the Software Subcommittee's recommendations. Such perfunctory participation certainly tends to support the Harbridge House view as to the interest of the independents.

On this point, the WIPO experience strikingly parallels CONTU's. Alastair J. Hirst writes that a one-sided approach in the WIPO search

> was more or less inevitable, given the composition of the Group. It is important to distinguish between the names shown on the list of participating organizations, and the individuals who were most active in directing and moulding the discussion as it proceeded. Of the latter, the most frequent and the best informed grouping was that composed of patent agents and lawyers in the employ of the large computer companies such as ICL and IBM. Even amongst those representing the computer industry, there was a singular lack of representation from the smaller independent software houses, who were intended to be the chief beneficiaries of the new software right: those who had the most influence on the discussions were in fact the representatives of the large companies who are in many ways the economic adversaries of these intended beneficiaries. 160/

Congress is urged to take careful note of this difference. Why do the large industrial corporations press for copyright, while it seems to be a matter of much less concern to the small independents? Is it not evident, from the testimony CONTU received, that the big companies want, by availing themselves of every possible form of protection, to lock their software into their own hardware, while the independents want to be able to sell their programs for use in all the major lines of hardware?

Thus a warning appears to be in order that the copyrighting of the machine phases of programs would be likely to strengthen the position

---

160/   Supra, note 148.

of the large firms, to reinforce the oligopoly of these dominant companies, and to inhibit competition from and among small independents.

The country has lately seen an alarming trend toward the concentration of economic power in all the communications industries. One company dominates telephonic communication. One company (IBM) dominates the computer hardware field, while three others (Burroughs, Honeywell and Sperry-Univac) join with IBM to manufacture over 85% of large-scale computers. One company (Xerox) dominates photocopying, and again three other companies (IBM, Kodak and 3M) outstrip all others. Three networks dominate television. There are now but six major film distributors. Paperback publishing has become the backbone of the book industry, and there are now but seven leading paperback lines. Industrial conglomerates are buying up these communications leaders horizontally: e.g., Gulf and Western owns both Paramount Pictures and Simon and Schuster, which in turn owns Pocket Books.

If there are social benefits to our nation, as we have always believed, in pluralism, in diversity, in lively competition in the market-place, and in the rights of the individual to maximum freedom of choice within the limits of the social contract, and above all to maximum freedom of speech, then this increasing concentration of corporate power in that most sensitive area in a democracy -- the area of communication from one human being to another, from leaders to citizens and vice versa -- should surely be a matter of greatest concern.

COMMUNICATION -- HUMAN AND MECHANICAL

The aim of all writing, be it for art or use, is communication. Up to this time, as we have seen, copyright has always protected the means of expression of various forms of "writing" which were perceived, in every case, by the human sense for which they were intended: written words by the human eye, music by the ear, paintings by the eye, and so on. Here, for the first time, the protection of copyright would be offered to a "communication" with a machine.

This pollution of copyrighted "writings" with units of mechanical work would affect not only creators but also the general public. Placed beside such traditional end products as books, plays, motion pictures, television shows, dance, and music, under the aegis of copyright, what end products of computer programs would we find?

The overwhelming majority of program applications are mechanical and industrial: the monitoring of an assembly line in a factory; micro-processors in an automobile; the aiming device of a weapons system; the coordination of approach patterns at an airport. An entire branch of the program industry is devoted to systems software -- new techniques for more efficient uses of machines, for more efficient industrial processing.

Progress is progress, and we can guess that we must have all these products of human ingenuity to keep one jump ahead of entropy. It can rea-sonably be argued, as the Commission Report does, that they reduce the load of human labor. But a definite danger to the quality of life must come with a blurring and merging of human and mechanical communication.

As one step in its education, this Commission has had the benefit of a book written by one of our witnesses, Professor Joseph Weizenbaum of M.I.T., entitled Computer Power and Human Reason -- a work which is both intricately technical and profoundly humanistic. Something that Professor Weizenbaum keeps emphasizing over and over again is the extent to which computer scientists, especially those who have worked on so-called artificial intelligence -- "and large segments of the general public as well" -- have come to accept the propositions "that men and computers are merely two different species or a more abstract genus called 'information processing systems,'" that reason is nothing more than logic, and "that life is what is computable and only that." (pp. 158, 240).

A society that accepts in any degree such equivalences of human beings and machines must become impoverished in the long run in those aspects of the human spirit which can never be fully quantified, and which machines may be able in some distant future to linguistically "understand" but will never be able to experience, never be able to bring to life, never be able therefore to communicate: courage, love, integrity, trust, the touch of flesh, the fire of intuition, the yearning and aspirations of what poets so vaguely but so persistently call the soul -- that bundle of qualities we think of as being embraced by the word humanity.

This concern is by no means irrelevant to the issue of whether computer programs should be copyrighted. It is the heart of the matter.

RECOMMENDATION

The logical conclusion of this dissent, then, is a recommendation to Congress that

> The Act of 1976 should be amended to make it explicit that copyright protection does not extend to a computer program in the form in which it is capable of being used to control computer operations.

Congress could obtain any technical advice necessary to assist it in reaching an appropriate definition of the cutoff point, the point at which a program ceases being a copyrightable writing and becomes an uncopyrightable mechanical device.

In our discussions, several possibilities have presented themselves: (1) the moment of transformation from "source" to "object" program; (2) the moment of input into a computer or micro-processor; or (3) at the point where a program goes from "natural language," which any expert reader can at once grasp, to higher-level, formal computer language -- this last deriving from Professor Weizenbaum, who writes "A higher-level formal language is an abstract machine." (Op. cit., p. 103). With rapidly advancing technology, natural language does in some programs already reach to the very moment of entry into the computer. In every case, however, Professor Weizenbaum makes clear, a transformation to a machine state takes place, with a result that when the program is run, communication as we understand it ceases and what he calls "behavior" -- an opening and closing of electronic gates -- sets in. Where his book is most eloquent, for our purposes, is in its powerful warning of our loss of humanity if we come to believe, as many already do, that anything like human communication is still taking place, or ever can take place, after this mechanical stage has set in.

Congress should weigh most carefully the heavy responsibility of breaking with tradition and enabling, by law of the land, for the first

time ever, copyright protection for communication, not with our fellow human
beings, but with machines -- thus equating machines with human beings
as the intended recipients of the distribution that copyright was designed
to foster.

Surely it is especially vital, in a time of hurtling and insa-
tiable technology, that the nation's laws reflect, whenever possible,
a distinction between the realm and responsibility of human beings
and the realm and responsibility attributed to machines.

i.   Dissent of Commissioner Karpatkin

Throughout the Commission's deliberations on computer software,
Commissioner Hersey has advocated the point of view expressed in his dissent.
While a majority of the Commission has not been persuaded, Commissioner
Nimmer shares a number of Mr. Hersey's doubts and concerns and the
late Commissioner Dix, who passed away before the Commission's Final
Report, indicated that he shared them as well.

The Commission has respectfully considered and discussed
Commissioner Hersey's views. In the course of the many discussions, I
have been persuaded that Commissioner Hersey has raised important issues
and that they merit serious consideration. Whether that consideration
tilts in the direction of a dissent or concurrence is less important
than the fact that the issues raised are serious.

Without agreeing with the entire text of Commissioner Hersey's
dissent I share his doubts and concerns sufficiently to lead me to add my
dissent to his.

2.   Computer Data Bases

a.   Background

The automated data base represents a new technological form of a
type of work long recognized as eligible for copyright. Dictionaries,
encyclopedias, and tables of numeric information are all forms of data bases
which long antedate the computer, and for which copyright protection has been,

and will continue to be, available under the copyright law. Under the new
law a data base is a compilation and thus a proper subject for copyright. [161]
This entitlement to copyright is not diminished by the fixation of the data
base in a medium requiring the intervention of a computer to communicate
its information content. [162] Accordingly, a data base, whether printed in
traditional hard copy or fixed in an electromagnetic medium, is protected
by copyright under the terms of the new law. [163]

Computer-readable data bases do differ, of course, from their
hardcopy counterparts. Some of these differences raise copyright issues
and related policy considerations. [164] Copyright applied to data bases should
encourage the development and dissemination of useful stores of information
to make this information readily available to the public. In addition
data base proprietors should be encouraged to publish and register their
copyrighted works, thereby creating a public record of the existence of

---

161/ 17 U.S.C. § 101 defines "compilation" as

> [a] work formed by the collection and assembling of
> preexisting materials or of data that are selected,
> coordinated, or arranged in such a way that the resulting
> work as a whole constitutes an original work of author-
> ship. The term "compilation" includes collective works.

162/ 17 U.S.C. § 102(a) provides that

> Copyright protection subsists, in accordance with
> this title, in original works of authorship fixed in
> any tangible medium of expression, now known or later
> developed, from which they can be perceived, reproduced,
> or otherwise communicated, either directly or with the
> aid of a machine or device. [emphasis added].

163/ The following language makes clear the congressional intent to include
computer-readable data bases within copyright by explaining that:

> The term "literary works" does not connote any criterion
> of literary merit or qualitative value: it includes
> catalogs, directories, and similar factual references,
> or instructional works and compilations of data. It
> also includes computer data bases.... House Report,
> supra note 1 at 54.

164/ Maximization of public access to information contained in automated data
bases is cited as a significant goal of a national information policy in the
Report to the President of the United States on National Information Policy,
70 (1976), prepared by the Domestic Council Committee on the Right of Privacy,
under the chairmanship of then Vice President Nelson Rockefeller.

the works and, in turn, make possible public awareness and utilization
of their works.$^{165/}$

b. Recommendations

Section 117 of the Copyright Act of 1976 should be repealed.

The New Copyright Act, in the absence of the limited moratorium
imposed by Section 117, deals effectively with questions related to copyright protection for automated data bases. For example, under the provisions
of Section 106 the copying or input of a data base or any other work of authorship embodied in a computer-readable medium is an exclusive right of the copyright owner. Other questions as to the scope of protection to be afforded
such works by copyright can and should be repealed upon completion of the
Commission's work as was apparently the legislative intent.$^{166/}$

The Register of Copyrights should adopt appropriate registration
and deposit regulations.

Regulations for registration and deposit of data bases and other
works first fixed in computer-readable media should permit and encourage
registration and periodic updating of identifying material rather than
actual data bases.   There appears no reason to tailor any notice
requirements specifically to computer-readable works; general principles
contained in the new law seem adequate without being particularly burdensome. Notice appearing on the initial display of any extract or extracts
obtained from the data base pursuant to a search should comply with the
intent of the statutory notice requirement. A copyright notice can easily
be included on the initial display extracted from a data base, and a human-
readable notice can also appear on the packaging.

c. The Case for Copyright Protection for Data Bases

The following discussion explains the Commission's agreement with

---

165/ Registration and deposit regulations have been adopted by the Copyright
Office, see 37 C.F.R. § 202 in Appendix J, pp. 17-22.

166/ House Report, supra note 1 at 116.

the legislative intent of the new copyright law to grant copyright protection
to computer data bases equivalent to the protection accorded compilations
in traditional hard-copy format. The problem areas identified and discussed
are: (1) What copyright consequences attach to the "input" into a computer
of a copyrighted work (perhaps better described as the fixation of a work
in a medium capable of use within a computer system)? (2) What rights does
the proprietor of copyright in a data base have with regard to the use of
extracts provided in response to authorized searches or inquiries made of
the data base? and (3) What constitutes publication of a data base, and
what legal consequences attach to publication? ^{167/}

The Input Issue

The issue whether copyright liability should attach at the input
or output stage of use in conjunction with a computer, that is to say,
at the time a work is placed in machine-readable form in a computer
memory unit or when access is sought to the work existing in computer
memory, has been the primary source of disagreement regarding copyright
protection for works in computer-readable form. This issue provided the
major impetus for the introduction of Section 117 into the copyright
revision bill.^{168/} It appears, nevertheless, that the provisions of the

---

167/ It should be clear that the same principles which apply to data bases
apply also to any copyrightable works embodied in a format for reproduction
and use within a computer. See pp. 104-08, infra.

168/ 17 U.S.C. § 117 provides as follows:

> Notwithstanding the provisions of sections 106 through 116 and 118,
> this title does not afford to the owner of copyright in a work any
> greater or lesser rights with respect to the use of the work in
> conjunction with automatic systems capable of storing, processing,
> retrieving, or transferring information, or in conjunction with any
> similar device, machine, or process, than those afforded to works
> under the law, whether title 17 or the common law or statutes of a
> State, in effect on December 31, 1977, as held applicable and con-
> strued by a court in an action brought under this title.

This section was first introduced in the copyright revision bill in 1969, see
S. 543, 91st Cong., 1st Sess. [Committee Print], (December 10, 1969), at which
time the impact of the computer, and particularly the "input-output" question,
was causing great concern on the part of copyright proprietors. Section 117
was agreed upon by interested parties as a means of permitting passage of the
revision bill without committing the Congress to a position on the computer-
related issue until more study could be undertaken.

new copyright law offer appropriate and sufficient guidance to determine
what acts create copyright liability in this area. The protection afforded
by Section 106 of the new law seemingly would prohibit the unauthorized
storage of a work within a computer memory, which would be merely one form
of reproduction, one of the exclusive rights granted by copyright.[169/]

     Considering the act of storing a computerized data base in the
memory of a computer, as an exclusive right of the copyright proprietor,
appears consistent both with accepted copyright principles and with considerations of fair treatment for potentially affected parties. Making a
copy of an entire work would normally, subject to some possible exception
for fair use, be considered exclusively within the domain of the copyright
proprietor. One would have to assume, however, that fair use would
apply rarely to the reproduction in their entirety of compendious works,
such as data bases.[170/] If a copy of the work is to be stored in a computer
and subsequently made accessible to others, its creation would have
to be properly authorized by the copyright proprietor. That only one
copy is being made, or even that the owner of the computer system intends
to exact no fee for providing access to the work, would no more insulate
the copies from liability for copyright infringement than would similar
circumstances insulate a public library which made unauthorized duplications
of entire copyrighted works for its basic lending functions.[171/]

     Under normal circumstances, the transfer by sale or lease of a
copyrighted work in computer-readable form, such as a data base, would be a
meaningless transaction unless implicit in the transfer was the authorization

---

169/ It may be that the use of the term "input" to describe the act to
which copyright liability attaches has been misleading. A more accurate
description of the process by which a work may be stored in a computer
memory would indicate that a reproduction is created within the computer
memory in order to make the work accessible by means of the computer.

170/ See 17 U.S.C. § 107 for statutory criteria governing "fair use."

171/ The example of a copyrighted work placed in a computer memory solely to
facilitate an individual's scholarly research has been cited as a possible
fair use. The Commission agrees that such a use, restricted to individual
research, should be considered fair. In order to prevent abuse of fair use
principles, any copy created in a machine memory should be erased after
completion of the particular research project for which it was made.

to place or reproduce a copy in the memory unit of the transferee's computer. Any limitations on the use to be made of the copy would be a matter to be negotiated between private parties, guided by applicable public policy considerations. 172/ The proprietor of a work in computer-readable form would, under any foreseeable circumstances, be able to control by contract the future disposition of machine-readable copies of his proprietary work. The proprietor of copyright in such a work would always have a valid cause of action, arising either under copyright or contract, if a reproduction of the work were entered into a computer without the proprietor's authorization, or if a transferee authorized a third party to enter a copy into the memory unit of a computer in violation of the terms of a valid agreement with the proprietor. That copyright would not provide the sole right and remedy for unauthorized use of a protected work is neither unique to the protection of proprietary interests in computer-readable works, nor is it a situation to be considered undesirable. 173/

Accordingly, the Commission believes that the application of principles already embodied in the language of the new copyright law achieves the desired substantive legal protection for copyrighted works which exist in machine-readable form. The introduction of a work into a computer memory would, consistent with the new law, be a reproduction of the work, one of the exclusive rights of the copyright proprietor. The

---

172/ Outright sale by a copyright proprietor of a copy of a protected work, rather than a lease under which the proprietor retains ownership of a copy which the lessee may use in accord with negotiated terms and conditions, normally results in a complete loss of control over the copy which has been sold. This reflects the unwillingness of courts to enforce restrictions on the alienation of property once a complete transfer of ownership interest in any item of property has been accomplished.

173/ Remedies for breach of contract, if the right being protected is not equivalent to copyright, would not be preempted under the provisions of Section 301 of the new law, and would accordingly be available to one who, on the strength of a copyright interest, granted permission to another to make certain uses of the copyrighted work only to have the terms of the authorization violated. There continues to be some scope for state enforcement of proprietary rights in intellectual property under the new copyright law. See House Report, supra note 1, at 130-33. That state law rather than federal, would be involved presents few real problems. The existence of parallel, but not equal, rights under state and federal law reflects advantages as well as disadvantages inherent in a federal polity, and generally both claims could be joined in the same federal cause of action under principles of pendent jurisdiction.

unauthorized transfer of an existing machine-readable embodiment of a
work could subject the violators to remedies for breach of contract. Principles of fair use would be applicable in limited instances to excuse an
unauthorized input of a work into computer memory. Exemplifying such fair
uses could be the creation of a copy in a computer memory in order to prepare a concordance of a work, or to perform a syntactical analysis of a
work, which but for the use of a computer would require a prohibitive
amount of human time and effort. To satisfy the criteria of fair use,
any copies created for such research purposes should be destroyed upon
completion of the research project for which they were created. Should
the individual or institution carrying on this research desire to retain
the copy for archival purposes or future use, it should be required to
obtain permission to do so from the copyright proprietor.

Scope Of Copyright In a Data Base

A computer-readable data base derives its value in large part from
the ease with which a user may retrieve from it data conforming to certain
specifications. That ease is the product of several factors -- the organization of the data, the sophistication of the program which assists in the
searching and retrieving, and the skill of the searcher in articulating the
search criteria. The difference between a data base in hard copy and one
in computer-readable form is that the use of the former is passive and the
latter may be used interactively, 174/ in the language of the industry.
Thus a student who searches the Reader's Guide to Periodical Literature
(a copyrighted data base) must not only know what is sought but must also
painstakingly read much unsought material in numerous volumes and updates to obtain the desired information. If, however, an interactive
bibliographic data base is used, only the topic(s) of interest need be
expressed in order to receive citations to apparently pertinent literature
and, frequently, abstracts of that literature to allow further evaluation
of its utility. One important question for the Commission's purposes
concerns what rights the proprietor of a computer-readable data base has

in the information obtained pursuant to a user's request to, or search of, such a data base.

There is little doubt that one who obtained access to a copyrighted data base by normal commercial methods -- paying the proprietor or the proprietor's authorized agent for the right to search the data base and retrieve from it information or data responsive to the search request -- would infringe an existing copyright by retrieving the entire data base and marketing an exact duplicate in competition with the copyright proprietor. Such activity would beyond question be unauthorized copying in violation of a valid copyright. Purchasing access to information contained in a data base no more entitles one to make and employ copies for commercial purposes than would purchasing a copy of a copyrighted directory entitle one to produce and disseminate copies of the directory.

Two complications arise in attempting to define the scope of protection in a computerized data base. First, such works are not static; rather, they are constantly being updated by the addition of current data and the deletion of that determined obsolete. Second, the question as to what rights a copyright proprietor has in extracts of information retrieved pursuant to an authorized search of the data base must be addressed. Provisions applicable to both issues are found in the text and legislative reports of the new law.

The dynamic process by which a data base changes need not affect the entitlement of the data base to copyright protection. This process raises two concerns: (1) that deposit of a new embodiment of the data base to reflect every modification of the data contained in it would be both extremely expensive for the proprietor and cumbersome for the Library of Congress; and (2) that a proprietor, by virtue of the constant updating of the data base, could claim copyright in the work in perpetuity, in disregard of the "limited times" provision of the Constitution and the statutory term of 75 years applicable to data bases under the new

---

174/ An "interactive" data base is one with which a user, aided by a computer can "converse," i.e., the user frames questions to which the data base, controlled by a computer, provides responses.

statute.   Neither of these concerns need cause serious problems.

The deposit requirement should prove no bar to providing effective copyright protection for dynamic data bases.   Deposit is not a precondition to copyright under the new law.   Sections 407(c) and 408(c) of the new copyright law authorize the Register of Copyrights to exempt categories of material from the deposit requirements by regulation, or to require alternative forms of deposit.   Computer data bases seem well-suited for this exemption, for the deposit of an identifying form would achieve the statutory purpose of "providing a satisfactory archival record of a work without imposing practical or financial hardships on the depositor...."   Nor [175/] would a dynamic data base necessarily obtain protection for a longer period than constitutionally or legislatively authorized, any more than would a telephone directory be given perpetual protection by virtue of its being updated annually.   The proprietor of a data base would have to register for copyright each update of the work, just as the proprietor of a telephone directory obtains copyright in new editions of a work.

Similar also to a telephone directory, copyright in a dynamic data base protects no individual datum, but only the systematized form in which the data is presented.   The use of one item retrieved from such a work -- be it an address, a chemical formula, or a citation to an article -- would not under reasonable circumstances merit the attention of the copyright proprietor.   Nor would it conceivably constitute infringement of copyright. The retrieval and reduplication of any substantial portion of a data base, whether or not the individual data are in the public domain, would likely constitute a duplication of the copyrighted element of a data base and would be an infringement.   In any event, the issue of how much is enough to constitute a copyright violation would likely entail analysis on a case-by-case basis with considerations of fair use bearing on whether the unauthorized copying of a limited portion of a data base would be held noninfringing.   Fair use should have very limited force when an unauthorized copy of a data base is made for primarily commercial use.   Only if

---

175/   17 U.S.C. § 407(c).

information of a substantial amount were extracted and duplicated for re-distribution would serious problems exist, raising concerns about the enforcement of proprietary rights.

It appears that adequate legal protection for proprietary rights in extracts from data bases exists under traditional copyright principles as expressed in the new law, supplemented by still-available relief under common law principles of unfair competition. The unauthorized taking of substantial segments of a copyrighted data base should be considered infringing, consistent with the case law developed from infringement of copyright in various forms of directories.[176] In addition, common law principles of misappropriation which, according to the legislative reports accompanying the new law, are not preempted with regard to computer data bases,[177] are available to enforce proprietary rights in these works.

Publication

"Publication" is defined in Section 101 of the new law as:

> the distribution of copies or phonorecords
> of a work to the public by sale or other
> transfer of ownership, or by rental, lease,
> or lending. The offering to distribute
> copies or phonorecords to a group of persons
> for purposes of further distribution, public
> performance, or public display, constitutes
> publication. A public performance or dis-
> play of a work does not of itself constitute
> publication.

According to Sections 401 and 407 of the new law, after publication the copyright owner is required to place copyright notice upon all publicly distributed copies of a work, and to deposit two copies of the work for the Library of Congress. If a proprietor wishes also to register the work in accordance with Section 408, the deposit required by Section 407 must be

---

176/ See, e.g., Leon v. Pacific Tel. & Tel. Co., 91 F.2d 484 (9th Cir. 1937); Jeweler's Circular Pub. Co. v. Keystone Pub. Co., 281 F. 83 (2d Cir. 1922), cert. denied, 259 U.S. 581 (1922), aff'g 274 F. 932 (S.D.N.Y. 1921); New York Times Co. v. Roxbury Data Interface, Inc., 434 F.Supp. 217, 194 U.S.P.Q. 371 (D.N.J. 1977).

177/ House Report, supra note 1, at 132, discussing the preemption provisions of Section 301.

accompanied by the prescribed registration application and fee. Although

the failure to deposit copies will not result in forfeiture of copyright,

the failure to place notice on published copies may. 178/   Accordingly, it

is of considerable importance to know what acts constitute publication

of any copyrighted work. Computerized data bases are no exception.

The definition cited above, and further discussed in the legis-

lative reports accompanying the new law, provides a reasonably clear bench-

mark for determining when a data base used in conjunction with an automated

storage and retrieval system, a computer, is published for the purposes of

the copyright law. The House Committee Report thoroughly discusses the

concept of publication in the context of considering the duration of copy-

right under the new law. It states that,

> Under the definition in section 101, a
> work is "published" if one or more copies
> or phonorecords embodying it are distributed
> to the public -- that is, generally to persons
> under no explicit or implicit restrictions
> with respect to disclosure of its contents --
> without regard to the manner in which the
> copies or phonorecords changed hands. The
> definition ... makes plain that any form
> of dissemination in which a material object
> does not change hands -- performance or
> displays on television, for example -- is
> not a publication no matter how many people
> are exposed to the work. On the other hand,
> the definition also makes clear that, when
> copies or phonorecords are offered to a
> group of wholesalers, broadcasters, motion
> picture theaters, etc., publication takes
> place if the purpose is "further distribution,
> public performance, or public display." 179/

178/   Under the new law, the most significant effect of the act of publication is the requirement that copyright notice be affixed to all copies
of the work distributed thereafter. Omission of notice may result, in
accord with the provisions contained in Section 405, in the forfeiture
of copyright. Section 405 of the Act of 1976 provides that omission
of notice will not invalidate copyright if notice is omitted from a relatively small number of publicly distributed copies, if the work is registered within 5 years of publication and reasonable efforts are made to
add notice to publicly distributed copies, or if omission of notice
violates terms set by the proprietor for authorizing public distribution
of copies of the work. Section 406 deals with errors in contents of
the notice with like flexibility. The failure to include notice may,
at least temporarily, deny the proprietor his full rights in a copyrighted
work, i.e., to prevent and collect damages for unauthorized copying.

179/   House Report, supra note 1, at 138, and Senate Report, supra
note 1, at 121.

Accordingly, a data base proprietor, by display alone, could make the data base available to users, without having published the data base. The same would be true where the proprietor leased a tape containing the data base directly to a user and placed that user under explicit restrictions prohibiting disclosure or transfer. Under these circumstances, the failure to place copyright notice on the data base, or to register with the Copyright Office, would jeopardize no rights the proprietor might have. If, however, the proprietor authorized transferees to distribute copies or make available displays of the data base, publication would be accomplished and the notice and registration requirements of the law would take effect. Many data bases are marketed in exactly this way, with the proprietor authorizing the broker to distribute or display extracts from the data base.

Certain consequences flow from the publication of any work. Publication of a work activates the requirement of deposit under Section 407, and a proprietor might choose not to publish and, thereby, avoid the need to affix notice to all copies and deposit two copies for the Library of Congress. The doctrine of fair use may be applied more narrowly to unpublished than to published works. The Senate Report accompanying the new law indicates that "[t]he applicability of the fair use doctrine to unpublished works is narrowly limited since, although the work is unavailable, this is the result of a deliberate choice on the part of the copyright owner." [180/] Accordingly, the proprietor of a work may have somewhat greater rights in unpublished as opposed to published works.

Certain remedies for infringements may be made available to one who publishes and registers a work which would be denied to the proprietor of an unpublished, unregistered work under the provisions of Section 412 of the Act of 1976. One who successfully prosecutes a copyright infringement action may be entitled, under Section 504 of the new law, to an award of statutory damages in spite of an inability to prove actual damages.

180/   Senate Report, supra note 1, at 64.

The proprietor may also be entitled to an award of attorney's fees under the provisions of Section 505. Section 412 provides that the proprietor of copyright in a work neither published nor registered at the time of the infringement is not entitled to these remedies; the proprietor of a published work, however, may register the work within three months after publication without forfeiting these remedies for infringing acts occurring after publication. While the key factor in determining the availability of these remedies is registration, there exists the three-month grace period after publication for registering copyright, during which period the lack of registration will not preclude availability of statutory damages and attorney's fees for infringements then occurring. No such grace period exists for registering works which are unpublished. Consistent with this thrust of the new law, proprietors of data bases are encouraged to publish and register their works and create a public record of the information available through their proprietary works.

3. New Works

The Commission was specifically assigned the responsibility to study and compile data on the creation of new works by the application or intervention of computers, and to recommend any changes in copyright law or procedure necessary to preserve public access to such works and to recognize the rights of copyright owners.[181] This matter appears to have been included within the Commission's mandate because of questions raised in the mid-sixties during early debates and hearings leading to the new law. For instance, in the 1965 Report of the Register of Copyrights it was stated:

> The crucial question appears to be whether the "work" is basic-ally one of human authorship, with the computer merely being an assisting instrument, or whether the traditional element of authorship in the work (literary, artistic or musical expression or elements of selection, arrangements etc.) were actually conceived and executed not by man but by a machine. [182]

181/ Pub. L. No. 93-573 (1974).

182/ Copyright Office, Sixty-Eighth Annual Report of the Register of Copyrights 5 (1965).

This discussion may have stemmed from a concern that computers either had or were likely to soon achieve powers that would enable them independently to create works that, although similar to other copyrightable works, would not or should not be copyrightable because they had no human author. The development of this capacity for "artificial intelligence" has not yet come to pass and, indeed, it has been suggested to this Commission that such a development is too speculative to consider at this time. [183/] On the basis of its investigations and society's experience with the computer, the Commission believes that there is no reasonable basis for considering that a computer in any way contributes authorship to a work produced through its use. The computer, like a camera or a typewriter, is an inert instrument, capable of functioning only when activated either directly or indirectly by a human. When so activated it is capable of doing only what it is directed to do in the way it is directed to do it.

Computers may be employed in a variety of ways in creating works that may be protected by copyright. Works of graphic art may consist of designs, lines, intensities of color and the like selected and organized with the assistance of a computer. [184/] A computer may be used to assist an artist in filling in numerous frames in an animation sequence, thus reducing the amount of time and effort otherwise needed to prepare an animated work. [185/]

In the case of computer music, a program may be designed to select a series of notes and arrange them into a musical composition, employing various tonal qualities and rhythmic patterns. The computer may also be used to simulate musical instruments and perform the music so composed. [186/]

183/ Letter to the Commission, February 1978, from John McCarthy, Director, Stanford University Artificial Intelligence Laboratory.

184/ Computer graphics and other pictorial art forms have also drawn much attention. See, e.g., H. Franke, Computer Graphics - Computer Art (1971); D. Davis, "The Artist and the Computer," 78 Newsweek (Sept. 13, 1971). Recently appearing in The New York Times was an article describing the possible future impact of computer and related technology on the creation and dissemination of works, such as musical compositions, dance and the dramatic arts, that are potentially protectible by copyright. A. Greene, "The Coming Impact of Technology on the Arts -- Computer Violins and the Electronic Palette" The New York Times, Feb. 26, 1978.

185/ For examples of such applications, see Transcript, CONTU Meeting No. 18 at 2-10.

In other instances, a computer may be used to manipulate statistical information to produce an analysis of that information. The resulting work may bear little similarity to the original form or arrangement of the work being analyzed, as in the case of an economic forecast produced by the manipulation of raw economic data. A computer may, on the other hand, be employed to extract and reproduce portions of a work.[187/] In every case, the work produced will result from the contents of the data base, the instructions indirectly provided in the program, and the direct discretionary intervention of a human involved in the process.

To be entitled to copyright a work must be an original work of authorship. It must be a writing within the meaning of that term as used in the Copyright Clause of the Constitution.[188/]   The Supreme Court has interpreted this requirement to include "any physical rendering of the fruits of creative intellectual or aesthetic labor."[189/] The history of the development of the concept of originality shows that only a modicum of effort is required. In Alfred Bell & Co. Ltd. v. Catalda Fine Arts, Inc. a federal Court of Appeals, speaking through Judge Frank observed:

> All that is needed to satisfy both the Constitution
> and the statute is that the "author" contributed
> something more than a "merely trivial" variation,
> something recognizably "his own" .... No matter
> how poor artistically the "author's" addition,
> it is enough if it be his own. 190/

Thus it can be seen that although the quantum of originality needed to support a claim of authorship in a work is small, it must

---

186/   See, e.g., the following works on computer music: H. Howe, Jr., Electronic Music Synthesis (1975); M. Mathews, The Technology of Computer Music (1969); L. Hiller, Jr. and L. Isaacson, Experimental Music (1959). See also, D. Keziah, "Copyright Registration for Aleatory And Indeterminate Musical Compositions," 17 Bull. Cop. Soc. 311 (1970).

187/   For a discussion of the copyright status of directories produced by computer use, see: M. Oberman. "Copyright Protection for Computer Produced Directories," 22 ASCAP Copyright L. Symp. 1 (1977).

188/   U.S. Const., Article I, § 8, cl. 8.

189/   Goldstein v. California, 412 U. S. 546, 561 (1973).

190/   191 F. 2d 99, 102-03 (2d Cir. 1951); but cf. Batlin v. Snyder, 536 F.2d 486 (2d Cir. 1976).

nevertheless be present. $\underline{191/}$ If a work created through application of computer technology meets this minimal test of originality, it is copyrightable. The eligibility of any work for protection by copyright depends not upon the device or devices used in its creation, but rather upon the presence of at least minimal human creative effort at the time the work is produced.

Computers are enormously complex and powerful instruments which vastly extend human powers to calculate, select, rearrange, display, design and do other things involved in the creation of works. However, it is a human power they extend. The computer may be analogized to or equated with, for example, a camera, and the computer affects the copyright status of a resultant work no more than the employment of a still or motion-picture camera, a tape-recorder or a typewriter. Hence, it seems clear that the copyright problems with respect to the authorship of new works produced with the assistance of a computer are not unlike those posed by the creation of more traditional works.

Needless to say, computers, like typewriters and other instruments, can be used to produce writings that lack the degree of originality held necessary to copyright. The statement "2 + 2 = 4" is, of course, not copyrightable, whether generated by a computer or written with a pencil. But the criteria that determine if a work is sufficiently original to qualify for copyright are already well established, and the intervention of the computer should not affect them.

Finally, we confront the question of who is the author of a work produced through the use of a computer. The obvious answer is that the author is one who employs the computer. The simplicity of this response may obscure some problems, though essentially they are the same sort of problems encountered in connection with works produced in other ways.

191/ For example, arranging the layout of an answer sheet within the rigid confines imposed by its use in an optical reading device for computer input has been held to constitute sufficient originality. Harcourt Brace & World, Inc. v. Graphic Controls Corp., 329 F. Supp. 517 (S.D.N.Y. 1971).

One such problem is that often a number of persons have a hand in the use of a computer to prepare, for example, a complex statistical table. They may have varying degrees and kinds of responsibility for the creation of the work. However, they are typically employees of a common employer, engaged in creating a work-for-hire, and the employer is the author. When the authors work together as a voluntary team and not as employees of a common employer, the copyright law with respect to works of joint authorship is as applicable here as to works created in more conventional ways, and the team itself can define by agreement the relative rights of the individuals involved.

In order to be used in the creation of a work, a computer must be controlled by a program and must ordinarily utilize data input from other sources. Both the program and the data may be copyrighted works or parts of copyrighted works. The question has been raised whether authorship or proprietorship of the program or data base establishes or may establish a claim of authorship of the final work. It appears to the Commission that authorship of the program or of the input data is entirely separate from authorship of the final work, just as authorship of a translation of a book is distinct from authorship of the original work. It is, of course, incumbent on the creator of the final work to obtain appropriate permission from any other person who is the proprietor of a program or data base used in the creation of the ultimate work. The unlawful use of a program or data base might limit or negate the author's claim of copyright in the ultimate work, just as the failure of a translator to obtain a license from the proprietor of the translated work might prevent securing copyright in and making use of the translation.[192] But this is not a question of authorship itself, and the author of the original work does not become the author of a translation merely because it is made from the original book without permission. Here, too, the situation with respect to works produced by the use of a computer does not appear to differ from that with respect to works otherwise created.

192/ See 17 U.S.C. § 103(b).

This approach is followed by the Copyright Office today in conducting examinations for determining registrability for copyright of works created with the assistance of computers. [193/] It comports with the rather summary conclusions reached by the Whitford Committee's investigation of copyright problems in the United Kingdom. [194/] It is supported by the comment of experts in the fields of computer art and music and computer science with whom the Subcommittee has consulted. [195/]

However, the Commission recognizes that the dynamics of computer science promise changes in the creation and use of authors' writings that cannot be predicted with any certainty. The effects of these changes should have the attention of the Congress and its appropriate agencies to assure that those who are the responsible policy makers maintain an awareness of the changing impact of computer technology on both the needs of authors and the role of authors in the information age. To that end, the Commission recommends that the Congress, through the appropriate committees, and the Copyright Office, in the course of its administration of copyright registrations and other activities, continuously monitor the impact of computer applications on the creation of works of authorship. The subject should be considered by the Congress as part of any hearings held on the general topic of the role of the computer in society. And the Copyright Office, in the course of its regular activities, should report to the Congress if the impact of computers is found to raise questions of copyright law or policy requiring legislative attention.

193/ The Performing Arts Section of the Examining Division, for example, requests specific information about the authorship of a musical composition submitted for registration when the composition has been created with a computer. The work will be registered only when it is shown that the applicant exercised sufficient control over the production of the work to be considered its author.

194/ Copyright and Designs Law: Report of the Committee to consider the Law on Copyright and Designs 132-33 (1977).

195/ These include Milton Babbitt, Professor of Music at Princeton University; Kenneth Knowlton, a computer scientist and computer artist at Bell Laboratories; Joseph Weizenbaum, Professor of Computer Science at Massachusetts Institute of Technology; and John McCarthy, Professor of Computer Science at the Artificial Intelligence Laboratory at Stanford University.

The Commission, therefore, concludes that no special problem
exists with respect to the "creation of new works by the application or
intervention of such automatic systems or machine reproduction;" that
existing statute and case law adequately cover any questions involved; and
that no action by the Congress is necessary at this time.

IV. MACHINE REPRODUCTION - PHOTOCOPYING

A.   Introduction

The Congress created the National Commission on New Technological
Uses of Copyrighted Works, in part, to assist it in resolving a problem
that had proven especially difficult in the revision of the 1909 Copyright Act: drawing a proper balance between the rights of copyright
owners, whose works were easily reproduced through the use of advanced
reproduction technologies, and the general interests and needs of members
of the public who were coming more and more to rely on photocopying as an
important auxiliary form of access to copyrighted works. According to the
legislation that authorized its establishment, the Commission was required

> to study and compile data on:
>
> (1) the reproduction and use of copyrighted works
>   of authorship --
>   * * *
> (B) by various forms of machine reproduction, not
>   including reproduction by or at the request of
>   instructors for use in face-to-face teaching
>   activities 196/

The Commission was also charged with making recommendations "as to such

changes in copyright law or procedures that may be necessary to assure ...

access to copyrighted works, and to provide recognition of the rights of

copyright owners." 197/

196/ Pub. L. No. 93-573 §201(b), 93d Cong., 2d Sess. (1974). See Appendix
B-1. The term "machine reproduction" in its mandate was recognized as being
susceptible to various interpretations. The Commission's legislative history has clear indications that the Congress had contemplated a study of
photocopying and related methods of reproduction -- rather than videotape
reproduction and other emerging technologies -- when it created the Commission. Accordingly, the Commission determined to concentrate its efforts on
photoduplication and closely related means of reproduction.

197/ Id., at §201(c).

Because the Congress was actively considering photocopying in connection with the general revision bill at the time the Commission began its deliberations, the Commissioners decided at their second meeting to defer hearing witnesses on photocopying issues until the Congress finally agreed upon the provisions of the general revision bill directly related to that subject. Chairman Fuld, however, appointed three members of the Commission to prepare an initial report on the issues related to photocopying that was considered at the December 1975 meeting.

The Commission sponsored a number of studies to gather data on photocopying. [198/] The Commission contributed funding for a study conducted by King Research, Inc., [199/] designed to provide data on how much photocopying of copyrighted works actually occurred in libraries throughout the country. The Public Research Institute prepared a study that compared the costs of subscribing and storing periodicals with the costs of borrowing to fulfill patron requests. [200/] The Indiana University Graduate Library School conducted a survey of publishers of periodical literature. [201/]

During the year in which these studies were conducted, the Commission heard testimony from representatives of authors, publishers, libraries government agencies, educators and others concerning current and future photocopying practices and their views on whether the 1976 Act needed amendment. Also during that year, the Commission assisted representatives of publisher, author, librarian and educator groups in formulating guidelines defining which interlibrary loan practices would comport with the provisions of Section 108(g)(2) of the new copyright law prohibiting

---

198/ Summaries of these reports appear in Appendix H. Copies of the reports are available from the National Technical Information Service, Springfield, Va. 22161.

199/ King Research, Inc. Library Photocopying in the United States (1977) PB 278 300. Also available from the Superintendent of Documents No. 052-003-00443-7. [Hereinafter cited at King Study.]

200/ V. Palmour, M. Bellassai and R. Wiederkehr. Costs of Owning, Borrowing, and Disposing of Periodical Publications (1977) PB 274 821. [Hereinafter cited as Palmour Study.]

201/ B. Fry, H. White, and E. Johnson. Survey of Publisher Practices and Current Attitudes on Authorized Journal Article Copying and Licensing (1977) PB 271 003. [Hereinafter cited as Fry/White/Johnson Study.]

libraries from engaging in "systematic reproduction" of copyrighted
works.
<u>202/</u>

     This Report sets forth the Commission's recommendation to the
Congress for legislative action, and its suggestions to the interested
parties for possible adjustments in practices related to photocopying
and document delivery. After setting forth this recommendation and
these suggestions, this Report discusses the effect of the new copyright
law on a broad range of photocopying practices and reviews the evidence
that the Commission considered in reaching its conclusions.

B.   Commission Recommendations

     The Commission's investigations and the testimony it heard sup-
port the determination that, with one exception, the Commission need not
recommend changes in the provisions of the Copyright Act of 1976 affecting
photocopying. The one exception deals with photocopying by organizations
that are in the business of making copies. The Commission also suggests
certain matters that should be studied by the Register of Copyrights in
preparing the first five-year report assessing how effectively the
interests of copyright proprietors and users are balanced under the
photocopying provisions of the new law. Also suggested are certain
actions that could be taken voluntarily by other interested parties
to facilitate access to copyrighted works in photocopy form within the
framework of the Copyright Act of 1976.

1. The 1976 Act should be amended only to provide specific guidance to
    organizations engaged in photocopying for profit and their customers.

     At present no persuasive evidence exists that the provisions of
the Copyright Act of 1976 affecting photocopying are inadequate to serve the
dual purposes of copyright: to reward creators of and facilitate public
access to works of authorship. There can be no directly applicable evidence
without some experience with the new law, now only a few months in effect.

<u>202/</u> The "CONTU guidelines" are set out and discussed in Section IV-D of this
Report at pp. 134-137, <u>infra</u>.

The importance of this absence of experience is accentuated by the fact that (1) photocopying received much attention during the debates preceding enactment of the new law; (2) the legislative process has produced two statutory sections dealing with photocopying; [203/] (3) representatives of publishers, author and library groups have agreed on a set of formal guidelines interpreting how these statutory provisions apply to inter-library lending; [204/] and (4) both government and private organizations are adapting their photocopying activities to the requirements of the new law.

Developments that have taken place since the new law came into effect on January 1, 1978, strongly support a wait-and-see attitude toward recommending major changes in its photocopying provisions. The National Technical Information Service (NTIS) is offering a service to provide its 13,000 deposit account customers with photocopies of scientific, technical and professional literature from several thousand domestic and foreign journals. The price of the service includes a copying fee for the copyright proprietor. [205/] The Copyright Clearance Center, Inc. (CCC) has been developed through the joint efforts of the Authors League and the Association of American Publishers (AAP), scientific societies and user organizations to provide a licensing and clearing mechanism for the photocopying of copy-righted periodical literature, initially encompassing primarily scientific and technical journals. [206/] The National Commission on Libraries and Information Science (NCLIS) has proposed the establishment of a nonprofit National Periodicals Center to provide the public with copies, including photocopies on demand from a comprehensive collection of periodical literature. [207/] The operation of all these services within the framework

---

203/ 17 U.S.C. §§ 107 and 108, which appear, along with other selected Sections of the 1976 Act, in Appendix J.

204/ See discussion of Commission Guidelines in Section IV-D of this Report, pp. 134-137, infra.

205/ The Institute for Scientific Information and University Microfilms described at p. 155 of this Report, infra, have long offered similar services from their collections.

206/ See pp. 154 and 163, infra.

207/ See pp. 159-160, infra.

of the new law may affect the balance of interests between copyright proprietors and users desiring photocopies of copyrighted works. Discretion
would seem to require that these services operate under the new law for
a reasonable period of time before any modifications are suggested.

No significant evidence has been presented to the Commission to
support an argument that major legislative changes are necessary at this
time. There is no immediate, measurable crisis in the publication of
periodical journal literature — which is, by all accounts, the segment
of publishing most directly affected by photocopying. No persuasive evidence exists that journals for which there is significant demand are going
out of existence because of photocopying. Nor is there a reliable means of
separating the effects of photocopying from those of the pressures of rising
costs and limited demand on the viability of individual journal titles. On
the other hand, there is no evidence that the payments requested and the
procedure for obtaining authorization to make photocopies not permitted
as fair use under Section 107 of the Act or as a specific exemption under
Section 108 will impose unacceptable burdens on individuals and organizations wishing to copy.

Furthermore, there has been no strong support for modifying the
statutory provisions of the 1976 Act among those most directly affected by
the regulation of photocopying; neither library groups, publisher and
author interests, nor members of the general public have seriously urged
the Commission to recommend legislative action at this time. Although the
library associations and author and publisher associations considered the
advisability of further defining some terms in Section 108 and clarifying
the application of fair use to photocopying, they made no proposals to the
Commission for legislative changes.²⁰⁸/   Should such interest develop as a
result of experiences gained from operating under the present provisions
of the 1976 Act, nothing would prevent these groups, acting individually or
in concert, from pursuing these concerns with the appropriate Congressional
committees. All of these considerations seem to counsel against major legis-

---

208/ Transcripts CONTU Meetings No. 17 and 21.

lative action at present. Such action should await an assessment of the effects of the new law and private arrangements made in regard to its provisions.

The one area in which some legislative change is recommended in the 1976 Act concerns copying done by commercial organizations in the business of making copies for profit. The 1976 Act and legislative history, including the educational copying,[209] music copying,[210] and CONTU interlibrary loan guidelines, provide extensive guidance to those educational institutions, libraries and archives engaged in copying, and to individuals requesting copies from such institutions. The statute requires that two warning notices be prescribed by the Register of Copyrights and posted in libraries and archives in which copying is done. One regulation, promulgated pursuant to Section 108(d), prescribes the form of copyright warning that is to appear on the order form for obtaining copies and at the place where these orders are accepted. The second regulation, promulgated pursuant to Section 108(e), prescribes the form of the notice that is to appear on the order form and at the place where requests are made to copy entire copyrighted works or substantial parts thereof.[211]

Neither the statute, the two sets of regulations, nor the three guidelines provide particular guidance as to what may be copied by commercial organizations that make copies for customers or by individuals buying copying services from such organizations. The Commission suggests that the Congress require the posting of a notice in commercial copying organizations, both to describe that copying which in most cases would not constitute fair use, and to warn prospective customers of the liability they might incur for copying in violation of the copyright law.

The proposed statutory amendment would retain the present language of Section 107 renumbered as Section 107(a) and a new Section 107(b), as follows.

209/ House Report, supra note 1, at 68.

210/ Id., at 70.

211/ See Appendix J for the texts of these subsections of Section 108.

§ 107(b) For the purpose of this title, those who make
or supply copies or phonorecords to customers on demand
in the regular course of their commercial business activity
are referred to as "commercial copiers". Commercial copiers
shall be required to display prominently, at any location
where orders for copies or phonorecords are solicited
or accepted, a notice advising the public of restrictions
on reproduction of copyrighted works created by this title.
Displaying the notice does not in itself constitute a fair
use defense for a commercial copier, but failure by a
commercial copier to display the prescribed notice shall
result in the denial to such commercial copier of fair use
as a defense to any copyright infringement action arising
from copying done in the absence of the notice, and a
trebling of any monetary amounts awarded a copyright
owner who prevails in a copyright infringement action
against a commercial copier. Such notice shall read as
follows:

WARNING CONCERNING COPYRIGHT RESTRICTIONS

The copyright law of the United States (Title 17, United
States Code) governs the making of reproductions of copyrighted
works. If a work is protected by copyright, in most cases it
is copyright infringement, even for purposes of private study,
to reproduce more than one article or other contribution to a
copyrighted collection or periodical, or more than a small part
of any other copyrighted work, or to make at the same time or at
different times, more than one copy of any such article, contribution or small part. Copying in violation of copyright may subject
you to an action for money damages under the copyright law.

2. Recommendations concerning the five-year review of photocopying practices

A review procedure is prescribed in Section 108(i) of the 1976

Act for assessing the adequacy of the new law with regard to photocopying,

and for recommending solutions to problems resulting from any inadequacy. [212/]

The Register of Copyrights is to undertake a study and report to the Congress

by January 1, 1983, and at five year intervals thereafter, "setting forth

the extent to which this section [108] has achieved the intended statutory

balancing of the rights of creators, and the needs of users." [213/]   Although

Section 108 primarily concerns photocopying by libraries and similar insti-

tutions, the language can be interpreted to enable the Register also to in-

vestigate the impact of photocopying performed by for-profit organizations

and by individuals, either on publicly available coin-operated machines or

_____

212/   17 U.S.C. § 108(i).

213/   Id.

through commercial copying services. The "intended statutory balancing of the rights of creators, and the needs of users," the sought-after statutory standard, can be attained only if all these activities are evaluated. The Register's report to the Congress is to "describe any problems that may have arisen, and present legislative or other recommendations, if warranted."[214/] Preparation of such a report would require that the study undertaken look beyond photocopying by libraries in order to accomplish its statutory purpose.

Having commissioned research, conducted investigations, and heard numerous witnesses on the photocopying issues related to current practices in and out of libraries, the Commission believes it can make helpful recommendations to the Register on how the first five-year study should be conducted.

The research effort should attempt to determine the impact of copying fees on the health of the publishing industry, with special emphasis on the publication of scientific, technical and medical journals. In particular, the study should attempt to determine (1) whether the imposition of copying fees contributes to the viability of individual journal titles; (2) what impact, if any, the imposition of copying fees has on journal subscriptions and library acquisitions; and (3) what information about the use of individual journal titles and their contents is provided by the numbers of photocopies for which payments are made.

The Register of Copyrights should construe Section 108(i) broadly and not confine the five-year studies to the provisions of Section 108 relating to library photocopying. The Register should examine how the educational and music copying guidelines have worked out in practice, and how the statute has operated with respect to organizations that are not educational institutions, libraries or archives, including organizations doing copying for a fee. All these types of copying have a potential impact on the creation and distribution of copyrighted works.

214/ Id.

The Register should begin immediately to plan and implement the collection of data necessary to complete the required study. The Commission recommends that the Register convene representatives of the interested organizations to ascertain problems that appear unresolved by the 1976 Act and receive their suggestions on the conduct of the first five-year study. If the parties and the Register can agree on these matters, the collection of data and the usefulness of the data assembled can be improved and costs of the study reduced.

The regular periodic surveys of public, academic, school, federal and special libraries conducted by the National Center for Education Statistics (NCES) will include at the Commission's request survey questions to determine, for the years 1978 and 1979, the gross amount of photocopying being done in the United States, broken down between periodicals and other copyrighted works and between copying for local use and for interlibrary loan. Similar data can be collected for 1980 and 1981. In addition consideration should be given to collecting data in these NCES surveys from the records on copying for interlibrary loan that libraries are required to keep under the CONTU guidelines. Also, the Register should obtain and publish data for the calendar years 1978, 1979, 1980 and 1981 on the operations of organizations such as the Copyright Clearance Center, Inc. (CCC), National Technical Information Service (NTIS), University Microfilms International (UMI) and the Institute for Scientific Information (ISI), which license or supply authorized photocopies of copyrighted works.

The Register should also consider updating the 1976 Fry/White Study 215/ of the economics of libraries and scholarly journals and incorporating some of the features of the King Study of 1977. 216/ The Fry/White Study for the National Science Foundation provides economic data concerning libraries and scholarly journal publishing in the period 1969-73. The King Study measured the type and volume of library

---

215/ B. Fry and H. White. Publishers and Libraries: A Study of Scholarly and Research Journals. (1976). [Hereinafter referred to as Fry/White Study.]

216/ See note 199, p. 118, supra.

photocopying in 1976. A combination of the two, with some additional
features designed to measure the impact of the specific photocopying provisions of the 1976 Act on libraries and journal publishing, repeated for
the calendar year 1981, would provide a means of assessing the economic
status of library and journal publishing for a thirteen year period, the
last four years of which would be after the effective date of the 1976
Copyright Act.

3. Recommendations to publishers

Publishers, especially publishers of journals, in cooperation
with the library community, the Copyright Office and the Library of Congress, should exert every effort to facilitate the determination of the
copyright status of both current and older issues of their publications.
A large portion of periodical issues copyrighted under the provisions of
the 1909 Act have not been renewed and are in the public domain. In addition, the Fry/White/Johnson Study <u>217/</u> undertaken for the Commission
showed that publishers of many scholarly journals are willing to permit
libraries — especially nonprofit libraries — to photocopy beyond the
limits established by Sections 107 and 108 of the 1976 Act.

There are several ways that publishers could inform the public of
the copyright status of journal issues. Publishers of journals could display prominently the copyright notice if they wish to protect their copyright and could include information in their current issues about the copyright status of back issues. Whether or not published with a copyright
notice, every journal issue could carry a statement of policy with respect
to copying. For example, several of the journals published by the American
Library Association carry the following statement:

> All material in this journal subject to copyright by
> the American Library Association may be photocopied
> for the noncommercial purpose of scientific or educa-
> tional advancement.

It would be helpful if the Register of Copyrights and the National Commis-

---

217/ See, p. 152, <u>infra</u>.

sion on Libraries and Information Science could bring together representatives of journal publishers, authors and library organizations to work out various forms of standard language providing the type of information suggested.

Every issue of a journal could display prominently a statement of participation (or nonparticipation) in copying clearance arrangements such as the Copyright Clearance Center, Inc., and could, in addition, indicate where and at what cost copies of articles or back issues may be obtained. If the publisher permits copying beyond that allowed by the 1976 Act, the publisher should so include that information in the statement.

Each issue of a journal should contain the International Standard Serial Number (ISSN) assigned by the Serial Records Division of the Library of Congress. This inclusion would facilitate the determination of the copyright status of periodical articles by computerized on-line systems. [218/] Users of copyrighted works will also benefit if organizations that authorize copying for a stated fee, such as the Copyright Clearance Center, Inc. include in their catalogues information on the copyright status of older issues similar to that suggested for incorporation in each journal issue; and information concerning where and at what cost authorized copies may be obtained. [219/]

4. Recommendations to government agencies

The Library of Congress, the Copyright Office and the National Commission on Libraries and Information Science, in consultation with the library associations, journal publishers and library consortia, should explore the possibility of including in the Conservation of Serials (CONSER) project — a data base of information on serials, including the

---

218/ The Copyright Office registration form TX for periodical issues published after December 31, 1977, includes a place for the insertion of the International Standard Serial Number; and the United States Postal Service and the Library of Congress have agreed as a general rule to have the ISSN printed in each issue of second-class publications instead of the separate and different Postal Service identification number now used by the Postal Service. 43 Fed. Reg. 29943.

219/ The Chairman of the Copyright Clearance Center, in a letter dated April 14, 1978, informed the Commission that the Center intended to "request publishers for information on the copyright status of older journals, and include information received in catalogues to be published in the future."

title, the publisher and the International Standard Serial Number --
information about the copyright status of journal issues, both current and
older issues; whether the publisher permits copying beyond that permitted
by the statute; whether the journal is in the Copyright Clearance Center
or other clearance systems; and what, if any, sources of authorized copies
exist. The Library of Congress, or any other organization planning to
establish a nonprofit periodicals copying center, should consider the
discussion of such centers in Part F of this report. 220/

C. Provisions of the 1976 Copyright Act Affecting Photocopying

Sections 107 and 108 of the Copyright Act of 1976 govern photocopying activities. 221/ An understanding of these sections and their
legislative history is necessary to analyze the needs of copyright proprietors and those who seek access to printed works by means of photocopying.

The 1976 Act deals with photocopying in four different ways:

(1) Copying for teaching purposes is dealt with, not by specific
statutory exemptions, but rather by a list of permissible practices held to
be fair use under Section 107. This is done by means of the so-called
educational guidelines, the "Agreement on Guidelines for Classroom Copying
in Not-For-Profit Educational Institutions," which were negotiated by
educational, author and publisher organizations and accepted by the
Congressional Committees. 222/ They will not be dealt with here in any
further detail because of the explicit exclusion from the jurisdiction
of the Commission of copying done in connection with face-to-face
teaching activities.

220/ See pp. 151-164, infra.

221/ For the full text of these Sections, see Appendix J of this Report.
Appendix J also contains the text of two other provisions relating
to photocopying: Section 504(c)(2) relating to the possible remission
of statutory damages for infringement by employees or agents of nonprofit
educational institutions, libraries or archives acting within the scope
of their employment; and Section 602(a)(3) relating to the importation
of copies by nonprofit scholarly, educational and religious organizations.

(2) Permissible copying of music for educational use is also dealt with in guidelines which were negotiated between music publishing organizations and organizations representing music users. The House Committee Report sets forth these guidelines.[223/]

(3) Specific exemptions for photocopying by libraries and archives are set forth in Section 108 of the Act and are discussed in detail in the following parts of this chapter.

(4) By implication, since they are the subject of no specific exemptions or guidelines, the following classes of copiers may engage in only fair use copying under the four general standards set forth in Section 107 of the Act:[224/]

    (a) individuals doing their own copying;

    (b) libraries and archives not qualifying for the privileges of Section 108; and

    (c) organizations which are not libraries or archives, including for-profit organizations charging fees for copying

Section 108 permits copying of most materials[225/] without authorization by libraries or archives for themselves and for their users in specified circumstances provided that: (1) the library or archives is open to the public or available to specialized researchers; (2) the reproduction or distribution includes a notice of copyright; and (3) the reproduction or distribution is made without any purpose of direct or indirect commercial advantage. This third limitation is interpreted in the House Report to mean that "direct or indirect commercial advantage" is an intention to profit directly from the sale of copies, rather than to profit from the use of the reproduced material in the business of the organization.[226/]

222/ House Report, supra note 1 at 68-70.

223/ Id., at 70-72.

224/ See Appendix J for the text of Section 107.

225/ Section 108(h) excludes "a musical work, a pictorial, graphic or sculptural work, or a motion picture or other audiovisual work other than an audiovisual work dealing with news...."

226/ House Report, supra note 1, at 74.

Libraries and archives qualifying for the privileges of Section 108 are permitted to make copies for themselves (as opposed to making copies for their patrons or users) only in two cases. Section 108(b) permits a library or archives to reproduce an unpublished work for purposes of preservation, security or research use in another library if the copy or phonorecord is currently in the collections of the library or archives. Section 108(c) permits libraries and archives to reproduce damaged, deteriorated, lost or stolen copies if, after a reasonable effort, an unused replacement can not be obtained at a "fair price."

Libraries and archives are given more extensive privileges of making copies for users both from their own collections and by securing copies from other sources. The principal privilege is conferred by Section 108(d) which permits the making of not more than one copy of an article from a periodical, or other contribution to a copyrighted collection, or a small part of part of any other copyrighted work, for purposes of private study, scholarship or research, provided that the library displays prominently at the place where orders are accepted and includes in its order forms the warning of copyright prescribed by regulation of the Register of Copyrights.

Libraries and archives also have the right under Section 108(e) to make a copy for a user of an entire copyrighted work, or a substantial part of it, or to secure a copy from another source, if (1) determination has been made that a copy cannot be obtained at a fair price; (2) the purpose of the requester is private study, scholarship or research; and (3) the prescribed warning by the Register of Copyrights is displayed and included on the order form.

All of the rights to make copies that are enumerated in Section 108 are limited by the prohibition in Section 108(g) against "the related or concerted reproduction ... of multiple copies ... of the same material," and the "systematic reproduction or distribution" of periodical articles or other small portions of copyrighted works. This prohibition against systematic reproduction and distribution, however, is in turn limited by the proviso in Section 108(g)(2) which states "[t]hat nothing in this clause prevents a library or archives from participating in interlibrary arrangements that do not have, as their purpose or effect, that the library or archives receiving such copies or phonorecords for distribution does so in such aggregate quantities as to substitute for a subscription to or purchase of such work." The aggregate quantities that constitute a substitution for a subscription or purchase of a work are defined in the CONTU Guidelines, which are described in the next section.

D. The CONTU Guidelines on Photocopying Under Interlibrary Loan Arrangements

The CONTU guidelines were developed to assist librarians and copyright proprietors in understanding the amount of photocopying for use in interlibrary loan arrangements permitted under the copyright law. In the spring of 1976 there was realistic expectation that a new copyright law, under consideration for nearly twenty years, would be enacted during that session of Congress. It had become apparent that the House Subcommittee was giving serious consideration to modifying the language concerning "systematic reproduction" by libraries in Section 108(g)(2) of the Senate-passed bill[227/] to permit photocopying under interlibrary arrangements unless such arrangements resulted in the borrowing libraries obtaining "such aggregate quantities as to substitute for a subscription to or purchase of" copyrighted works.

The Commission discussed this proposed amendment to the Senate bill at its meeting on April 2, 1976. Pursuant to a request made at that meeting by the Register of Copyrights, serving in her _ex officio_ role, the Commission agreed that it might aid the House and Senate Subcommittees by offering its good offices in bringing the principal parties together to see whether agreement could be reached on a definition of "such aggregate quantities." This offer was accepted by the House and Senate Subcommittees and the interested parties, and much of the summer of 1976 was spent

---

227/ S. 22, 94th Cong., 2d Sess. (1975).

by the Commission in working with the parties to secure agreement on "guide-

lines" interpreting what was to become the proviso in Section 108(g)(2)

relating to "systematic reproduction" by libraries. The pertinent parts of

that section, with the proviso added by the House underscored, follow:

> (g) The rights of reproduction and distribution under this
> section extend to the isolated and unrelated reproduction or
> distribution of a single copy or phonorecord of the same
> material on separate occasions, but do not extend to cases
> where the library or archives, or its employee --

> * * *

> (2) engages in the systematic reproduction or distribution
> of single or multiple copies or phonorecords of material
> described in subsection (d): <u>Provided, That nothing in this
> clause prevents a library or archives from participating in
> interlibrary arrangements that do not have, as their purpose
> or effect, that the library or archives receiving such copies
> or phonorecords for distribution does so in such aggregate
> quantities as to substitute for a subscription to or purchase
> of such work.</u>

Prior to enactment of the new copyright law, the principal library,

publisher and author organizations agreed to the following detailed guide-

lines defining what "aggregate quantities" would constitute the "systematic

reproduction" that would exceed the statutory limitations on a library's

photocopying activities.

PHOTOCOPYING-INTERLIBRARY ARRANGEMENTS

INTRODUCTION

> Subsection 108(g)(2) of the bill deals, among
> other things, with limits on interlibrary arrangements
> for photocopying. It prohibits systematic photocopying
> of copyrighted materials but permits interlibrary
> arrangements "that do not have, as their purpose or
> effect, that the library or archives receiving such
> copies or phonorecords for distribution does so in
> such aggregate quantities as to substitute for a
> subscription to or purchase of such work."
>   The National Commission on New Technological Uses of
> Copyrighted Works offered its good offices to the House and
> Senate subcommittees in bringing the interested parties
> together to see if agreement could be reached on what a
> realistic definition would be of "such aggregate quantities."
> The Commission consulted with the parties and suggested the
> interpretation which follows, on which there has been
> substantial agreement by the principal library, publisher,
> and author organizations. The Commission considers the
> guidelines which follow to be a workable and fair inter-
> pretation of the intent of the proviso portion of subsection
> 108(g)(2).
>   These guidelines are intended to provide guidance in the
> application of section 108 to the most frequently encountered

interlibrary case: a library's obtaining from another library, in lieu of interlibrary loan, copies of articles from relatively recent issues of periodicals — those published within five years prior to the date of the request. The guidelines do not specify what aggregate quantity of copies of an article or articles published in a periodical, the issue date of which is more than five years prior to the date when the request for the copy thereof is made, constitutes a substitute for a subscription to such periodical. The meaning of the proviso to subsection 108(g)(2) in such case is left to future interpretation.

The point has been made that the present practice on interlibrary loans and use of photocopies in lieu of loans may be supplemented or even largely replaced by a system in which one or more agencies or institutions, public or private, exist for the specific purpose of providing a central source for photocopies. Of course, these guidelines would not apply to such a situation.

GUIDELINES FOR THE PROVISO OF SUBSECTION 108(g)(2)

1. As used in the proviso of subsection 108(g)(2), the words "... such aggregate quantities as to substitute for a subscription to or purchase of such work" shall mean:

(a) with respect to any given periodical (as opposed to any given issue of a periodical), filled requests of a library or archives (a "requesting entity") within any calendar year for a total of six or more copies of an article or articles published in such periodical within five years prior to the date of the request. These guidelines specifically shall not apply, directly or indirectly, to any request of a requesting entity for a copy or copies of an article or articles published in any issue of a periodical, the publication date of which is more than five years prior to the date when the request is made. These guidelines do not define the meaning, with respect to such a request, of "... such aggregate quantities as to substitute for a subscription to [such periodical]."

(b) With respect to any other material described in subsection 108(d), (including fiction and poetry), filled requests of a requesting entity within any calendar year for a total of six or more copies or phonorecords of or from any given work (including a collective work) during the entire period when such material shall be protected by copyright.

2. In the event that a requesting entity —

(a) shall have in force or shall have entered an order for a subscription to a periodical, or

(b) has within its collection, or shall have entered an order for, a copy or phonorecord of any other copyrighted work, material from either category of which it desires to obtain by copy from another library or archives (the "supplying entity"), because the material to be copied is not reasonably available for use by the requesting entity itself, then the fulfillment of such request shall be treated as though the requesting entity made such copy from its own collection. A library or archives may request a copy or phonorecord from a supplying entity only under those circumstances where the requesting entity would

have been able, under the other provisions of section
108, to supply such copy from materials in its own collection.
3. No request for a copy or phonorecord of any material ·
to which these guidelines apply may be ·fulfilled by the
supplying entity unless such request is accompanied by
a representation by the requesting entity that the request
was made in conformity with these guidelines.
4. The requesting entity shall maintain records of all
requests made by it for copies or phonorecords of any
materials to which these guidelines apply and shall maintain
records of the fulfillment of such requests, which records
shall be retained until the end of the third complete
calendar year after the end of the calendar year in which
the respective request shall have been made.
5. As part of the review provided for in subsection 108(i),
these guidelines shall be reviewed not later than five years
from the effective date of this bill.

These guidelines were accepted by the Conference Committee and

were incorporated into its report on the new Act.   228/   During the ensuing

twenty months, both library and publisher organizations have reported con-

siderable progress toward adapting their practices to conform with the

CONTU guidelines.

The guidelines specifically leave the status of periodical ar-

ticles more than five years old to future determination. Moreover,

institutions set up for the specific purpose of supplying photocopies

of copyrighted material are excluded from coverage of the guidelines.

E. The volume of library photocopying in 1976

Enactment of the 1976 Act was one prerequisite to the Commission's

formulation of recommendations concerning photocopying; another was access

to data about the incidence of photocopying and its impact, both real and

perceived, on the activities of authors, publishers and those seeking ac-

cess to works of authorship. Two studies published in 1976 and 1977 pro-

vided most of the data that was utilized by the Commission for these purposes.

Comprehensive quantitative data on the photocopying of copyrighted

materials in the United States is provided by the 1977 report of King

---

228/ Conference Report, supra note 1 at 71-73.

229/
Research, Inc.,   which was based primarily on sample surveys of photo-

copying conducted on supervised machines by public, academic, federal govern-
230/
ment and special libraries.   Records of 130,000 interlibrary loan trans-

actions in 1976 in the Minnesota Interlibrary Telecommunications Exchange

(MINITEX), a network of libraries in Minnesota and surrounding states,
231/
supplemented the King Research survey sample.   An advisory committee

consisting of librarians, publishers and government agency officials

provided oversight for the project.

Although the study has furnished the most comprehensive body of

data on photocopying ever assembled in the United States, it did not cover

every kind of photocopying of copyrighted materials. It excluded, for

example: (1) copying in public and non-public elementary and secondary

school libraries; (2) copying for classroom use in nonprofit educational

institutions at all levels — elementary, secondary and higher — unless

the copying was done by the library of the institution; (3) copying on

unsupervised machines (including coin-operated machines in libraries and

elsewhere in organizations); (4) copying by government agencies other

than in their libraries; (5) copying by organizations other than libraries

or in organizations in units other than the libraries such as by business

organizations without libraries or departments of educational institutions;

and (6) copying by organizations selling copying services either as a major

or incidental part of their operations, such as commercial photocopying ser-

---

229/ See note 199, p. 118 supra. This study was conducted in 1976 and 1977
under contract with the National Commission on Libraries and Information
Science, with additional financial support from the National Science Foundation and CONTU. Such a study was recommended in 1975 by the Conference on
the Resolution of Copyright Issues, which consisted of representatives
of producers and consumers of copyrighted materials under the joint chairmanship of Frederick Burkhardt, Chairman of NCLIS, and Barbara Ringer,
Register of Copyrights.

230/ Special libraries generally are libraries other than public, school,
federal or academic. Included would be libraries located in business
corporations, trade associations, law firms, museums, hospitals, etc.

231/ The MINITEX records constituted the only existing comprehensive data on
interlibrary loan transactions for an entire year.

232/
vices and "information brokers."

    The overall volume of items of copyrighted materials estimated
to have been copied by the four types of libraries sampled in the King Study
233/
are shown in Table I which follows:

TABLE I

PHOTOCOPYING IN LIBRARIES FROM ALL COPYRIGHTED MATERIALS

Millions of Photocopied Items
(one or several pages)

Type of Use

Type of Library	Local Users *	Intrasystem Transactions*	Interlibrary Loan *	Total Copyrighted Materials	Copyright Status Unknown
Public	13.7	7.2	3.2	24.1	11.0
Special	11.0	5.6	1.2	17.8	2.6
Academic	3.5	3.1	1.3	7.9	3.1
Federal	2.7	1.0	0.4	4.1	0.3
Totals	30.9	16.9	6.1	53.9	17.3

* King Study, Tables 3.13, 3.15, 3.17 and 3.19

(Note: Rows and columns may not add exactly due to rounding.)

232/ See p. 157, infra.

233/ The volumes of photocopying discussed in the following section
may be significantly smaller than the estimated volumes which would have
resulted from a more comprehensive survey covering the exemptions noted
above. Such a survey would probably have been precluded by factors
such as cost, available time and the lack of an adequate statistical
universes (mailing lists).

An estimated total of 53.9 million items from copyrighted materials was copied on supervised machines in the 22,000 libraries in the universe sampled. Of this total 70% was copied from serials, 24% from books, and 6% from other copyrighted materials. The task of estimating what amount of this volume of copyrighted materials would be exempted under Sections 107 and 108 of the 1976 Act and what amount would require authorization to copy is complicated by the fact that the contract for the King Study came into effect in July 1976, three months before the new Copyright Act was enacted and its detailed provisions on photocopying were known. The data gathered, therefore, may not correspond exactly with the activities defined in the Act. Nevertheless, some rough estimates can be made for the types of libraries included in the survey. This analysis is undertaken in the following sections broken down into the three types of transactions and then broken down in each case by type of library.

1. Copying of copyrighted U.S. serials for interlibrary loan [234]

    The King sample survey collected more detailed data concerning copying for interlibrary loan arrangements than for any other category. Its data was supplemented and reinforced by the data on the 130,000 actual transactions in the MINITEX system. Table II, which follows, contains the King Study figures on the total volume of copying of United States copyrighted serials for interlibrary loan, and the two alternative estimates of the volume of copying that would require authorization under Section 108(g)(2) and the CONTU guidelines. [235]

---

[234]   The definition of a serial used in the King Study was " A publication issued in successive parts bearing numerical or chronological designations, which is intended to be continued indefinitely and which may be identified by an ISSN (International Standard Serial Number). Serials include periodicals, newspapers, and the journals, memoirs, proceedings, transactions, etc. of societies. Serials are subject to subscription prices paid in advance. (This eliminates publications that appear annually or less frequently.)" King Study, supra note 199, at ix.

[235]   The King Study provides no similar breakdown for books or other copyrighted materials, nor for serials not published in the United States.

TABLE II

PHOTOCOPYING FROM U.S. COPYRIGHTED SERIALS FOR INTERLIBRARY LOAN

Millions of Photocopied Items
(one or several pages)

Conditions Affecting Need for Authorization to Make Copies

	1	2	3	4
Type of Library	No. of Items Copied *	No. Exempt for Classroom Use, Replacement and Under 5 copies per title *	No. Needing Authorization w/o Time Limit (=col. 1 – col. 2)*	No. Needing Authorization w/5-year Time Limit*
Special	1.25	.63	.62	.22
Academic	1.13	.47	.66	.14
Public	1.01	.53	.48	.09
Federal	.38	.22	.17	.06
Totals	3.77	1.85	1.93	.51

* King Study, Table 4.14, and page 71.

The King Study data suggest that from 505,000 to 1,925,000 of the items from United States serials photocopied for interlibrary loan in 1976 would have required authorization from the copyright proprietor, had the provisions of the 1976 Act been applicable.[236/] To this number, however, must be added some portion of the 1,200,000 copies made from copyrighted books, some portion of the 600,000 photocopies made from other copyrighted materials, and some portion of copies of foreign serials and the materials for which copyright status was not reported. Appropriate deductions from all of these categories must be made to take into account copying for classroom use and for replacement. A portion of that copying may be exempted from copyright liability under Sections 107 and 108. These figures in turn should be reduced by the number of single-page photocopied items made for interlibrary loan, which likely fall under the definition of fair use.

236/ The total figure would depend on how articles from journals over five years old — those not covered by the CONTU guidelines — were treated.

Information on one-page and two-page items is available in the King Study only for periodicals and other serials, but not for books or other copyrighted material. That information indicates that 16% of the filled requests were for one page. If 16% is deducted from the figures in Columns 3 and 4 of Table II, the number of copies of domestic serial items photocopied for interlibrary loan and requiring authorization would be reduced to 420,000 copies for articles less than six years old and 1,621,000 copies of articles irrespective of age.

2. Photocopies made for local use

Copying for local use as defined in the King Study includes copying both by public library borrowers, students and faculty of colleges and universities, and employees of libraries and the institutions in which they are located, including corporate employees. The number of copies for local use will also include those permitted under the fair use provisions of Section 107 which permit the making of one copy of an article or a small portion of other works for purposes of private study, scholarship or research, as well as those permitted under the provisions of Section 108(d). The King Study provides no direct data on these types of exempted copying, but an approximation appears in Table III, which follows, arrived at by distinguishing single and multiple copies and by applying estimates of the number of photocopied items consisting of but one page.

TABLE III

PHOTOCOPYING FROM ALL COPYRIGHTED SERIALS FOR LOCAL USE

Millions of Photocopied Items
(one or several pages)

Conditions Affecting Need for Authorization to Make Copies

	1	2	3	4	5
Type of Library	No. Copies Made From All Serials*	No. Copies Not Made for Replacement or Classroom Use **	No. of Single Copies***	No. of One-Page Items	No. of Copies Needing Author. (col. 2- col. 3 + 4)
			****		
Special	9.7	9.6	1.8	0.9	0.9
Public	7.6	7.2	3.8	0.7	2.7
Federal	2.5	2.4	0.8	0.2	1.4
Academic	2.0	1.8	1.5	0.2	0.1
Totals	21.7	21.0	13.9	2.1	5.1

*   King Study, Table 4.19
**   King Study, Table 4.23. Does not include 4,560,000 items for
      which the purpose of the request is unknown or unreported.

***   King Study, Table 4.26
****   Composed of an estimated 4.3 million in for-profit institutions
        and 3.6 million in non-profit institutions

(Note: Rows and columns may not add exactly due to rounding.)

At first glance it appears that only some 5,100,000 photocopied items made for local patrons would require authorization. To this number there must be added some portion of the 4,260,000 single items photocopied by libraries in for-profit organizations to take into account photocopies by those libraries that do not avail themselves of the benefits of Section 108(d) because their collections are not open to the public or specialized researchers.

3. Photocopies made for "intrasystem" use

The second highest volume of copying of copyrighted materials in the types of libraries surveyed by King Research was for "intrasystem loan."

This volume was almost as great as copying for local patrons and more than twice as great as copying for interlibrary loan. "Intrasystem loan" was defined in the King Study as "borrowing or lending or library materials carried on between branches or departments within the same library system as determined by common funding." [237/]   No definition was provided for "library system," but a "library" was defined to include "both the central library/ headquarters and the branch libraries/departments of your library system or archives." [238/]

The problem of estimating what portion of the intrasystem photo-copying of copyright materials falls within fair use under Section 107 or within the exceptions in Section 108 is further complicated by the lack in either the 1976 Copyright Act or its legislative history of definitions of the terms "library" or "archives." It is necessary to estimate what portion of "intrasystem loan" copies is governed by Section 108(d) -- single copies for patrons of articles or other small portions of copyrighted works -- and what portion of the copies is governed by the limitations in Section 108(g)(2) on copying for interlibrary loan. Presumably the Congress intended that individual instances of copying would fall under one or the other of these provisions, but not under both.

The estimates made in the analysis which follows are based upon the assumption that copying for intrasystem use is copying within a "library" as that term is used in the statute. For example, it is assumed that a large city's central or headquarters library and its numerous branches constitute one library, and, therefore, any library patron in that city may go to the headquarters or any branch to secure a single copy of an article from any periodical subscribed to by any library unit in that city -- pro-vided that the requests for the copies are isolated, unrelated and not a part of a concerted or systematic scheme — without incurring liability to the copyright proprietor in accord with Section 108(d). Conversely, secur-ing such a copy would not count as an interlibrary loan under the provisions

237/   King Study, supra note 199, at viii.

238/   Id., at 216

of Section 108(g)(2) and the CONTU guidelines. The corollary of this interpretation is that if the periodical is not subscribed to by any unit in the
city system, all requests for copies of articles made to any unit in the
city which were met from sources not in the city system would count against
the quota of five copies in the CONTU guidelines. This interpretation seems
to fit best with usual library practice, wherein only requests for copies
that cannot be met within a city system are counted as interlibrary loans.

Table IV, which follows, applies this assumption in attempting to
estimate what portion of the volume of photocopying shown in the King Study
as intrasystem use requires authorization.

TABLE IV

PHOTOCOPYING FROM ALL COPYRIGHTED SERIALS FOR INTRASYSTEM LOAN

Millions of Photocopied Items
(one or several pages)

Conditions Affecting Need for Authorization to Make Copies

	1	2	3	4	5
Type of Library	No. Copies from all Serials	No.Copies for Replacement or Classroom Use *	No. Single Copies **	No. Copies Needing Author. w/o Limit on Length Col.1−Col.2+3	No.Copies Needing Authorization w/ One-Page Copies Exempt
Special	4.78	NA	2.10	2.68	1.47
Public	4.68	0.18	2.53	1.97	.80
Academic	1.63	0.23	1.29	0.11	.00
Federal	0.86	0.05	0.78	0.03	.00
Totals	11.95	0.45	6.70	4.80	2.27

** King Study, Table 4.34.
** Donald King estimate, telephone conversation December 22, 1977

An examination of Table IV suggests that some 2,270,000
items copied for "intrasystem loan" would require authorization. To
this number, however, should be added some portion of the 2,100,000 single
copies made by special libraries, shown in column 3, in order to account

for intrasystem copying by libraries in for-profit organizations that do not avail themselves of the privileges of Section 108.

Table V, which follows, recapitulates estimates of the minimum number of items copied from copyrighted materials on unsupervised machines in libraries that would require consent of the copyright proprietor.

TABLE V

For interlibrary loan	420,000	From domestic serials under six years old
For local use	5,100,000	From serials only
For intrasystem loan	2,270,000	From serials only
Total	7,790,000 *	

*Note: The estimates in Table V are minimal because they do not include copies for interlibrary loan made from serials over five years old; single copies made for local use or intrasystem use in libraries in for-profit organizations which do not wish to make themselves eligible for the provisions of Section 108; copies made from books and other copyrighted materials; issues of foreign serials copied for interlibrary loan; and copies made in institutions not covered by the King Study.

F. Means of Obtaining Permission to Make Photocopies or to Obtain Authorized Copies Under the 1976 Copyright Act

The complexities of the new copyright law and the data compiled in the several studies discussed in Part IV-G, highlight the importance of ascertaining the copyright status of works and the need for easily obtaining permission to copy. Because the 1976 Copyright Act became effective on January 1, 1978, it is too early to know all the various arrangements that may come into existence for obtaining consent to make or to receive copies of copyrighted works not permitted under the new law -- either as fair use under Section 107, or pursuant to the various exemptions in Section 108. However, some of the principal methods and mechanisms for obtaining authorization and making payments are known and may be briefly discussed.

1. Publisher may notify public that photocopying certain works for individual use is permissible

The absence of copyright notice on any work subject to copyright normally may be relied on by the public as evidence, in the absence of knowledge to the contrary, that a work may be copied.[239]

Various ways exist to notify the public that a proprietor grants consent for photocopying beyond that permitted under Sections 107 and 108 of the 1976 Act. One method is to print in each issue a specific license stating what copying may be done without individual authorization. Some periodical publishers are likely to adopt liberal copying policies on photocopying and will publish such policies in each issue of the periodicals. A variety of such policies are conceivable: (1) general permission to copy except for resale; (2) permission to copy (single or multiple copies) by non-profit organizations; and (3) permission to copy from older issues before a certain date.

The 1977 Fry/White Johnson Study, a report prepared for the Commission in 1977 by Bernard Fry, Herbert S. White and Elizabeth Johnson of the Indiana University Graduate School, Survey of Publisher Practices and Present Attitudes on Authorized Journal Article Copying and Licensing, throws some light on the extent to which periodical publishers may wish to adopt such policies.[240] Approximately 20% of the 974 responding journals were willing to permit copying by non-profit organizations beyond that authorized in the law (and to permit copying to a lesser extent by for-profit organizations). The journals surveyed were more liberal in permitting copying from older issues than from more recent issues. Copyright Office records indicate that of the 1485 journals not responding in this study approximately 600, or 40%, did not register claims to copyright under the 1909 Act, which may indicate that a considerable portion of the journals not registering in the past may be willing to permit copying beyond that which is permissible under Sections 107 and 108 of the 1976 Act.

239/ Section 405(b) of the 1976 Act offers considerable, although not absolute protection to "an innocent infringer" who copies in reliance on the absence of a copyright notice. For the text of this section see Appendix J.

240/ Fry/White/Johnson, supra note 201.

A considerable number of older issues fall into the public domain when copyright is not renewed at the expiration of the first twenty-eight year period of protection under the 1909 Act.[241/]   Unfortunately there exists no simple and inexpensive method to determine whether these older issues are still under copyright. The Copyright Office has published annually a Catalog of Copyright Entries for periodicals that indicates what serial titles are registered for copyright under the 1909 Act, including renewal registrations, and will continue to publish data on renewal registrations. Obtaining access to and using these catalogs, however, is a rather cumbersome way of checking the copyright status of older periodical issues. At least three methods can be conceived to simplify the process.

(a) A statement published in current issues of periodicals that issues more than twenty-eight years old regularly are (or are not) under copyright.

(b) A statement in the catalog of journals participating in the Copyright Clearance Center that older issues are (or are not) under copyright, or, alternatively, an indication that copying fees will not be requested for older issues.

(c) A statement on the copyright status of individual journal titles in the on-line bibliographic data on periodicals available through library networks. It might well be possible for those responsible for the CONSER[242/] project to add copyright status to this computerized data base at a one-time cost that would be minimal when spread over libraries throughout the country.

241/ In 1974, issues of 475 periodical titles out of approximately 4900 titles eligible for renewal were, in fact, renewed. When renewals were filed it was usually for all issues of the title for the year. Of these 475 titles which renewed, 14% were in the fields of science and technology and 9% in law and the social sciences. Historically, then, a relatively small minority of copyrighted periodical material is renewed.

242/ See p. 130, supra.

2. Clearance mechanism for obtaining consent to photocopy

The Copyright Clearance Center, Inc. (CCC) is a not-for-profit New York corporation created under the sponsorship of publisher and author organizations. After December 31, 1977, persons or organizations wishing to copy material entered into the Center's system -- initially predominantly scientific, technical and medical journals -- for which consent must be obtained from copyright proprietors may do so by paying the Center the copy-ing fee per article or periodical page printed in the publication or for pre-1978 issues listed in the CCC catalog. 243/

Publishers have the option of designating the Copyright Clearance Center, Inc. as their agent to authorize the making of photocopies. Publish-ers who elect this option are also free to enter into agreements directly with individuals or organizations to authorize the making of photocopies. The Copyright Clearance Center provides, accordingly, but one mechanism of securing authorization to photocopy copyrighted works.

3. Suppliers of authorized photocopies

The great majority of photocopies of material that libraries do not possess and thus must secure from other sources will continue to be supplied through traditional interlibrary loan channels, pursuant to the proviso in Section 108(g)(2) of the 1976 Act as further defined in the "CONTU Guidelines.' However, there will be a small, but significant, portion of requests for photocopies of materials that will require securing authorized copies from institutions prepared to furnish photocopies on demand. 244/ Some of the principal suppliers will be described briefly.

243/ The Copyright Clearance Center reports that as of June 30, 1978, there were 1,633 United States and foreign publications, mostly periodicals, participating in the system; that 591 organizations were registered as users; and that the range of copying fees for articles published before 1978 was from zero to $12.25, with a median fee of somewhere between $2.00 and $2.50. The Center has estimated that in the 1978 calendar year 1,000,000 copying transactions will be authorized by use of its system.

244/ **See pp.** 142-44, <u>supra</u>.

Institute for Scientific Information (ISI) $\underline{245/}$

      The Institute for Scientific Information in Philadelphia, has been furnishing various bibliographic information services and providing tearsheets or authorized photocopies of journal articles to its clients for some twenty years. This tearsheet/photocopy service is called Original Article Tear Sheets (OATS).

      Copies of articles in the most recent five years from more than 5,000 scientific, technical and social science journals are available through OATS. ISI supplied more than 100,000 tearsheets or photocopies of articles in 1977, and volume has been growing at a rate of 10% a year.

      During 1978, ISI will add about 800 arts and humanities journals and 3,000 published scientific proceedings to its collections. When feasible OATS service will be extended to these new materials, thereby providing access to more than 180,000 additional items a year.

University Microfilms

      University Microfilms International in Ann Arbor, Michigan, a subsidiary of the Xerox Corporation, has contracts with publishers of several thousand serials authorizing it to sell microform copies of full year volumes. The bulk of its business has been with libraries, which substitute the microfilm copies for the original paper issues in order to save storage space and binding costs. University Microfilms' contracts with publishers permit it to supply on demand single or multiple copies of articles from about 8,000 serials (usually in full size). The periodical titles for which University Microfilms has contracts for the most part do not duplicate those journals from which ISI supplies copies. University Microfilms publishes a catalog so that libraries and other users may determine the periodical titles from which University Microfilms is authorized to photocopy. Unlike the Institute for Scientific Information, however,

---

245/ See pp. 156-58, infra, for a comparison of authorized copy delivery services.

University Microfilms ordinarily can supply copies of articles from all issues of its serials, back to the start of publication.

4. Secondary suppliers of authorized copyright-fee-paid copies

There are or will be a number of what may be called "secondary suppliers" of authorized copies of copyrighted materials. The National Technical Information Service (NTIS), for one example, is an agency of the Department of Commerce established to make the results of research reports and other materials prepared in or for federal agencies more readily available to industry, business and the general public. It operates a large facility in Springfield, Virginia, a suburb of Washington, D.C., which stores these documents and supplies full size or microform copies of hundreds of thousands of documents annually. NTIS publishes catalogs of documents and also enters them into a bibliographic data base to which on-line access is available through some of the commercial data base services. NTIS instituted a means of ordering and paying for authorized copies of articles from 5,300 non-government journals in May 1978, and estimates that by mid-summer of 1978, it will have completed arrangements for supplying copies from 8,000 to 9,000 journals.

Another source of copies of articles are so-called "information on demand" or "information broker" companies. These companies are organized to do research and supply information on a wide variety of topics to anyone interested in such services. 247/ There are also organizations which provide computerized access to approximately 360 bibliographic data bases. 248/ Subscribers to certain of these services may electronically order copies of documents from these bibliographic data bases of certain materials and from certain suppliers for delivery by mail. Convenience and the increased

247/ In the past these organizations have often provided copies of copyrighted materials without authorization from copyright proprietors. A number of these organizations, however, have indicated to the Commission that they will begin to obtain authorization for any copies they supply their customers in the course of their business.

248/ R. Christian, The Electronic Library 1 (1978).

speed of document delivery make it likely that this kind of electronic
ordering of documents will increase in volume.

The Table on the following page summarizes and compares the
authorized copy delivery services provided by the Institute for Scientific
Information, Inc., University Microfilms International, and the National
Technical Information Service.

THREE AUTHORIZED COPY DELIVERY SERVICES

Characteristic	Institute for Scientific Information (OATS) 1/	University Microfilms 2/	National Tec Information Serv (NTIS/JACS)
Number of Titles	5000 science, social science journals (For last five years) 1000 humanities journals (1978) 3000 proceedings volumes (1978)	10,000 serials (all issues) 80,000 monographs	8000-9000 (est (time coverage varies)
Serials Included			
Science/Technology	yes	yes	yes
Social Sciences	yes	yes	yes
Humanities	yes (1978 -)	yes	a few
Monographs Included	no	yes	no
Proceedings Included	yes (1978 -)	no	no
Base price range/ transaction	$3.50 + air mail postage	$ 6.00/article 3/ (first copy) 10.00/issue monograph price varies entire work entire work only	$ 6.00-13.50 (6.50 for majority)
Method of ordering	mail, telex, on-line, telephone	mail telephone	TWX, telex on-line or telephone
Processing time	48 hours + delivery	24 hours + delivery	2 days + delivery
Method of payment	prepaid stamps cash	cash with order credit card deposit accounts	deposit account only

1/ Approx. 4000 titles from I.S.I. are also available through NTIS.
2/ UM. titles generally are not available through NTIS.
3/ Journals listed in Current Index to Journals in Education are $4.00/
    article (first copy).

5. Possible nonprofit periodicals copying centers

In April 1977, the National Commission on Libraries and Information Science (NCLIS) published a task force report which proposed a national system for providing libraries with better access to copies of periodical materials not in their collections, based on three levels of supply, as follows:

> Level 1 - Local, state and regional library systems responsible for meeting a substantial portion of routine needs for periodicals.
>
> Level 2 - A comprehensive periodicals collection dedicated for lending and photocopy service to meet the majority of unfulfilled requests derived from Level 1. Initially, a single National Periodicals Center would be developed, but experience and demand may warrant more than one.
>
> Level 3 - Existing national libraries and other unique collections to back up the first two levels.

The report was approved by the National Commission on Libraries and Information Science in June 1977. $\underline{249/}$

Levels 1 and 3 already exist for the most part and only need to be tied into the total system. The local, state and regional library systems would be expected to provide access in Level 1 to most heavily used periodicals, estimated to consist of some 2000 titles. Level 2 in this system would be a new National Periodicals Center, designed to supply copies of periodical articles from some 55,000 periodicals in the middle range of use. In Level 3 access to very rarely used periodicals would be provided by the three national libraries and other special collections.

The NCLIS report makes the following statement with respect to the status of such a Center under the 1976 Copyright Act:

> The impact of the new copyright law, effective January 1, 1978, on the National Center is unclear at this time. Should the law be interpreted in light of the suggested CONTU guidelines, the responsibility rests on the individual

---

249/ Task Force on a National Periodicals System, National Commission on Libraries and Information Science, Effective Access to the Periodical Literature: A National Program 38 (1977). Superintendent of Documents Stock No. 052-003-00353/8.

borrowing libraries to account for their borrowing activities
in accordance with the guidelines. This would seem to
imply that a library would have to account for its combined
borrowing activities from both the National Center and from
other sources. The guidelines are expressed in terms of
borrowing on a title by title basis. It would only be
possible for the Center to do the accounting for libraries
using the Center on a title by title basis.

King Research, Inc., in their photocopy study for
the NCLIS, NSF, and CONTU, will investigate alternatives for
royalties payment mechanisms. The results and recommendations
of this study are expected to provide direction for the
Center on the copyright issue.

The Library of Congress has indicated that it would be willing

to operate such a Center, if the library community wanted it to do so, and

if the initial funding for setting up the system is supplied by non-federal

sources. The Council on Library Resources, using funds of its own and

other foundations, is making a further study of how such a Center might

be operated, either by the Library of Congress or by some other organization,

existing or to be created. This further study is expected to be completed

by the late summer of 1978.

This Report is being published in advance of the completion of

the additional study of a National Periodicals Center discussed above.

Therefore the Commission does not know what the study may recommend.

Since it seems possible, however, that one or more such centers may come

into existence within the next few years, the Commission has considered how

they might operate and how they would fit in with other means of securing

copies of copyrighted material not in hand.

The Commission agrees with the basic recommendation of the NCLIS

report that improved methods of securing copies of periodical articles not

in hand are needed, since the traditional interlibrary loan arrangements

tend to be slow, inefficient and costly, but the Commission does not take a

position about the merits of non-profit centers as opposed to other methods

of achieving the objectives sought.

The experience of the British Library Lending Division (BLLD) in
Boston Spa [250/] shows that a centralized and specialized source of supply
can provide a very rapid service at a relatively low cost. In addition,
the existence of such centers in the future might provide a means for
the on-demand publishing of short documents as an alternative to, or
a supplement to, traditional journal publishing. Publishers could supply
documents to these centers, which would sell copies in full size or microform, much as the National Technical Information Service now sells copies
of government reports.

The status of such non-profit centers with respect to the 1976
Copyright Act is unclear. Can such non-profit copying centers be considered
a "library or archives" entitled to the benefits of the various exemptions
in Section 108 of the 1976 Act. More specifically, Section 108(d) permits
libraries and archives to make copies for users of single articles and small
portions of other works for the purpose of "private study, scholarship and
research," either from works in their own collections or "from that of
another library or archives." Section 108(g)(2) prohibits the "systematic
reproduction or distribution of single copies" of materials covered by Section
108(d) except that a proviso states that

> nothing in this clause prevents a library or archives
> from participating in interlibrary arrangements that do
> not have, as their purpose or effect, that the library
> or archives receiving such copies or phonorecords for
> distribution does so in such aggregate quantities as to
> substitute for a subscription to or purchase of such work.

The "aggregate quantities" constituting a substitute for subscriptions or
purchases are defined in the CONTU guidelines, described in Part IV D of
this Report. [251/]

250/ This organization is set up to supply photocopies of periodical articles, one copy to a customer and not more than one article per issue, to
British and overseas organizations. It lends physical volumes of books.
BLLD currently supplies about 1.5 million copies of articles per year and
subscribes to approximately 55,000 periodicals.

251/ See pp. 134-37, supra.

Neither "library" or "archives" is defined in the 1976 Act. However, the American Library Association Glossary of Library Terms contains the following two definitions of a library:

> Library. 1. A collection of books and similar material organized and administered for reading, consultation, and study. 2. A room, a group of rooms, or a building, in which a collection of books and similar material is organized and administered for reading, consultation, and study. 252/

If such nonprofit copying centers are not libraries or archives within the meaning of the 1976 Act, other libraries would not have the benefits of Section 108(d) and its extension in the Section 108(g)(2) proviso and the CONTU guidelines in securing photocopies of articles from them. In addition, the introduction to the CONTU guidelines, included in the Conference Report on the bill that became the 1976 Act, contains the following explicit statement:

> The point has been made that the present practice on interlibrary loans and use of photocopies in lieu of loans may be supplemented or even largely replaced by a system in which one or more agencies or institutions, public or private, exist for the specific purpose of providing a central source for photocopies. Of course, these guidelines would not apply to such a situation. 253/

Taking these factors into consideration, the Commission believes that non-profit centers established for the specific purpose of providing copies would be required to secure authorization from copyright owners to make and distribute full scale copies of periodical articles from the original issues as well as to make microform copies. The two major alternatives seem to be (1) to secure licenses to copy from copyright proprietors, or (2) to pay royalties on individual transactions through a mechanism similar to that established by the Copyright Clearance Center, Inc.

In view of the uncertainties of whether one or more non-profit periodical copying centers will be established and the lack of specific information as to how they might operate, the Commission does not believe that it is in a position to recommend any change in the 1976 Copyright Act

---

252/ A.L.A. Glossary of Library Terms 80 (1943).

253/ Conference Report, supra note 1, at 72.

directed at the operation of such centers. The Commission is of the opinion, however, that such arrangements are probably not entitled to the benefits of Section 108 of the 1976 Act.

6. Periodical centers in general

The Commission believes that arrangements that can supplement and in part take over copying services now provided through interlibrary loan systems could have great potential benefits, some examples of which are:

Providing comprehensive access to periodical literature;

Providing, in cooperation with publishers, more efficient distribution of materials after initial distribution in traditional periodical form;

Insuring preservation in at least one copy of periodical literature;

Making possible, in cooperation with publishers, the utilization of new technologies to develop alternative publishing and distribution methods for material for which there is a limited demand; and

Assisting local libraries to rationalize their collection development and maintenance plans.

Such arrangements may include non-profit centers especially created to serve this function, existing institutions, and various private enterprise undertakings. Central information sources or switching services to direct those seeking materials to the most efficient source of supply will no doubt be an important element.

Careful study will be required to determine the most effective array of resources, public and private, to meet these needs and the best modes of their operation. The Commission believes that the appropriate Congressional Committees, and the Register of Copyrights in monitoring developments preparatory to the mandatory first five-year report on the operation of Section 108 of the 1976 Act, should carefully follow the evolution of plans for such centers during the next few years.

G. The Interrelated Economics of Publishing and Libraries and the Impact of Copying Fees

Many assertions were made about the economic impact of photocopying on journal publishing during the debates in the Congress' twenty-year
effort to revise the copyright law, but little statistical or other factual
evidence to substantiate these assertions was presented, either by librarians
or by publishers and authors.

Librarians took the position that copying did not and would not
significantly reduce the volume of sales of printed publications, and that
librarians strive to purchase little-used materials rather than subject
their patrons to the inconvenience and delay of interlibrary loan. In part,
publisher and author concerns were not so much for the present as for the
future, at which time they believed various means of photocopying might
become increasingly cheaper relative to the cost of acquiring printed
publications. They also believed that they should secure some revenue
from copying as a contribution to the "first copy" costs of publications,
such as editorial, typesetting and business overhead.

The General Relationship of Journal Publishing to Library Budgets

The most complete study on library and journal publishing economics
and their relationship to one another is the 1975 Fry/White Study [254] sponsored by the National Science Foundation covering the years 1969, 1971 and
1973. Pertinent data were obtained through questionnaires filled out by a
sample of United States scholarly and research journals and by a sample
of academic, public and special libraries. [255]   The periodicals included in

---

254/ Fry/White, supra note 215. A further study by Fry and White repeating
the library portions of the 1976 study and covering the years 1974, 1975,
1976 has been delivered to the National Science Foundation and will be made
available through the National Technical Information Service: Impact of
Economic Pressures on American Libraries and Their Decisions Concerning
Scholarly and Research Journal Acquisition and Retention (NSF Grant
Number DSI 76-23592). The second study shows a continuation of the
1969-1973 trends in library budgets and practices but at slower rates.
In the 1974-1976 period funds were still being shifted from books
to periodical purchases and the total number of periodical subscriptions
was still rising.

255/   Federal, state and local government libraries were not surveyed in
the Fry/White Study except those that may have been included in the sample
of special libraries. Elementary and secondary school libraries, both public
and private, were not covered.

the survey were approximately 2,500 United States scholarly journals, of which about 150 furnished extensive usable data. The study provides data separately for four categories of journals by publisher: commercial publishers, professional societies, university presses, and other non-profit publishers.

1. Library acquisition budgets -- 1969-1973

During the period from 1969 to 1973 when prices rose sharply for both periodicals and books, expenditures for periodicals and the number of subscriptions increased in all three types of libraries included in the Fry/White Study. Although the total dollar expenditure for books also increased somewhat, the number of books purchased decreased. These trends were more sharply accentuated in academic libraries, the largest purchasers of periodicals, than in public and special libraries. For example, the median percentage increase in acquisition expenditures for periodicals and books from 1969 to 1973 in large libraries of all three types were as follows:

Type of Library	Expenditure Increase 1969-73	
	Periodicals	Books
Large Academic	75%	3%
Large Public	73%	28%
Large Special	89%	29%

Large academic libraries, which had allotted 67% of their acquisition budgets to books and 33% to periodicals in 1969 by 1973, were allotting 54% of the acquisition budgets to books and 46% to perioodicals.

The overall percentage increases in the number of periodical subscriptions by large libraries during the same 1969-73 period were: academic libraries, 18%; public libraries, 22%; and special libraries, 6%.

2. Borrowing and photocopying through interlibrary loan

All types and sizes of libraries increased their borrowing of periodicals through interlibrary loan during the 1969-1973 period. The median

number of interlibrary loans and the percentage increases were as follows for
large academic libraries, medium-sized public libraries and large special
libraries:

Median Number of Interlibrary Borrowings for Libraries

Type of Library	1969	1971	1973	Increase 1973 over 1969
Large Academic	1583	1907	1910	21%
Medium public	1730	1553	1950	13%
Large Special	1214	1145	1441	19%

(The above statistics are for borrowing periodical articles, but since the overwhelming proportion of interlibrary lending of articles consists of photocopies,
this is also a reasonable measure of the increase in securing photocopies through
interlibrary loan).

3. The effect of borrowing on periodical subscriptions

Despite the frequent debate concerning whether library photocopying from journals substitutes for subscriptions, little data has been
available to help resolve it. When Fry and White asked librarians whether
whether photocopying had this effect on subscriptions, they received the
following responses:

Types of effects

Type of Library	Total Percentage affected by Photocopying	Dropped Duplicates	Dropped Subscriptions	Added Fewer	Added More	Not Specified
Large academic libraries	42%	15%	24%	26%	7%	5%
Large public libraries	27%	9%	14%	9%	7%	2%

(Note: The percentages in the "affected" categories are not additive because
         multiple responses were possible).

Thus, while most libraries reported their purchase of journals were unaffected
by photocopying practices, a substantial minority said otherwise. Although
many libraries reported increasing subscriptions, the net effect on subscriptions seemed clearly negative in this study. Evidence from another study,
however, indicates that in the State of Minnesota the total number of

periodical subscriptions by 53 academic libraries in the MINITEX system

increased by about 25% from 1970/71 to 1976/77 following the establishment

of this state-wide interlibrary loan network in 1971. [256/]

4. Scholarly journal subscriptions and library budgets

The Fry/White Study also dealt with the economics of United States

scholarly journal publishing and the significance of the library market for

such journals. Libraries constitute the largest market for scholarly jour-

nals. These journals are also the type of periodical most copied in or by

libraries in relation to the size of circulations. The universe of 2459

United States scholarly journals surveyed by Fry and White was broken

down as follows:

256/ A 1977 British study, conducted by Aslib with the cooperation
of the British Library and the Scientific, Technical and Medical group
of the International Publishers Association, indicated little impact
on periodical subscriptions in British libraries due to the availability
of a quick and inexpensive source of photocopies from the British Library
Lending Division. Since Britain's interlibrary photocopy service is
superior to that in the United States, one would expect a greater depress-
ing effect on circulation levels there. However, only 15% of the British
academic, public, and special libraries surveyed indicated that an effective interlibrary loan service enabled them "to reduce subscriptions
by a significant amount without damaging the service". The British
study also concluded that only about 3% of the photocopies secured
from other libraries (or borrowing the periodical volume and photocopying the article on receipt) constituted "replacement borrowing",
which is defined as securing photocopies of current materials from BLLD
from periodicals which were once, but no longer, subscribed to by the
borrowing library.

The author of this British study concludes that "the total
number of subscriptions entered by all libraries is beginning to decline
in 1976-1977," but he attributes this to causes other than photocopying,
such as the stringency in library budgets and the inflation of periodical
and other library materials prices. The more general conclusion of
the Aslib study was that no evidence was presented that "a direct causal
relationship exists whereby increased interlibrary lending leads to
an overall decrease in periodical subscriptions by virtue of its
associated photocopying."

A.M. Woodward, Factors Affecting the Renewal of Periodical
Subscriptions: A Study of Decision-Making in Libraries with Special
Reference to Economics and Inter-Library Lending, London: Aslib R & D
Department, November 1977.

Subject Area	Commercial	Society	By Type of Publisher University Presses	Other Not-for-Profit	Total
Pure Science	147	209	40	77	473
Applied Science & Technology	276	356	9	76	717
Humanities	40	84	28	147	299
Social Sciences	182	424	50	314	970
Total	645	1073	127	614	2459
Percentage of Total	26.2%	43.6%	5.2%	25.0%	100.0%

The journals responding to the questionnaire reported that the number of copies circulated increased in the period 1969-1973, but generally this was the result of increases in the number of foreign subscribers and institutional subscribers, and decreases in the number of individual subscribers. The following table presents data by type of publisher:

Percentage Changes in Circulation 1969-1973 257/
By Type of Publisher

Type of Subscription	Commercial	Society	University Presses	Other Not-for-Profit
Total	4.2%	2.3%	9.2%	27.2%
Total U.S.	-0.9%	-0.3%	-3.6%	NA
Institution	0.9%	12.5%	6.3%	11.6%
Individual	-2.7%	-4.0%	-12.9%	54.3%
Foreign	11.5%	20.6%	74.7%	4.0%

These figures are consistent with the general trend in the Fry/White survey data which showed an increase in periodical subscriptions by libraries from 1969-1973. These journal subscription data do not correspond exactly with the library data because, among other reasons, U.S. libraries subscribe to foreign journals and serial materials other than scholarly journals.

257/ Fry and White are skeptical about the figures in the above table for other not-for-profit publishers and indicate that these reported results do not agree with other data supplied for journals published by this category of publisher.

The data also show that United States institutions -- principally libraries -- account for about one third of the circulation of scholarly journals published by commercial presses, university presses, and other not-for-profit periodicals, and over 20% of the circulation of journals of professional societies which provide subscriptions to their own members as part of general membership fees. The complete data on the proportion of subscriptions by type of subscriber follow:

Percent Circulation Distribution 1973

Type of Publisher

Type of Subscriber	Commercial	Society	University Press	Other Not-for-Profit
Total U.S. subscriptions	56%	86%	74%	84%
Institutional	32	22	40	36
Individual	24	64	34	48
Foreign subscriptions	44%	14%	26%	16%

The publisher data shown in the following table indicate that in general the number of journals that had differential (usually higher) subscription rates for institutions and libraries increased markedly from 1969 to 1973.

Percent of Journals Having Institutional and Library Subscription Rates

Type of Subscription	Commercial		Society		University Presses		Other Not-for-Profit	
	1969	1973	1969	1973	1969	1973	1969	1973
Institutional	37%	50%	56%	67%	39%	58%	13%	30%
Library	2%	2%	20%	16%	6%	10%	10%	11%

In general the institutional (usually library) subscription rates, when they exist, increased substantially more than the individual subscription rates in the period 1969-1973. The figures are:

Percentage Increases in Individual and Institutional Subscription Rates

Type of Publisher	Rate	Median Subscription Rates			Percentage Change 1969-73
		1969	1971	1973	
Commercial	Individual	$16.61	$19.50	$22.39	35%
	Institutional	$31.75	$41.56	$54.16	71%
Society	Individual	$14.54	$17.83	$20.64	42%
	Institutional	$18.21	$20.87	$25.56	40%
University Presses	Individual	$ 7.41	$ 7.96	$ 9.27	25%
	Institutional	$ 9.70	$10.35	$12.85	32%
Other not-for-Profit	Individual	$ 6.05	$ 7.00	$ 8.64	43%
	Institutional	$ 9.71	$11.00	$14.14	46%

Taking all of the above data into consideration, it is clear that libraries and other institutions provided an increased share of the revenues of scholarly journal publishers in 1973 as compared with 1969. Institutions were buying a larger number of subscriptions, as well as an increased proportion of all subscriptions. In many cases, they were also paying institutional subscription prices which increased more than the subscription price for individuals. Unfortunately, direct data on the proportion of total revenues derived by scholarly journal publishers from institution and library subscriptions are not provided in the Fry/White Study. However, for many individual journals (except for society journals with high proportions of individual subscriptions), as well as for classes of journals, one-half or more of total subscription revenues, must have come from United States libraries or other institutions. If foreign sales are added (and these are predominantly to institutions) this proportion is still higher.

The Fry/White Study also collected data on the profitability of United States scholarly journal publishing. Statistically, this is the weakest part of the study because only ninety-two journals provided financial data. The data may be summarized as follows:

	Operating Income as a Percentage of Total Revenue	
	1969	1973
Type of Publisher		
Commercial	11%	14%
Society	3%	3%
University Presses	-4%	-7%
Other Not-for-Profit	-1%	-7%
All Journals	1%	4%

Operating income is defined as "all revenue minus costs of sales and operating expenses. It does not take into account such items as interest paid or received, capitalized expenditures, or taxes." Thus, for commercial publishers in 1973, the net profit after corporate income and other taxes would be about 6% of total revenue. The society, university press, and other not-for-profit publishers would not, of course, be subject to Federal and state corporate income taxes. Although libraries in the 1969-1973 period were subscribing to more scholarly journals and paying higher prices for subscriptions, especially when they had to pay institutional subscription rates, the net effect was not a windfall for the publishers of scholarly journals. Fry and White concluded that the price-budget imbalance did not result from excessive returns to publishers. Commercial publishers had profits no better than average, and societies had barely enough capital to launch new journals. They described the condition of university press journal publishing as "disastrous."

5. Estimates of possible additional costs to libraries for copying fees

Using the estimates made from the King Research data in Part IV-E of this Report on the number of photocopied items from serials that would require authorization, and assuming a certain average level of photocopying fees, it is possible to arrive at estimates of additional annual costs to libraries resulting from copying fees under the new copyright act. These estimates are valid only if libraries do not change their copying practices

as a result of the 1976 Act. It is likely, however, that libraries may
alter their practices. The analysis uses the three categories of copying
in the King Study (interlibrary loan, local use and intrasystem use) and
breaks down the copying by type of library. These amounts are then compared
with the available data on total annual library expenditures for library materials to arrive at some estimate of the comparative magnitudes of these new
costs as compared with the existing acquisition costs for library materials.
In the absence of comprehensive statistical data at this time, an average
copying fee to publishers per article of $1.25 will be assumed. This is
higher than the $.60 paid by ISI and the $.50 paid by NTIS under direct contracts with publishers. It may, however, be less than the weighted average
price which will be paid to the Copyright Clearance Center. The 1977 Fry/
White/Johnson Study for the Commission on journal publishing indicated that
some 53% of the journals responding to a question relating to appropriate
fees to be paid by agents or clearinghouses for copying articles set $1.00
or less as an appropriate fee. 258/

Copying for Interlibrary Loan

Table II in Part IV-E and the discussion following the table presented estimates of the volume of copying of periodicals for interlibrary
loan for items not more than five years old that would not be exempt either
under the CONTU guidelines, the exceptions in Section 108 for replacement
of copies, or under Section 107 for classroom use. At an average of $1.25
the additional annual costs to libraries would be:

Type of Library	Additional Costs (thousands)
Academic	$147
Public	$ 94
Special	$231
Federal	$ 63
TOTAL	$ 535

258/ Fry/White/Johnson, supra note 201, at 112.

These estimates may in some respects overstate the additional costs because they do not take into account the following: (1) libraries reaching their limit of five copies for a title might subscribe to the journal,[259] or tell patrons that their requests could not be met, or that they charge an additional fee for copying; (2) many journals may adopt more liberal copying policies than is required by law; and (3) authorized royalty-paid copies might cost the borrowing library the same as or less than conventional interlibrary loans.

Data compiled from a special survey of interlibrary loan charges by members of the Association of Research Libraries (ARL) in 1976 showed that the libraries in this group that charged for photocopies had a weighted average price of $3.50 for a ten-page article -- excluding those cases in which special lower rates were charged to libraries in the same state (or consortium), or in which interlibrary loans were subsidized by the state. If this $3.50 figure is taken as a base, and there is added to it an internal borrowing cost of $6.00, the total average cost to the borrowing library becomes $9.50. Six dollars is selected as an internal borrowing cost; this is somewhat less than the average of the internal borrowing costs in 1977 in the three libraries for which such costs were calculated in the Palmour Study contracted for by the Commission.[260]

These combined costs compare with an out-of-pocket direct cost to a borrowing library of securing a ten-page article from the Institute of Scientific Information of $3.50 (higher with special services); the $4.00 - $6.00 cost of securing a single copy from University Microfilms; and the price of a copy through NTIS, which will vary somewhat, but may average $7.00. These comparisons do not take into account the internal costs to the lending library, over and above the fees charged.

259/ The Palmour Study, supra note 200, shows that as the number of photocopies of articles from a single title secured from other libraries increases above five, in many cases it will be less costly for a library to subscribe rather than to continue to secure photocopying through interlibrary loan.

260/ Id.

6. Copying for local use

   Table III in Part IVE presented estimates of the number of copies for local use by type of library requiring authorization. Applying the the same assumed $1.25 average copying fee, the additional annual costs for various types of libraries would be:

Type of Library	Copying Fees (thousands)
Academic	$ 125
Public	3,375
Special	1,125
Federal	1,750
Total	$6,375

   As in the case of copying for interlibrary loan, these figures may in some respects be an overstatement of additional costs for some (but not all) of the reasons mentioned for interlibrary loan copying: (1) patrons might be informed that copies could not be made, or that they would have to pay an additional copying fee; (2) many journals may adopt more liberal copying policies than is required by law; and (3) many older issues of journals will be out of copyright because they were not renewed for a second term. On the other hand, the estimate for academic libraries may be low because the King data on classroom use included all copying for classroom use, not copying for classroom use permissible under the educational copying guidelines.

7. Copying for Intrasystem use

   Table IV in Part 1V-F presents estimates by types of library of the number of copies made for intrasystem use that would require authorization. Applying the same average $1.25 copying fee, the following would be the additional annual costs for various types of libraries:

Type of Library	Copying Fees (Thousands)
Academic	$ 00
Public	1,000
Special	1,837
Federal	00
TOTAL	$2,837

These figures may be an overstatement of additional costs for the same reasons given in the discussion of copying for local use.

Estimates of Total Additional Costs for Libraries

Based upon the above discussion and calculations, the estimated costs for various types of libraries may be aggregated as shown in the following table. Data from the National Center for Education Statistics on the total expenditures of three types of libraries for library materials are also included.

Possible Annual Additional Costs to Libraries in Copying Fees for Periodicals as Compared with Expenditures for Library Materials (figures rounded)

	1	2	3
Type of Library	Additional Costs (thousands)	Total Library Materials Expenditures 261/ (millions)	Percentage Column 1 of Column 2
Academic	$ 272	(1976) $337	0.1%
Public	4,469	(1974) 165	2.7%
Special	3,193	NA	–
Federal	1,813	(1972) 44	4.1%
Total	$ 9,747		

261/   Source: National Center for Education Statistics published reports.

There are no reliable data on expenditures for materials by special libraries. The National Center for Education Statistics has contracted with the Special Libraries Association for a preliminary study of special libraries in commerce and industry, including the expenditures for materials. The results of this study may be be available before the end of 1978.

The preceding table has some unexpected aspects. The net estimated increased costs for academic libraries constitute an insignificant percentage of the current expenditures of these libraries for materials. The estimated copying fees of almost 3% of public library material expenditures constitute a very much higher percentage of materials expenditures than for academic libraries, but the dollar amounts are not large.

The special library estimates may reflect the amount of multiple copying done in many of these libraries for their research, professional and executive personnel. The federal agency library estimates are not particularly surprising, given the nature of most of their operations, which are more similar to special libraries than to either of the other two types of libraries.

If these estimates of copying fees are approximately correct, the impact on academic libraries as a class would be minimal and should not present any significant budget problems. Copying fees, which would go mostly to journal publishers, would not be great enough to do more than accentuate very slightly the trend in academic libraries of spending more of their acquisition funds on serials and less on books. For public libraries the impact of photocopying would be proportionately much greater, with copying fees amounting to almost 3% of total acquisition budgets in 1974. Since the bulk of the copying fees would be paid to periodical publishers, in the case of public libraries this might modestly accentuate existing trends of shifting funds from book to periodical purchases.

For special libraries at least two different situations exist: one for libraries in business and industrial establishments or related organizations such as trade associations, and the other for special libraries in nonprofit organizations. In the first category information is used for the purpose of increasing the revenues or reducing the costs of the business. Copying fees would also be a tax-deductible cost of doing business. As compared to all other costs of doing business, copying fees would be small. Special libraries in nonprofit organizations are extremely varied, and it is difficult to state generally what the impact of copying fees would be on their operations, especially since no statistical data exist either on their costs of operations as a class or their expenditures for periodicals, books and other materials.

The federal library situation is somewhat similar to that of libraries in business and industrial establishments. Information is used in carrying out the work of federal agencies. Copying fees would represent another operating cost, and should not in general be of such a magnitude compared to other operating costs as to present unmanageable budget problems.

8. Potential copying fees compared with publishers revenues -- periodicals

Data on the total revenues from periodical publishing are collected approximately every five years by the Bureau of the Census in the Census of Manufactures, and estimated each year based on a sample survey in the Annual Survey of Manufactures. Unfortunately, the Bureau of the Census divides periodicals into only four classes -- farm periodicals, specialized professional and business periodicals, general periodicals and "other" periodicals (excluding shopping news, directories and catalogs). Specialized professional and business periodicals, with estimated total 1976 revenues of $407 million from subscriptions and $946 million from advertisements[262] are those most likely to be photocopied. It is clear that this broad category of periodicals is very different from the 2459 scholarly periodicals surveyed in the 1975 Fry/White study, the 1973 total annual revenues which were estimated at $170 million, of which less than 10% was from advertising. If we compare total annual copying fees for periodicals, estimated to be about $10 million, with the total 1973 revenues of the scholarly journals surveyed by Fry and

---

262/ U.S. Bureau of the Census. Annual Survey of Manufactures 1976: Value of Product Shipments. 12 (1977).

White, revenues from copying fees appear to be a minor but still significant source of revenue for some of these journals. While not comparable with revenues from subscription charges, income from authorized photocopying could be, in some cases, more significant than such current sources of revenue as advertising, page charges or a variety of subsidies. [263/]

9. The economics of book publishing, the library market for books, and photocopying

Libraries account for a very much smaller proportion of the total sales of United States books than they do of sales of scientific, technical and scholarly journals, and the kinds of books which are photocopied in libraries fall into a few limited classes. The most copied classes and the industry estimates of total dollar receipts in 1977 of United States publishers (including exports) for these classes were as follows: [264/]

Technical and Scientific Books	$266.8 million
Business and Other Professional Books	195.2 million
Medical Books	97.0 million
University Press Books	53.5 million

The library and institutional market is particularly important to university press books, constituting well over half of university press sales within the United States. [265/] The King Study clearly indicates that in 1976 the volume of photocopying from copyrighted books in libraries

---

263/ Some comment needs to be made here as to the impact of copying fees on individual journals. The journals most copied by the British Lending Library Division (BLLD) in Boston Spa have, in general but not uniformly, been journals with larger circulations. The King Study tabulations of the MINITEX data do not seem to reflect the same correlation between the volume of copying and circulation size. It is probably fair to say that the amount of copying from journals will vary greatly from one journal to another, and that the importance of copying fees relative to other revenues will also vary greatly. In economic terms, this would be a "good" result: the revenue of journals would be related not only to their subscriptions but also to the extent that they are copied, reflecting in each case the market value placed on journals by subscribers and other users.

264/ Association of American Publishers, 1977 Industry Statistics. Washington, D.C. (1977).

265/ Id.

was considerably less than the volume of copying from copyrighted serials. The respective proportions were: 70% of the items copied in libraries were from serials; 24% from books; and 6% from other copyrighted materials. These data are consistent with data from other studies, and also are consistent with the general practice of libraries, which is to lend the physical book to their patrons for local use and also for interlibrary loans and intrasystem loans rather than to make photocopies. The bulk of the copying from books in libraries has probably occurred in two ways:

(1) The library patron may make a copy of some part of a book on a coin-operated machine;

(2) Library employees or others in educational institutions may make copies in order to place chapters or other portions of books on reserve for the use of students; or the instructor may have copies of portions of books made for classroom use.

Because of the ambiguity of the 1909 law there also had been a certain amount of copying to create anthologies or substitute textbooks by putting together photocopies of chapters of books and periodical articles for use in specific courses.

The Congress dealt with copying for educational use by including in the House Report the "educational copying guidelines."[266/] These guidelines place definite limitations on the amount and character of copying for teachers and for classroom use that can be regarded as fair use under Section 107. It is unlikely that the educational copying permissible within these guidelines will have much adverse affect on the economic viability of book publishing.

The amount of copying from books that is permissible under the 1976 Act either as fair use under Section 107 and the educational copying guide lines, or the exemptions in Section 108 for library copying would seem to have no appreciable effect on the economics of book publishing at this time or in the next few years. There will undoubtedly be some

---

266/ House Report, supra note 1, at 68.

copying of books in violation of the 1976 Act that will substitute for
the purchase of books. The amount of such copying is probably small, however, and is inhibited by cost factors, in particular the current frequently
higher per-page cost of making copies as compared with the cost of buying
the book. Furthermore, there are whole categories of books for which photocopies are not acceptable substitutes for the original product, such
as paperback books, book club books, and art books.

The book publishing industry, although not highly profitable as
compared with some other industries, has been in a fairly stable condition
in the past few years. There has been a growing dollar volume of sales,
much of which is a reflection of inflation and higher prices with little
or no increase in the number of copies of books sold. There is no question,
however, that a problem exists with respect to the production and sale
of scholarly books, most of which are now published in the United States
by university presses. This problem is primarily due to inflation, limitations on the amount of support that universities are prepared to give
their presses, and library budgets which have not kept pace with rising
prices of periodicals and books. As discussed earlier, the data in the
1976 Fry/White report show the decline of the physical volume of book
purchases by libraries because of the shift of acquisition funds from
books to periodicals. For the next few years, at least, it does not
appear that the photocopying of books under the conditions imposed by the
1976 Act will have any significant impact on any branch of book publishing.

10. Economic analyses of the impact of photocopying charges

The Commission sought the assistance of several economists
in assessing the likely consequences of imposing and collecting fees for
photocopying copyrighted works, primarily periodical articles. Professors
Fritz Machlup and William Baumol, each affiliated with Princeton and New
York Universities, presented testimony and Dr. Allen Ferguson, President of
the Public Interest Economics Center in Washington, D.C., prepared a study
for the Commission entitled, An Analysis of Computer and Photocopying

Copyright Issues from the Point of View of the General Public and the Ultimate
Consumer.[267]

Professor Machlup suggested that the imposition of copying fees
would be economically sound only if the burden of paying the fees fell on
the actual users and the collection of fees provided additional revenues
that would hold down subscription prices or assist journals to survive.
He expressed skepticism whether any of these effects, given the volume
of photocopying for which payments would be made at this time and administrative costs, would be realized by collections of fees for photocopying.[268]

Professor Baumol viewed copying fees as economically beneficial
if they served to spread the costs of publication, including a reasonable
return on capital, over a broader base of actual users of copyrighted works.
He questioned, however, whether publishers' revenues for photocopying would
significantly exceed the cost of collecting the fees. Unless fees provided
additional net revenues, their imposition would not have a desirable
economic effect.[269]

In his study, Dr. Ferguson concluded that the imposition of copying fees would not serve the interests of the general public.[270]   Such fees
might inhibit user access to valuable information, he suggested, and would
not necessarily hold down subscription rates significantly. He suggested
that the Commission recommend broad exemptions from copyright liability for
photocopying done by individuals and tax-exempt not-for-profit corporations.
Copying done for resale by the copier, however, should not be exempted. He
also suggested that publishers could practice price discrimination among
different classes of subscribers to reflect factors, such as photocopying,
as a means of increasing revenues. Periodical publishers can and often

---

[267]/ Transcript, CONTU Meeting No. 15 164 (1977).

[268]/ Id. at 9.

---

[269]/ Id. at 52.

[270]/ Id. at 167.

do charge libraries higher subscription prices than they charge individuals,
but higher institutional subscription charges have not carried with them
authorization to copy. 271/

The possibility, suggested by Dr. Ferguson, that photocopying
privileges could be attached to higher prices charged to institutional
subscribers, is one of three ways in which publishers could use the subscription price mechanism to authorize reproduction and to increase revenues.
Other methods include an optional surcharge on the subscription price for
blanket internal copying, and the provision of lower multiple subscription rates. Although neither of the first two methods is in general
use, two major newsletter publishers, the Bureau of National Affairs and
Knowledge Industries Publications, offer lower multiple subscription rates.
Furthermore, the optional subscription surcharge is the chief method
used by the photocopying royalty collection agency in the Federal Republic
of Germany. These considerations prompt a consideration of the relative
merits of photocopying fees based on actual transactions and surcharges
on subscription prices permitting photocopying.

A transaction-based system, such as that of the Copyright Clearance
Center, Inc. offers the greatest exactitude in payments from users to publishers and authors. In such a system the payment falls directly on users
and is proportional to the amount of reproduction. At the same time it
imposes greater administrative burdens and higher collection costs. Authorization through subscription pricing has the opposite characteristics:
the payments are less proportional to the amount of copying but the
administrative burdens and costs of the system are very low. Hence, one
can easily understand why, out of eight possibilities, authorization

271/ The 1976 Fry/White Study showed that in 1973, 1754 out of the 2459 journals
in their universe of scholarly journals were practicing price discrimination
between institutional and individual subscribers. By categories the percentage
of journals practicing such price discrimination were:

Commercially published journals	52.2%
Society published journals	82.9%
University press journals	9.7%
Journals published by other non-profit organizations	38.4%

to make copies via subscription pricing was the single most popular alternative among the libraries surveyed in the King Study. From the publishers'
point of view, subscription revenues offer the advantage of providing
revenues before publication, whereas copying fees provide delayed payments
with a discounted present value.$\underline{272/}$

It is important to realize that these two systems are complementary rather than exclusive. A library with significant photocopying
activity might wish to acquire authorization for copying for local and
intrasystem uses through higher subscription prices in some cases and
to use clearance systems such as the Copyright Clearance Center, Inc.
in others. In some instances the subscription price alternative may
work to the mutual advantage of both the publisher and the subscriber.
These considerations of complementary and mutual advantage call for further
consideration and exploration of flexible subscription pricing with photocopying privileges as an alternative to transaction-based systems of
licensing photocopying of material which the copiers have in their possession.

> H. Legislation and Systems Relating to
> Photocopying in Other Countries

The executive bodies responsible for the administration of the
two international copyright conventions, The Berne Union and the Universal
Copyright Convention, have studied copyright problems raised by photocopying for several years. They decided at a joint meeting in December 1975
that the subject was not yet ripe for international treatment, but should be

---

272/ Under the 1976 Copyright Act both the transaction-based and subscription
surcharge systems will require authors to transfer photocopying rights to the
publisher. Section 201(c) of the Act provides that unless otherwise specified
by contract, authors retain the rights to their individual contributions to
a collective work and the publisher merely has a copyright in that
collective work. In a transaction based system, such as the CCC, authors
may contract with the publisher to pay them a portion of the revenues
derived from the photocopying rights to their individual contribution to
collective works, which can be identified. In a subscription surcharge
system, however, it would be impossible to determine what part of the
photocopying revenues were due to individual authors because there would
be no record of the amount of photocopying of specific contributions.

left for the time being to national consideration. When the two committees
met again in November and December of 1977, this earlier decision was
allowed to stand, and no further consideration has been given to adding
to the international conventions specific provisions relating to photocopying.

Meanwhile, active study of problems presented by photocopying has
been undertaken in a number of countries. The discussion which follows will
concentrate on four of these countries: Great Britain, Canada and Australia --
all of which have published official reports -- and the Netherlands, where
the copyright law of 1972 and subsequent administrative decrees have
established a compulsory license and various schedules of fees for photocopying. Some consideration is also given to developments in France and
the Federal Republic of Germany. Sweden operates a system under which the
government makes payments to Swedish publishers for domestic materials copied
for classroom use in the elementary and secondary schools.

In Great Britain a special committee on general copyright revision
reported its findings and recommendations in March 1977 in a publication
entitled Copyright and Designs Law: Report of the Committee to consider
the Law on Copyright and Designs,[273/] commonly referred to as the "Whitford
Committee Report" after its Chairman, Justice Whitford. With respect to
photocopying the Whitford Committee recommended that the British copyright
law of 1958 -- which, among other things, generally permits the making
of single copies of articles from periodicals without authorization --
be amended. The recommended amendments would permit no photocopying
without authorization of the copyright proprietor, but this change would not
take effect until authors and other copyright proprietors, with the approval
of the government, (under a so-called umbrella statute), had set up one or
more collecting societies to collect copyright fees under blanket licenses.
The fees to be charged by the collecting societies would be subject to review by a copyright tribunal.

273/ See note 53, supra.

The Canadian Department of Consumer and Corporate Affairs published a working paper in April 1977 entitled Copyright in Canada -- Proposals for a Revision of the Law, by A. A. Keyes and C. Brunet. The Department has requested interested Canadian organizations to submit written comments on this report and oral testimony is expected to be heard in 1979. The recommendations of the Keyes-Brunet report are somewhat similar to those of the Whitford Committee. Keyes and Brunet believe, however, that the present Canadian law adequately covers photocopying, and recommend no changes in the statute. They propose that authors and other copyright proprietors form a collective or collectives, similar to those existing in Canada for the collection of music performance fees, to license photocopying under the supervision of a government tribunal.

In Australia a special committee headed by Justice Franki published in October 1976 a report limited to the photocopying question entitled, Report of the Copyright Law Committee on Reprographic Reproduction, frequently referred to as the Franki Report. That Committee was set up largely as a result of an Australian Supreme Court decision which held that universities were liable for unauthorized photocopying of copyrighted materials, including copying done on unsupervised coin-operated machines on their premises where no copyright warning was posted. The Franki Committee's recommendations differ greatly from those of the Whitford Committee and of Keyes and Brunet. The Franki Report recommended that the Australian Copyright law be amended to permit extensive single copy photocopying of "reasonable portions" of copyrighted works by or on behalf of students in educational institutions and patrons of public libraries, and up to six copies for classroom use in nonprofit educational institutions. For copying beyond these limitations a compulsory licensing scheme for nonprofit educational institutions was proposed.

In the Netherlands, the Copyright Law of 1972 established liability for certain photocopying and provided for a compulsory licensing scheme covering both Dutch and foreign works. The implementation of the general provisions was spelled out in a Royal Ordinance of 1974. In general,

articles and short excerpts may be copied freely for private use. Commercial
enterprises and public institutions may also make copies by paying fees to
copyright owners. In the case of commercial enterprises the payment is required to be "equitable." The copying fee for public authorities, universities
and public libraries is set at ten Dutch cents per page and for schools, two
and a half Dutch cents per page. Libraries, however, may make single copies
of articles for patrons and for interlibrary loan without liability.

A Dutch collecting society representing authors and publishers
has been established but seems not to have progressed very far as yet in collecting copying fees. The one exception has been that the Dutch government
paid 100,000 guilders for its copying in the years 1975 and 1976, and is
negotiating for the payment of fees for the years 1977-1979. The collecting
society proposes to negotiate several blanket license agreements with
industry, universities, schools, libraries and local governments. The fees
collected will ultimately be distributed to the copyright proprietors
whose works are copied, based on sampling and estimates. Until these arrangements can be made, any funds collected are to be distributed on an approximate basis by types of works, such as newspapers, books and periodicals.

As a result of a lawsuit in the Federal Republic of Germany, later
reinforced by the enactment of Section 54(2) of that country's Copyright
Act of 1965, a partial scheme for collecting fees for the photocopying
of German scientific, technical and professional journals was set up several
years ago. Corporations wishing to copy articles of this type published
by members of the Boersenverein (short designation of the publishers
and booksellers association) pay for copies they make on a sliding schedule
of fees. Small amounts of copying may be paid for by the purchase of
stamps from an operating affiliate of the Boersenverein. A corporation may
pay for larger amounts of copying in selected journals by means of a 30%
surcharge on vhe subscription price. Alternatively, blanket copying privileges may be obtained by paying a 20% surcharge on all journals purchased.
After the deduction of rather modest charges to cover administrative
expenses the fees are distributed, with one-half going to publishers of

journals and one-half to various professional societies whose members are frequently the authors of articles in the journals covered. Although this system has been in operation for some years, it has continued to be limited in scope, with only about 100 large companies paying copying fees on some 1200 journals. The total annual gross revenues to the collection agency are currently less than 1,000,000 German marks.

Following a court decision in France, the CNRS (<u>Centre National de la Recherche Scientifique</u> -- National Center for Scientific Research) has confined its photocopy services to single copies of articles for "research use" supplied by two installations in Paris. Research use includes research in for-profit corporations. However, these two copying centers will not supply photocopies or microfiche of articles from issues of periodicals that are less than three months old.

There has also been a tax on the sale of photocopying machines in France since 1976. This tax, however, is not related to what is copied on the machines. The yield of the tax is not paid to authors and other copyright proprietors, but is distributed to French libraries for the purchase of French publications.

I.   Recommendations of Interested Organizations

On October 21, 1977 and April 28, 1978, representatives of the principal library, author and publisher organizations concerned with photocopying, other than for classroom use, appeared before the Commission to make recommendations to the Commission regarding the Commission's final report.[274] Testimony was presented by representatives of the Council of National Library Associations' Ad Hoc Committee on Copyright Practice and Implementation, which includes represrntatives of the following library organizations: Special Libraries Association, Music Library Association, Medical Library Association, Association of Research Libraries, American Library Association, and American Association of Law Libraries. On the

---

274/ Transcript, CONTU Meeting No. 17 and No. 21.

same days, representatives of the Authors' League of America and the
Association of American Publishers also testified. All three groups stated
that they wished to see how the provisions relating to photocopying in the
1976 Copyright Act would work out in practice. They stated that they did
not wish to suggest amendments to the 1976 Act at this time, but preferred
to make such recommendations, if any, to the Register of Copyrights under
the provisions of Section 108(i) which requires the Register of Copyrights
to report to the Congress in 1983 on how Section 108 has worked out in
practice.

Two organizations with which the Commission had contracts to
prepare studies on copyright issues from the point of view of consumers
and the general public recommended changes in the 1976 Copyright Act at
the July 1977 Commission hearings.[275/] The Public Interest Economics Center
and the Public Interest Satellite Association recommended that the 1976
Act be amended to remove all restrictions on photocopying except copying
for commercial resale. The full text of their recommendations may be found
in the reports of the two organizations cited in Appendix H.

J. The Effects of Future Technological Change

The Commission has given attention to the prospects of technological changes that may affect both the creation and the distribution
of information (including copyrighted materials) which have been distributed
by conventional publishing methods in the past in order to determine whether
prospective changes in technology may require amendment of the copyright
law. An entire meeting of the Commission in November 1977[276/] was given
over to a discussion of this topic with several invited outside experts.

It is now technologically possible to distribute text, data and
graphics electronically rather than in traditional printed forms. The
limitations on the spread of this mode of distribution at the moment are

---

275/ Transcript, CONTU Meeting No. 15.

276/ Transcript, CONTU Meeting No. 18.

more in the cost of such technology and in user acceptance rather than in the technology itself, but costs are rapidly decreasing both for storage and for transmission. In addition, more and more textual materials appearing ultimately in printed form exist at some state in the production process in digital form on tapes and disks or other electronic storage devices. The full text of certain legal materials, such as court decisions, can already be displayed on computer terminals from distant data bases.

It seems to the Commission, however, that these present and prospective technological developments for the creation, storage and distribution of copyrighted materials do not in themselves call for any change in the copyright law other than those which have been recommended by the Commission to deal with copyright for computer software and for computer data bases. These technological developments may ease the problem which has been caused by the wide availability of photocopying machines capable of producing copies quickly and relatively inexpensively. If the copyright owner possesses material in digital form on tapes or other storage devices and sells access to such material by contracts with users, the copyright owner may have more effective control over unauthorized use than over information distributed in printed form. Even now, owners of bibliographic and other data bases make them electronically available to users who pay for this service, either directly or through intermediaries selling on-line access to a variety of data bases.

It seems to the Commission that the foreseeable developments in technology and reduction of costs do not warrant any present change in the copyright law relating to the "machine reproduction" of copyrighted materials. Furthermore, the provisions of Section 108(i) of the 1976 Act provide for a review of Section 108 in 1983 and every five years thereafter by the Register of Copyrights, after consultation with the affected parties. If changes in the copyright law relating to machine reproduction seem necessary or desirable because of technological developments five, ten or twenty-five years hence, this review provision provides a mechanism for timely consideration.

V. SUMMARY

This report has presented the recommendations of the Commission for the changes in copyright law and procedure needed to balance the interests of copyright owners and users of works created by the application of and used in conjunction with computers and reprographic systems. In developing these recommendations the Commission has sought to consider, as well, the ways in which the interests of the general public and the ultimate consumer may be affected. As is apparent from a reading of those recommendations and the accompanying expository material, the Commission believes that the new law, by and large, effectively deals with the interests of both proprietors and users and requires but little modification at this time. The Commission, however, believes that the Congress should immediately enact legislation to repeal Section 117 of the 1976 Act and should carefully consider the introduction of legislation dealing with computer software or programs in light of the controversy surrounding that area. Any legislation dealing with either computer or photocopying issues enacted and based upon these recommendations should be subject to a process of periodic review similar to that mandated for certain photocopying procedures in Section 108(i) of the Act of 1976. It is apparent to this Commission that technology will continue to pose new problems for the copyright system and this review will help keep the law in step with technological and economic development.

It is equally important to note that these recommendations do not deal with each and every technological issue affecting the interests of copyright users and owners. Specific topics may deserve congressional attention.
Indeed, two such have been raised before the Commission and deemed to be outside the scope of its mandate:

1) the off-the-air videotaping of television broadcasts
   of copyrighted works; and

2) protection for the topography or layout of microcircuit chips.

With respect to off-the-air videotaping, the Commission determined that it should not take up this subject since the legislative history clearly shows that Congress intended the mandate to study "machine reproduction" to apply to photocopying. Additionally, the Commission believed that the issues involved in off-the-air videotaping were essentially matters requiring public policy decisions not related to technology per se, and that these matters were being tested in a pending legal action. [277]

The question of copyright protection for the topography of microcircuit chips was raised by a manufacturer of these devices too late to be dealt with adequately by the Commission. [278] These chips are complex electronic circuits built up on silicon chips by steps involving a type of photographic reproduction on several layers, each similar to the preparation of a photoengraving. Layouts of the structures in each of these layers are produced at great expense and converted to a type of photographic plate, called a mask, to be used as a master in the successive photographic reproductions previously mentioned. It is asserted that the chips produced by use of these masks should be protectable by copyright since the masks can be readily duplicated either by outright copying or by disassembling and chemically treating a chip to expose each layer. The topography contained on these layers can then be photographed and used to prepare masks which duplicate those originally used to produce the chip, a result which the manufacturer claims would infringe its copyright as would the use of these masks to produce copies of the original chip.

Examples cited emphasize the need for the continued monitoring and oversight of technological developments not encompassed or antici-

---

277/ Universal City Studios, Inc. v. Sony Corporation of America, No. 76-3520F, C.D. Cal.

278/ Certain questions relating to this issue may be answered in another pending lawsuit, Intel Corp. v. Ringer, No. C-77-2848-RHS, N.D. Cal.

pated in the Copyright Act of 1976. Human ingenuity will continue to
develop new works which may be in themselves copyrightable and it
will employ existing copyrighted works in new ways in the production
of literary, artistic and even utilitarian works. If this process
of innovation and enrichment of our cultural heritage is to continue,
the rights of authors and creators of these works must be protected
and the public dissemination and use of these works encouraged. The
recommendations and considerations contained in this report are intended
to do just that and thereby promote the progress of science and the
useful arts for the advancement of the general public welfare.

APPENDIX A-1

A SUMMARY OF THE LEGISLATIVE HISTORY
OF COMPUTER-RELATED ISSUES

During the early discussions of copyright revision from 1961
through 1964, copyright questions with regard to computer programs and the
use of copyrighted works in conjunction with computers were largely ignored.

Section 5(a) of the Preliminary Draft for Revised U.S. Copyright
Law dealt with the exclusive rights to copy or record:

> § 5. Exclusive Rights Comprised in Copyright....
> (a) The right to copy or record. Copyright shall
> include the exclusive right to copy or record the work
> in any tangible medium of expression, now known or later
> developed, from which it can be visually or aurally per-
> ceived, either directly or with the aid of a machine
> or device. It shall include the right to reproduce the
> work in visual copies, to make or duplicate sound record-
> ings of it, to make a translation, adaptation, or any
> other derivative work from it, and to reproduce it in
> any form in the programming or operation of an informa-
> tion storage and retrieval system [emphasis added]. 1/

In addition, a proposed Section 6 2/ dealt with fair use.

During a meeting held at the Library of Congress on February 20,
1963, 3/ the relation of these two sections to the use of copyrighted works

---

1/ Copyright Law Revision, Part 3: Preliminary Draft for Revised U.S.
Copyright Law and Discussions and Comments on the Draft 4 (1964).

2/ See p. A-27, infra.

3/ Copyright Law Revision, Part 3, supra note 1, at 120.

in machine-readable forms was discussed. Throughout the period when the Preliminary Draft was being considered the primary concern seems to have been with this use of computers. Several interested parties suggested changes in Section 5 during the 1963 discussions[4/] and in statements submitted in the summer of 1964.[5/]

THE EIGHTY-EIGHTH CONGRESS

The 1964 Revision Bill

The three identical versions of the Revision Bill introduced in the Second Session of the 88th Congress[6/] had a modified Section 5:

> § 5. Exclusive rights in copyrighted works.
>   (a) General scope of copyright. -- Subject to sections 6 through 13, the owner of copyright under this title has the exclusive rights to do or to authorize any of the following:
>   (1) to reproduce the copyrighted work in copies or phonorecords;
>   (2) to prepare derivative works based upon the copyrighted work;
>   (3) to distribute copies or phonorecords of the copyrighted work to the public by sale or other transfer of ownership, or by rental, lease, or lending;
>   (4) in the case of literary, musical, dramatic, and choreographic works, pantomimes, and motion pictures, to perform the copyrighted work publicly;
>   (5) in the case of pictorial, graphic, or sculptural works, to exhibit the copyrighted work publicly. 7/

At a meeting held in New York City on August 6, 1964, Morton David Goldberg, Esq., raised these significant questions which might be paraphrased as 1) are computer programs "copyrighted works"; 2) does "the right to reproduce the copyrighted work" include reproduction, storage and retrieval devices;

4/ Id. at 374 (statement of Reed C. Lawlor, Esq.).

5/ Copyright Law Revision, Part 4: Further Discussions and Comments on Preliminary Draft for Revised U.S. Copyright Law 269 (statement of American Book Publishers Council and American Textbook Publishers Institute), 315 (Authors League); 392 (National Audio-Visual Assoc. Inc.) (1964).

6/ S. 3008 (July 20, 1974), sponsored by Senator McClellan, H. R. 11947 (July 20) sponsored by Rep. Celler, and H. R. 12354 (August 12), sponsored by Rep. St. Onge.

7/ Copyright Law Revision, Part 5: 1964 Revision Bill with Discussions and Comments 4 (1965).

3) is the fixation of magnetic impulses in the storage unit a derivative work; 4) are computer programs "literary works"; and 5) what are the performing rights of a computer program?[8]

The Register of Copyrights replied, "I don't think there are any more difficult or important problems than the ones you have raised ... we deliberately avoided any specific references to 'computers' or 'information storage and retrieval units' in this clause. We think that there are many developments that are going to come in the immediate future, and we think it safer to draft general language which can be interpreted by the courts to apply to particular usages."[9]

The General Electric Company made some specific suggestions on the copyright protection which should be extended to computer programs.[10]

In May, 1964, the Copyright Office announced that it had "taken the position that copyright registration for computer programs is possible under the present law," (i.e., the 1909 Act).

The announcement of the practice went to make the following statement:

> The registrability of computer programs involves two basic questions: (1) Whether a program as such is the "writing of an author" and thus copyrightable, and (2) whether a reproduction of the program in a form actually used to operate or be "read" by a machine is a "copy" that can be accepted for copyright registration.
> Both of these are doubtful questions. However, in accordance with its policy of resolving doubtful issues in favor of registration wherever possible, the Copyright Office will consider registration for a computer program as a "book" in Class A if:
> (1) The elements of assembling, selecting, arranging, editing, and literary expression that went into the compilation of the program are sufficient to constitute original authorship.
> (2) The program has been published, with the required copyright notice; that is, "copies" (i.e., reproductions of the program in a form perceptible or capable of being made perceptible to the human eye) bearing the notice have been distributed or made available to the public.

8/ Id. at 62.

9/ Id. at 63.

10/ Id. at 271.

(3) The copies deposited for registration consist of or include reproductions in a language intelligible to human beings. If the only publication was in a form that cannot be perceived visually or read, something more (e.g., a print-out of the entire program) would also have to be deposited. 11/

The 1965 Revision Bill

12/

When the 1965 Revision Bill was introduced in the 89th Congress

the Register of Copyrights explained the deletion of the granting of

an exclusive right "to reproduce [the work] in any form in the programming

or operation of an information storage and retrieval system" thusly:

> We became convinced...that it would be a mistake for the statute, in trying to deal with such a new and evolving field as that of computer technology, to include an explicit provision that could later turn out to be too broad or too narrow. A much better approach, we feel, is to state the general concepts of copyright in language, such as that in section 106(a), which would be general in terms and broad enough to allow for adjustment to future changes in patterns of reproduction and other uses of authors' works.
>   At the same time, we should emphasize here that, unless the doctrine of "fair use" is applicable in a particular case, the bill contemplates that certain computer uses would come within the copyright owner's exclusive rights. It seems clear, for example, that the actual copying of entire works (or substantial portions of them) for "input" or storage in a computer would constitute a "reproduction" under clause (1), whatever form the "copies" take: punchcards, punched or magnetic tape, electronic storage units, etc. Similarly, at the "output" end of the process, the "retrieval" or "print-out" of an entire work (or a substantial part of it) in tangible copies would also come under copyright control. 13/

The bill also specifically removed the "performance" aspects of

a computer from Section 106(b)(1), with the deletion explained as follows:

> A computer may well "perform" a work by running off a motion picture or playing a sound recording as part of its output, but its internal operations do not appear to us to fall within this concept. 14/

11/ Announcement SML-47 from the Office of the Reigster of Copyrights (May 1964), also Copyright Office Circular 31D (January 1965).

12/ H. R. 4347 and S. 1006, 89th Cong., 1st Sess. (1965).

13/ Copyright Law Revision, Part 6: Supplementary Report of the Register of Copyrights on the General Revision of the U.S. Copyright Law: 1965 Revision Bill 18 (1965).

14/ Id. at 22.

During hearings on the then pending revision bill,[15/] the following

individuals presented testimony on statements in computer related issues:

Page

Anthony J. Celebreeze, Dept. of Health,
    Education and Welfare. 1131-32
Alanson W. Willcox, Dept. of Health,
    Education and Welfare 1132-33
John V. Vinciguerra, Atomic Energy
    Commission 1135-36
John F. Banzhaf, Computer Program Library 1144-50
Larston D. Farrar, Farrar Publishing Company. . . 1150-51
Maxwell C. Freudenberg, Department of Defense . . 1163-72
Mark Carroll, Association of American
    University Presses 1216
Bella L. Linden, American Textbook Publishers
    Institute with Kenneth B. Keating, Esq.,
    and Lee Deighton 1420-49, 1455-59
Carl T. J. Overhage, M.I.T. 1455
Abraham L. Kaminstein, Register of Copyrights 1861
Graham W. McGowan, Electronic Industries Assoc. . 1898-99
Reed C. Lawlor, Esq. 1914-16

Hearings were held before the Senate Judiciary Subcommittee on

Patents, Trademarks and Copyright, on S. 1006, the companion bill, in August

1965. Alanson W. Willcox, General Counsel of the Department of Health,

Education and Welfare, submitted a statement which made several recommen-

dations with respect to the rights of libraries to duplicate, "by any process

now in existence or which may hereafter be developed, including such processes

as photocopying, sound recording, and computerization, any work in its col-

lections or in collections available to it ..." [emphasis added][16/] and

went on to outline specific conditions under which those copies could be made.

The House Committee on the Judiciary reported H. R. 4347 on

October 12, 1966, and made the following statements on the application of

the proposed law to computer systems on the right of public display:

> Clause (5) of section 106 represents the first
> explicit statutory recognition in American copy-
> right law of an exclusive right to show a copy-
> righted work, or an image of it, to the public.
> The existence or extent of this right under the
> present statute is uncertain and subject to chal-

15/ Copyright Law Revision; Hearings before Subcomm. No. 3, House Comm. on
the Judiciary H.R. 4347, H.R. 5680, H.R. 6381, H.R. 6835, 89th Cong., 1st Sess.
(1965).

16/ Copyright Law Revision; Hearings before the Subcomm. on Patents,
Trademarks, and Copyrights of the Senate Comm. on the Judiciary, on S. 1006,
89th Cong., 1st Sess. 50 (1965)

lenge. The bill would give the owners of copyright
in "literary, musical, dramatic, and choreographic
works, pantomimes, and pictorial, graphic, or
sculptural works" the exclusive right "to display
the copyrighted work publicly."

With the growing use of projection equipment,
closed and open circuit television, and computers for
displaying images of textual and graphic material to
"audiences" or "readers," this right is certain to
assume great importance to copyright owners. A
recognition of this potentiality is reflected in
the proposal of book publishers and producers of
audiovisual works which, in effect, would equate
"display" with "reproduction" where the showing
is "for use in lieu of a copy." The committee is
aware that in the future electronic images may
take the place of printed copies in some situations, and has dealt with the problem by amendments in sections 109 and 110, and without mixing
the separate concepts of "reproduction" and "display." No provision of the bill would make a purely
private display of a work a copyright infringement. 17/

....

The corresponding definition of "display," as amended,
covers any showing of a "copy" of the work, "either directly or by means of a film, slide, television image,
or any other device or process." The phrase "motion
picture" before the word "film" has been omitted to
avoid confusion. Since "copies" are defined as including the material object "in which the work is first fixed,"
fixed," the right of public display applies to original
works of art as well as to reproductions of them. With
respect to motion pictures and other audiovisual works,
it is a "display" (rather than a "performance") to show
their "individual images nonsequentially." In
addition to the direct showings of a copy of a
work, "display" would include the projection of
an image on a screen or other surface by any
method, the transmission of an image by electronic
or other means, and the showing of an image on a
cathode ray tube or similar viewing apparatus
connected with any sort of information storage
and retrieval system. 18/

On reproduction and uses for other purposes the Report stated that

The concentrated attention given the fair use provision in the context of classroom teaching activities
should not obscure its application in other areas.
The committee emphasizes again that the same general
standards of fair use are applicable to all kinds of
uses of copyrighted material, although the relative
weight to be given them will differ from case to
case.

For example, the doctrine of fair use would apply
to all stages in the operations of information storage

17/ H.R. Rep. No. 2237, 89th Cong., 2d Sess. 55 (1966).

18/ Id. at 57.

and retrieval systems, including input, and output in
the form of visual images or hard copies. Reproduction
of small excerpts or key words for purposes of input,
and output of bibliographic lists or short summaries
might be examples of fair use in this area. On the
other hand, because the potential capabilities of a
computer system are vastly different from those of a
mimeograph or photocopying machine, the factors to be
considered in determining fair use would have to be
weighed differently in each situation. For reasons
already explained, the committee does not favor any
statutory provision that would exempt computer uses
specially from copyright control or that would specify
that certain computer uses constitute "fair use." 19/

The 89th Congress adjourned without taking action on either

H. R. 4347 or S. 1006.

THE NINETIETH CONGRESS

In the 90th Congress Rep. Emmanuel Celler introduced a revision bill,

H. R. 2512, on January 17, 1967; a companion bill, S. 597, was introduced in

the Senate six days later.

The House Committee on the Judiciary reported H. R. 2512 on March 8,

1967. The Report deals with the use of copyrighted works in information storage

and retrieval systems in the following language:

Although it was touched on rather lightly at the
hearings, the problem of computer uses of copyrighted
material has attracted increasing attention and
controversy in recent months. Recognizing the
profound impact that information storage and retrieval
devices seem destined to have on authorship,
communications, and human life itself, the committee
is also aware of the dangers of legislating prematurely
in this area of exploding technology.
    In the context of section 106, the committee believes
that, instead of trying to deal explicitly with computer
uses, the statute should be general in terms and broad
enough to allow for adjustment to future changes in
patterns of reproduction and other uses of authors' works.
Thus, unless the doctrine of fair use were applicable,
the following computer uses could be infringements of
copyright under section 106: reproduction of a work
(or a substantial part of it) in any tangible form
(paper, punch cards, magnetic tape, etc.) for input
into an information storage and retrieval system;
reproduction of a work or substantial parts of it,
in copies as the "print-out" or output of the
computer; preparation for input of an index or abstract
of the work so complete and detailed that it would be
considered a "derivative work"; computer transmission or

19/ Id. at 64.

display of a visual image of a work to one or more
members of the public. On the other hand, since the
mere scanning or manipulation of the contents of a
work within the system would not involve reproduction,
the preparation of a derivative work, or a public
distribution, performance, or display, it would be
outside the scope of the legislation.

It has been argued on behalf of those interested
in fostering computer uses that the copyright owner
is not damaged by input alone, and that the development of computer technology calls for unrestricted
availability of unlimited quantities of copyrighted
material for introduction into information systems.
While acknowledging that copyright payments should
be made for output and possibly some other computer
uses, these interests recommended at least a partial
exemption in cases of reproduction for input. On
the other side, the copyright owners stressed that
computers have the potential, and in some cases
the present, capacity to destroy the entire market
of authors and publishers. They consider it indis-
pensable that input, beyond fair use, require the
consent of the copyright owner, on the ground that
this is the only point in computer operations at
which copyright control can be exercised; they
argue that the mere presence of an electronic
reproduction in a machine could deprive a publisher
of a substantial market for printed copies, and
that if input were exempted there would likewise
be no market for machine-readable copies.

In various discussions since the hearings, there
have been proposals for establishing voluntary
licensing systems for computer uses, and it was
suggested that a commission be established to study
the problem and recommend definitive copyright
legislation several years from now. The Committee
expresses the hope that the interests involved will
work together toward an ultimate solution of this
problem in the light of experience. Toward this
end the Register of Copyrights may find it appropriate
to hold further meetings on this subject after passage
of the new law. In the meantime, however, section 106
preserves the exclusive rights of the copyright owner
with respect to reproductions of his work for input
or storage in an information system. 20/

The House passed H. R. 2512, with several amendments, on April 11.

The Senate Judiciary Subcommittee held hearings on, the
compromise bill, S. 597, in March and April of 1967.[21] During the
course of those hearings the witnesses listed below expressed concern over
the provisions of the bill relating to computers and information storage

---

20/ H. R. Rep. 90-83, 90th Cong., 1st Sess. 24 (1967).

21/ Copyright Law Revision; Hearings before the Subcomm. on Patents,
Trademarks, and Copyrights of the Senate Comm. on the Judiciary,
on S. 597, 90th Cong., 1st Sess. (1967).

and retrieval systems. They addressed the specific problems of whether

copyright royalties should be levied at the input of copyrighted works into

automated retrieval systems or on output; whether computer programs should

indeed be copyrightable; and whether a clearinghouse for payment of royalties

on computerized use of copyrighted works might be feasible. A number of

these witnesses also urged the creation of a "study panel" or other body

to gather data and to deal with computer problems so that the legislative

process would not be delayed while Congress considered them.

The following witnesses testified on S. 597:

Written statements from the following individuals appear in the

Appendix to the Hearings:

THE NATIONAL COMMISSION

The Senate Subcommittee convened a meeting on July 25, 1967, to

discuss a draft bill to establish a national study commission. The attendees,

some 150 representatives of authors, publishers, librarians, educators,

computer users and government agencies, unanimously supported the creation

of such a commission. Senator McClellan made this statement when introducing

S. 2216:

> During the subcommittee hearings there was considerable
> testimony concerning the relationship between such tech-
> nologies as information storage and retrieval systems
> and various forms of machine reproduction, and the copy-
> right law. The Congress, at the present time, lacks
> sufficient information on which to base an informed judgment
> as to what changes in the copyright law may be necessary
> in the light of these scientific advances. On the other
> hand, the need for modernizing the copyright law is urgent
> and should not await the resolution of these new issues.
>   I, therefore, concluded that the most desirable course
> of action would be to proceed with the consideration of
> the pending copyright revision bill, but establish at
> the earliest opportunity a national commission to study
> the copyright implications of these technological
> advances and to make recommendations to the President
> and Congress concerning the need for any changes in our
> copyright law or procedure. 22/

The Report accompanying this bill amplifies further the necessity

for establishing the Commission.

> Prior to the introduction of copyright revision legislation
> in the Congress, exhaustive study was given by the Copyright
> Office and various interested groups to those issues that it
> was anticipated would require attention by the Congress during
> the revision program. The current or potential impact of
> computers and other information storage and retrieval systems
> on the copyright revision effort was not foreseen and conseq-
> uently the bill submitted to the Congress did not take into
> account the significance of this new technology.
>   The first extensive consideration of these matters in the
> Congress occurred during the hearings of this committee's
> Subcommittee on Patents, Trademarks, and Copyrights on S. 597,
> the general copyright revision bill. At the same time within
> the executive branch the Committee on Scientific and Technological
> Information of the Federal Council of Science and Technology
> was also exploring these problems. It became apparent during
> the subcommittee examination of this subject that if the
> Congress were to undertake at this time to make a final
> determination concerning the possible necessity of modifi-
> cations in the copyright law, because of various technological
> advances, it would delay for at least several years the
> enactment of a general copyright revision bill. Such a delay
> would be extremely undesirable in view of the obvious
> need for revision of the copyright statute, which is

22/   113 Cong. Rec. 20909 (1967).

essentially that enacted in 1909. More importantly,
sufficient information is currently not available
to provide the foundation for a sound judgment
concerning the future development of the technology
and the necessity for modification of the copyright
statute.
    Another important copyright issue arising from
technological developments is the reproduction of
copyrighted material by the use of various machines.
Photocopying in all its forms presents significant
questions of public policy, extending well beyond
that of copyright law. No satisfactory solutions
have emerged in the limited consideration devoted
to this problem during the current revision effort. 23/

The Report also contains a supporting statement from the

Librarian of Congress, who said, "As I see it, the goals of the National

Commission should be to seek and find genuine answers to what now promises

to develop into one of the most significant problems in the history of

copyright law." 24/

The Senate passed S. 2216 on October 12, 1967, but the 90th

Congress ended before the House of Representatives took any action on the bill.

THE NINETY-FIRST CONGRESS

On January 22, 1969, Senator McClellan introduced a bill which combined

most of the provisions of S. 597 and S. 2216 from the previous Congress.

In order to effect a compromise between those who proposed a 3-year moratorium

on copyright infringement for uses in computerized systems and those who adamantly

opposed such a moratorium, Section 117 was added to S. 543.

§ 117. Scope of exclusive rights: Use in conjunction
with computers and similar information systems

Notwithstanding the provisions of sections 106 through
116, this title does not afford to the owner of copyright in
a work any greater or lesser rights with respect to the use
of the work in conjunction with automatic systems capable
of storing, processing, retrieving, or transferring information, or in conjunction with any similar device, machine,
or process, than those afforded to works under the law,
whether title 17 or the common law or statutes of a State,
in effect on December 31, 1970, as held applicable and construed by a court in an action brought under this title. 25/

23/ S. Rep. No. 640, 90th Cong., 1st Sess. 2 (1967).

24/ Id. at 7.

25/ S. 543, 91st Cong., 1st Sess. [Committee Print], (December 10, 1969).

THE NINETY-SECOND CONGRESS

Senator McClellan introduced S. 644, a bill almost identical to S. 543 on February 18, 1971, but neither house took any action on it.

THE NINETY-THIRD CONGRESS

The Copyright Revision Bill was reintroduced as S. 1361 on March 26, 1973. The following witnesses testified at hearings held by the Senate Judiciary Subcommittee on July 31 and August 1:[26]

Statements from the following individuals and organizations appear in the Appendix:

The Report to accompany S. 1361 described Section 117 in the following manner:

> Use in information storage and retrieval systems -- As section 117 declares explicitly, the bill is not intended to alter the present law with respect to the use of copyrighted works in computer systems.[27]
> . . . .
> As the program for general revision of the copyright law has evolved, it has become increasingly apparent that in one major area the problems are not sufficiently developed for a definitive legislative solution. This is the area of computer uses of copyrighted works: the use of a work "in conjunction

---

26/ Copyright Law Revision; Hearings before the Subcomm. on Patents, Trademarks, and Copyrights of the Sen. Comm. on the Judiciary on S. 1361. 93d Cong., 1st Sess. (1973).

27/ S. Rep. No. 983, 93d Cong., 2d Sess. 112 (1974) [Star Print].)

with automatic systems capable of storing, processing, retrieving, or transferring information." The Commission on New Technological Uses established by Title II is intended, among other
things, to make a thorough study of the emerging patterns in
this field and, on the basis of its finding, to recommend definite copyright provisions to deal with the situation.

Since it would be premature to change existing law on
computer uses at present, the purpose of section 117 is to
preserve the status quo. It is intended neither to cut off
any rights that may now exist, nor to create new rights that
might be denied under the Act of 1909 or under common law
principles currently applicable.

The provision deals only with the exclusive rights of a
copyright owner with respect to computer uses, that is, the
bundle of rights specified for other types of uses in section
106 and qualified in Sections 107 through 116. With respect
to the copyrightability of computer programs, the ownership of
copyright in them, the term of protection, and the formal requirements of the remainder of the bill, the new statute would
apply.

Under section 117, an action for infringement of a copyrighted work by means of a computer would necessarily be a
federal action brought under the new Title 17. The court, in
deciding the scope of exclusive rights in the computer area,
would first need to determine the applicable law, whether
State common law or the Act of 1909. Having determined what
law was applicable, its decision would depend upon its interpretation of what that law was on the point on the day before
the effective date of the new statute. 28/

A section of the Report also deals with Title II of the bill "to
                                                              29/
establish a National Commission to study and compile data..." in language

similar to that of S. Rep. 90-640, cited above.

S. 1361 was referred to the Senate Commerce Committee on July 9,

1974, and then reported with several amendments on July 29, and was passed

by the Senate on September 9th of the same year.

Immediately after the Senate had passed S. 1361, Senator McClellan

introduced S. 3976, stating, "...[I]t is doubtful that the House of Representa-

tives will have time in this Congress to complete action on the copyright

revision bill which was just passed by the Senate. There are several pro-

visions of the omnibus bill which require action before the adjournment of this

Congress .... [I]t is desirable to establish this year the National Commission

which is provided for in title 2 of S. 1361 to prepare for the resolution of

---

28/   Id. at 154.

29/   Id. at 208.

the copyright issues which are arising from the rapid development of new technology." 30/

The Senate considered and passed the bill that same day, September 9, 1974.

The House Judiciary Subcommittee held a hearing on S. 3976 on November 26, at which the Register of Copyrights supported Title II of the bill:

> The inadequacy of the present law to deal with the problems arising from the use of copyrighted works in computer systems is certainly something that no one can deny. This is still in a developmental stage. We really have no experience with the copyright patterns -- the concepts and the needs that will arise from this new technology. In the many discussions that took place on this subject the feeling was that what was being expressed on both sides were fears rather than facts. As the result, there was a genuine emphasis on the part of both the users and the potential users on the one side, and the authors and the copyright owners on the other, to have a study of this subject, so that they could base their suggestions on facts rather than fears.
> The revision bill literally does nothing to solve this problem. The compromise, if you can call it that, was to specify expressly that the status quo would be preserved. In other words, whatever is the copyright law now with respect to computer uses of copyrighted works would remain the law. This is not very desirable as a legislative solution, but it was tied in directly with the understanding that a Commission would be operating in this area, and would be studying and recommending on a rather short deadline. 31/

The House Committee on the Judiciary amended Section 202(3) of Title II to include "that at least one of the four public members shall be selected from among experts in consumer protection affairs" and reported S. 3976 on December 12, 1974, with a dissenting view by Rep. Robert F. Drinan opposing the establishment of the Commission. 32/

The House of Representatives considered and passed S. 3976 on December 17, 1974, and President Gerald R. Ford signed the bill on December 31. 33/

30/   120 Cong. Rec. 30516 (1974).

31/   Copyright Miscellany; Hearing before the Subcomm. on Courts, Civil Liberties, and the Administration of Justice of the House Comm. of the Judiciary on S. 3976, 93d Cong., 2d Sess. 6 (1974).

32/   H.R. Rep. No. 1581, 93d Cong., 2d Sess. 17 (1974).

33/   Pub. L. No. 93-573 (1974).

THE NINETY-FOURTH CONGRESS

The Copyright Revision Bill came before Congress again early in the 94th Congress when Senator McClellan introduced S. 22 on January 15, 1975, and Representative Kastenmeier introduced H.R. 2223 on January 28. The bill was substantially the same as S. 1361, which had passed the Senate in the previous Congress. The Senate Judiciary Committee reported S. 22 on November 20, 1975.[34] The Senate unanimously approved S. 22 on February 19, 1976.

In the meantime the House Judiciary Subcommittee had been holding hearings on H.R. 2223,[35] during which the following witnesses discussed computer-related issues:

	Page
Bella L. Linden, Linden and Deutsch	311-13
Edwin Meell, Educational Media Producers Ass'n	321
Paul G. Zurkowski, Information Industry Association	332-40, 366-67

The Copyright Office submitted to the House Subcommittee a series of eighteen briefing papers on issues raised by H.R. 2223. The section on "Computer Uses of Copyrighted Works" outlines the background of the issue and includes summaries of the arguments for and against considering "input" as infringement, a statement of the tasks to be undertaken by the National Commissio on New Technological Uses of Copyrighted Works,[36] and an analysis of Section 117

The House Subcommittee then held public markup sessions on H.R. 2223 and reported the bill on August 3, 1976. The full Judiciary Committee of the House reported the bill without further amendment on September 3.[37]

34/ S. Rep. No. 473, 94th Cong., 1st Sess. (1975).

35/ Copyright Law Revision; Hearings before the Subcomm. on Courts, Civil Liberties, and the Administration of Justice, of the House Judiciary Comm. on H.R. 2223. 94th Cong., 1st Sess. (1975).

36/ Id. at 2075.

37/ H.R. Rep. No. 1476, 94th Cong., 2d Sess. (1976).

The Committee of Conference reconciled the different versions of the bill as it had been approved by the Senate and House of Representatives and issued its report on September 29, 1976. [38/]   Both Houses of Congress approved the Conference Committee version of S. 22 on September 30, 1976, and the Revision Bill finally became law when President Ford signed it on October 19. [39/]

APPENDIX A-2

A SUMMARY OF THE LEGISLATIVE HISTORY OF THE

PHOTOCOPY ISSUE

In 1955, the Copyright Office began sponsoring, prior to any legislative action on revising the existing 1909 law, a series of 34 studies on copyright law and practice for the Senate Judiciary Subcommittee on Patents, Trademarks, and Copyrights. Studies Number 14 and 15, "Fair Use of Copyrighted Works" by Alan Latman and "Photoduplication of Copyrighted Material by Libraries" by Borge Varmer, respectively, appeared in 1960. [40/]

After examining the status of fair use under American case law, previous proposals for legislative revision, and the laws of other nations, Latman summarized the issue as follows:

> 1. Should a statutory provision concerning fair use be introduced into the U.S. law?
> 2. If so:
> (a) Should the statute merely recognize the doctrine in general terms and leave its definition to the courts?
> (b) Should the statute specify the general criteria of fair use? If so, what should be the basic criteria?
> 3. Should specific situations be covered? If so, what specific specific situations? [41/]

Varmer followed the same format in his study on photoduplication and made the following summary of the basic issues:

38/ H.R. Rep. No. 1733, 94th Cong., 2d Sess. (1976).

39/ Pub. L. No. 94-553 (1976).

40/ Copyright Law Revision; Studies Prepared for the Subcomm. on Patents, Trademarks, and Copyrights of the Senate Comm. on the Judiciary. Committee Print, 86th Cong., 2d Sess. (1960)

41/ Id. at 34.

The following appear to be the primary questions to be considered.

1. Should the copyright statute provide expressly for the photocopying of copyrighted works by libraries? If so:

(a) Should the statute merely provide, in general terms, that a library may supply a single photocopy of any work to any person for his personal use in research and study?

(b) Should the statute specify limitations and conditions with respect to:

(1) the kinds of library institutions that may make and supply photocopies?

(2) the purposes for which they may make and supply photocopies?

(3) the conditions under which they may make and supply photocopies?

(4) the extent to which they may photocopy, under the specified conditions, the contents of (1) periodicals and (2) other publications?

(5) the kinds of published material, if any, which they may not photocopy?

(c) Should the statute provide for photocopying in general terms (as in (a) above) subject to limitations and conditions to be prescribed by administrative regulations?

2. Instead of a statutory prescription, would it be preferable to encourage the libraries, publishers, and other groups concerned to develop a working arrangement, in the nature of a code of practice, to govern photocopying by libraries? 42/

Comments on this study by the following individuals (with their affiliations when given) are appended to the text:

Sixteen years later, following numerous Congressional hearings and several attempts at revising the law, these questions were answered by the Copyright Act of 1976.

In July, 1961, the House Committee on the Judiciary issued a report containing "the tentative recommendations of the Copyright Office for revision of the law." It was "issued for the purpose of inviting all persons concerned to submit comments and suggestions...." 43/

42/ Id. at 66.

43/ Copyright Law Revision: Report of the Register of Copyrights on the General Revision of the U. S. Copyright Law. House Judiciary Committee Print, 87th Cong., 1st Sess. iii (1961) [footnote omitted].

The report dealt with photocopying by libraries in the following
language:

>Library photocopying. -- The report would permit a library to
make a single photocopy of material in its collections for research
purposes under explicit conditions. <u>44/</u>
>
>. . . .

2. PHOTOCOPYING BY LIBRARIES

a. <u>Statement of the problem</u>

The application of the principle of fair use to the making of a
photocopy by a library for the use of a person engaged in research is
an important question which merits special consideration. This question has not been decided by the courts, and it is uncertain how far a
library may go in supplying a photocopy of copyrighted material in
its collections. Many libraries and researchers feel that this uncertainty has hampered research and should be resolved to permit the
making of photocopies for research purposes to the fullest extent com
patible with the interests of copyright owners.

Scholars have always felt free to copy by hand from the works
of others for their own private research and study. Aside from the
impossibility of controlling copying done in private, the acceptance
of this practice may have been based on the inherent limitations of
the extent to which copying could be done by hand. But copying has
now taken on new dimensions with the development of photocopying
devices by which any quantity of material can be reproduced readily
and in multiple copies.

Researchers need to have available, for reference and study, the
growing mass of published material in their particular fields. This
is true especially, though not solely, of material published in
scientific, technical, and scholarly journals. Researchers must rely
on libraries for much of this material. When a published copy in a
library's collections is not available for loan, which is very often
the case, the researcher's need can be met by a photocopy.

On the other hand, the supplying of photocopies of any work to a
substantial number of researchers may diminish the copyright owner's
market for the work. Publishers of scientific, technical, and
scholarly works have pointed out that their market is small; and they
have expressed the fear that if many of their potential subscribers
or purchasers were furnished with photocopies, they might be forced
to discontinue publication.

b. <u>Approach to a solution: single photocopies for research use</u>

As a general premise, we believe that photocopying should not be
permitted where it would compete with the publisher's market. Thus,
when a researcher wants the whole of a publication, and a publisher's
copy is available, he should be expected to procure such a copy.

In situations where it would not be likely to compete with the
publisher's market, however, we believe that a library should be
permitted to supply a single photocopy of material in its collections
for use in research. Thus, when a researcher wants only a relatively
small part of a publication, or when the work is out of print,
supplying him with a single photocopy would not seriously prejudice
the interests of the copyright owner. A number of foreign laws permit libraries to supply single photocopies in these circumstances.

<u>44/</u>   Id. at v.

c. Multiple and commercial photocopying

The question of making photocopies has also arisen in the situation where an industrial concern wishes to provide multiple copies of publications, particularly of scientific and technical journals, to a number of research workers on its staff. To permit multiple photocopying may make serious inroads on the publisher's potential market. We believe that an industrial concern whould be expected to buy the number of copies it needs from the publisher, or to get the publisher's consent to its making of photocopies.

Similarly, any person or organization undertaking to supply photocopies to others as a commercial venture would be competing directly with the publisher, and should be expected to get the publisher's consent.

There has been some discussion of the possibility of a contractual arrangement whereby industrial concerns would be given blanket permission to make photocopies for which they would pay royalties to the publishers. Such an arrangement, which has been made in at least one foreign country, would seem to offer the best solution for the problem of multiple and commercial photocopying.

d. Recommendations

The statute would permit a library, whose collections are available to the public without charge, to supply a single photocopy of copyrighted material in its collections to any applicant under the following conditions:

(a) A single photocopy of one article in any issue of a periodical, or of a reasonable part of any other publication, may be supplied when the applicant states in writing that he needs and will use such material solely for his own research.

(b) A single photocopy of an entire publication may be supplied when the applicant also states in writing, and the library is not otherwise informed, that a copy is not available from the publisher.

(c) Where the work bears a copyright notice, the library should be required to affix to the photocopy a warning that the material appears to be copyrighted. 45/

A meeting convened by the Register of Copyrights to discuss

the Report took place on September 14, 1961. Comments on the photocopy

provisions quoted above are contained in Copyright Law Revision, Part 2. 46/

Written comments from the following individuals and organizations also

appear in the document:

45/ Id. at 25.

46/ Copyright Law Revision, Part 2: Discussion and Comments on Report of the Register of Copyrights on the General Revision of the U.S. Copyright Law. House Judiciary Committee Print, 87th Cong., 1st Sess. 31 (1963).

A third report in this series, issued in September, 1964, contains
the following proposed section.[47/]

    § 7. LIMITATIONS ON EXCLUSIVE RIGHTS: COPYING AND RECORDING
BY LIBRARIES. Notwithstanding the provisions of section 5, any
library whose collections are available to the public or to researchers
in any specialized field shall be entitled to duplicate, by any process
including photocopying and sound recording, any work in its collections other than a motion picture, and to supply a single copy or
sound recording upon request, but only under the following conditions:
    (a) The library shall be entitled, without further investiga-
tion, to supply a copy of no more than one article or other contribution
to a copyrighted collection or periodical issue, or to supply a copy or
sound recording of a similarly small part of any other copyrighted
work.
    (b) the library shall be entitled to supply a copy or sound
recording of an entire work, or of more than a relatively small part
of it, if the library has first determined, on the basis of a reasonable
investigation that a copy or sound recording of the copyrighted work
cannot readily be obtained from trade sources.

    (c) the library shall attach to the copy a warning that the work
appears to be copyrighted.

A discussion of Section 7 appears in the transcript of a meeting held
at the Library of Congress on February 20, 1963.[48/] The following organizations

and individuals submitted written responses to the Draft:

Those commenting on the proposed Section 7 found several phrases

disturbing: they questioned the definitions of "reasonable investigation"

and "readily be obtained from trade sources" in particular.

47/ Copyright Law Revision, Part 3: Preliminary Draft for Revised U.S.
Copyright Law and Discussions and Comments on the Draft. House Judiciary
Committee Print, 88th Cong., 2d Sess. 6 (1964).

48/ Id. at 159.

Additional responses to the proposed Section 7 appear in the fourth
49/
volume of the series:

THE EIGHTY-EIGHTH CONGRESS

The 1964 Revision Bill

During the Second Session of the 88th Congress three identical versions

of the 1964 Revision Bill were introduced: S. 3008 by Mr. McClellan, on July 20

1974, H. R. 11947 by Mr. Celler also on July 20 and H. R. 12354 by Mr. St. Onge

on August 12, 1964.

The text of the Bill and comments on it appear in Copyright Law Revision, Part 5. 50/   The Bill did not directly address photocopying by libraries;
Sections 5(a)(1) and 6 are pertinent to the matter, however.

§ 5. Exclusive rights in copyrighted works.
    (a) General scope of copyright. -- Subject to sections 6
through 13, the owner of copyright under this title has the exclusive rights to do or to authorize any of the following:
        (1) to reproduce the copyrighted works in copies or
phonorecords;

§ 6.   Limitations on exclusive rights: fair use.

Nothwithstanding the provisions of section 5, the fair use of
a copyrighted work to the extent reasonably necessary or incidental
to a legitimate purpose such as criticism, comment, news reporting,
teaching, scholarship, or research is not an infringement of
copyright.   In determining whether the use made of a work in
any particular case is a fair use, the factors to be considered
shall include:

    (1) the purpose and character of the use;
    (2) the nature of the copyrighted work;

49/ Copyright Law Revision, Part 4: Further Discussions and Comments on
Preliminary Draft for Revised U.S. Copyright Law. House Judiciary Committee
Print 88th Cong., 2d Sess. (1964)

50/ Copyright Law Revision, Part 5: 1964 Revision Bill with Discussions
and Comments. House Judiciary Committee Print, 89th Cong., 1st Sess. (1965).

(3) the amount and substantiality of the portion used in relation to the copyrighted work as a whole; and
(4) the effect of the use upon the potential market for or value of the copyrighted work.

The Register of Copyrights convened a meeting on August 6, 1964, in New York City at which brief testimony on photocopying was presented. [51/]
The General Electric Company also submitted a brief comment on photocopying. [52/]

The 1965 Revision Bill

In light of the comments received on the 1964 bill, two new bills (H. R. 4347 and S. 1006) were introduced in the 89th Congress on February 4, 1965. Copyright Law Revision, Part 6 [53/] contains the 1965 bill in summary. Appendix B is a comparative table showing the language of the then-current law, the 1965 and 1964 Revision Bills and the 1963 draft.

The Supplementary Report "represents an effort to state ... the thinking behind the language of the 1965 bill and, in many cases, the arguments for and against particular provisions." [54/]

In the portion of the Report on Fair Use the Register explained why, once again, the 1965 bill did not directly deal with photocopying: [55/]

> In a way the comments on section 7 of the preliminary draft represented an interesting case study. Opposition to the provision was equally strong on both sides but for exactly opposite reasons, with one side arguing that the provision would permit things that are illegal now and the other side maintaining that it would prevent things that are legal now. Both agreed on one thing: that the section should be dropped entirely. We also became convinced that the provision would be a mistake in any event. At the present time the practices, techniques, and devices for reproducing visual images and sound and for "storing" and "retrieving" information are in such a stage of rapid evolution that any specific statutory provision would be likely to prove inadequate, if not unfair or dangerous, in the not too distant future. As important as it is, library copying is only one aspect of the much larger problem of changing technology,

---

51/ Id. at 103.

52/ Id. at 270.

53/ Copyright Law Revision, Part 6: Supplementary Report of the Register of Copyrights on the General Revision of the U. S. Copyright Law: 1965 Revision Bill. House Judiciary Committee Print, 89th Cong., 1st Sess. (1965).

54/ Id. at viii.

55/ See p. A-25, supra.

and we feel the statute should deal with it in terms of broad
fundamental concepts that can be adapted to future developments.

The decision to drop any provision on photocopying tended
to increase the importance attached to including a general section on fair use in the statute. Thus, in the 1964 bill, further language was added to section 6 in an attempt to clarify
the scope of the doctrine of fair use but without freezing or
delimiting its application to new uses ....

This language elicited a large body of comments, most of
them critical. Without reviewing the arguments in detail, it
can be said in general that the author-publisher groups expressed fears that specific mention of uses such as "teaching,
scholarship, or research" could be taken to imply that any
use even remotely connected with these activities would be a
"fair use." On the other side, serious objections were raised
to the use of qualifying language such as "to the extent reasonably necessary or incidental to a legitimate purpose" and "the
amount and substantiality of the portion used * * *."

In addition to opposing this language as unduly restrictive,
a group of educational organizations urged that the bill adopt
a new provision which would specify a number of activities
involved in teaching and scholarship as completely exempt from
copyright control. In broad terms, and with certain exceptions,
the proposal as it evolved would permit any teacher or other
person or organization engaged in nonprofit educational activities to make a single copy or record of an entire work, or a
reasonable number of copies of "excerpts or quotations," for
use in connection with those activities. It was argued that
these privileges are a necessary part of good teaching, and
that it is unjustifiable to burden educators with the need
to buy copies for limited use or to obtain advance clearances
and pay royalties for making copies. These proposals were
opposed very strongly by authors, publishers, and other copyright owners on the ground that in the short run the reproduction of copies under this proposal would severely diminish
the market for their works, and that the ultimate result would
be to destroy the economic incentive for the creation and publication of the very works on which education depends for its
existence. It was suggested that a clearinghouse for educational materials, through which it would be possible to avoid
problems of clearances, is a practical possibility for the
near future.

For reasons we have already discussed at some length, we
do not favor sweeping, across-the-board exemptions from the
author's exclusive rights unless an overriding public need
can be conclusively demonstrated. There is hardly any public
need today that is more urgent than education, but we are convinced that this need would be ill-served if educators, by
making copies of the materials they need, cut off a large
part of the revenue to authors and publishers that induces
the creation and publication of those materials. We believe
that a statutory recognition of fair use would be sufficient
to serve the reasonable needs of education with respect to
the copying of short extracts from copyrighted works, and
that the problem of obtaining clearances for copying larger
portions or entire works could best be solved through a
clearinghouse arrangement worked out between the educational
groups and the author-publisher interests.

Since it appeared impossible to reach agreement on a
general statement expressing the scope of the fair use
doctrine, and since in any event the doctrine emerges from
a body of judicial precedent and not from the statute, we

decided with some regret to reduce the fair use section to
its barest essentials. Section 107 of the 1965 bill therefore provides:

> Notwithstanding the provisions of section 106, the fair
> use of a copyrighted work is not an infringement of copy-
> right.

We believe that, even in this form, the provision serves a
real purpose and should be incorporated in the statute.
   The author-publisher interests have suggested that fair
use should be treated as a defense, with the statute placing
the burden of proof on the user. The educational group has
urged just the opposite, that the statute should provide
that any nonprofit use for educational purposes is presumed
to be a fair use, with the copyright owner having the burden
of proving otherwise. We believe it would be undesirable to
adopt a special rule placing the burden of proof on one side
or the other. When the facts as to what use was made of the
work have been presented, the issue as to whether it is a
"fair use" is a question of law. Statutory presumptions or
burden-of-proof provisions could work a radical change in the
meaning and effect of the doctrine of fair use. The intention
of section 107 is to give statutory affirmation to the present
judicial doctrine, not to change it. 56/

Subcommittee No. 3 of the House Committee on the Judiciary held
hearings in May, June, and August of 1965. 57/ A number of witnesses presented

testimony and statements on photocopying issues:

	Page
Kenneth B. Keating, American Book Company, etc.	63-64
Lee Deighton, American Textbook Publishers Institute	68, 73
Elizabeth Janeway, Authors League	100-1
John Hersey, Authors League	103
Dan Lacy, American Book Publishers Council	120-1, 127
Horace S. Manges, American Book Publishers Council.	131, 139-40
Rutherford D. Rogers, Joint Libraries Committee on Copyright	448-49, 452
Charles F. Gosnell, American Library Association.	460-2, 471-2
Robert T. Jordan	464-65, 468-70
Robert H. Bahmer, General Services Administration.	1110-16
Anthony J. Celebrezze, Dept. of Health, Education and Welfare	1131-32
Alanson W. Willcox, Dept. of Health, Education and Welfare	1132-33
Julian P. Boyd, Society of American Archivists, etc.	1140-43
Maxwell C. Freudenberg, Dept. of Defense	1164
Mark Carroll, Association of American University Presses	1216
Bella L. Linden, American Textbook Publishers Inst.	1420 1430-2, 1435, 1438-52, 1460
Carl F. J. Overhage, M.I.T.	1455
Howard A. Meyerhoff with Gerald Sophar, Committee to Investigate Copyright Problems.	1471-83
Ralph H. Devan, Raymond H. Herzog and Charles Lauder, Minnesota Mining and Manufacturing.	1497-1508

56/ Copyright Law Revision, Part 6, supra note 52, at 26.

57/ Copyright Law Revision, Hearings before Subcomm. No. 3 of the House
Committee on the Judiciary on H.R. 4347, H.R. 5680. H.R. 6831, H.R. 6835.
89th Cong., 1st Sess. (1965).

Lyle Lodwick and Francis Old, Williams and Wilkins. . . 1511-18
Frederick Burkhardt and Martin F. Richman, American
        Council of Learned Societies 1550, 1555-57
Fred S. Siebert, Michigan State University. . . . 1563-64, 1566
Frank C. Campbell, Music Library Association 1575
Gerhard Van Arkel, International Typographical Union . . . 1650
Harry F. Howard, Book Manufacturers' Assoc. . . . 1666-67, 1674
Irwin Karp, Authors League 1755-61, 1765-69
Melville B. Nimmer, UCLA Law School. 1810-13, 1817-18
William D. Barns, West Virginia University. 1887-88
J. C. Wilson, Xerox Corporation 1930
                                        58/
During August 1965 hearings on S. 1006 were also being held,

at which the following individuals submitted statements or testimony on

photocopying:

                                                  Page
Alanson W. Willcox, Dept. of H.E.W. . . . . pp. 50-51
Abraham L. Kaminstein, Register of Copyrights 69-70
Harold E. Wigren, Ad Hoc Committee... 84-93
Harry N. Rosenfield, Ad Hoc
    Committee 118-27, 129, 132-36, 148-49
Charles F. Gosnell, American Library Association 136-38
Fred S. Siebert, American Council on Education 144
Mark Carroll, American Assoc. of University Presses 180
Kenneth B. Keating, representing publishers 219-20

On October 12, 1966, the House Committee on the Judiciary issued

                                          59/
a report to accompany H.R. 4347, the 1965 Revision Bill.   Several changes

relating to photocopying had been incorporated into the bill: Section

107 reinstated the "factors to be considered" in determining fair use from

Section 6 of the 1964 Revision Bill.

§ 107. Limitations on exclusive rights: Fair use
    Nothwithstanding the provisions of section 106, the fair use of
a copyrighted work, including such use by reproduction in copies or
phonorecords or by any other means specified by that section, for
purposes such as criticism, comment, news reporting, teaching,
scholarship, or research, is not an infringement of copyright. In
determining whether the use made of a work in any particular case
is a fair use, the factors to be considered shall include --
    (1) the purpose and character of the use;
    (2) the nature of the copyrighted work;
    (3) the amount and substantiality of the portion used in relation
to the copyrighted work as a whole; and
    (4) the effect of the use upon the potential market for or value
of the copyrighted work.

58/ Copyright Law Revision; Hearings before the Subcomm. on Patents, Trademarks, and Copyrights of the Senate Judiciary Comm. on S. 1006. 89th Cong., 1st Sess. (1965).

59/ H.R. Rep. No. 2237, 89th Cong., 2d Sess. (1966).

The analysis and discussion of this section [60] address fair use

within the classroom setting as had most of the testimony and discussion

prior to that time.

The House Report made this commentary on the subject of library copying:

> [B]oth the American Council of Learned Societies and the
> Department of Health, Education, and Welfare argued that the
> problem is too important to be left uncertain, and proposed
> adoption of a statutory provision allowing libraries to supply
> single photocopies of material under limited conditions.
>   As in the case of reproduction of copyrighted material by
> teachers for classroom use, the committee does not favor a
> specific provision dealing with library photocopying.
>   Unauthorized library copying, like everything else, must be
> judged a fair use or an infringement on the basis of all of the
> applicable criteria and the facts of the particular case. Despite
> past efforts, reasonable arrangements involving a mutual under-
> standing of what generally consititutes acceptable library practices,
> and providing workable clearance and licensing conditions, have
> not been achieved and are overdue. The committee urges all concerned
> to resume their efforts to reach an accommodation under which the needs
> of scholarship and the rights of authors would both be respected. [61]

This version of the Revision Bill added a new section dealing with

non-profit archives:

> § 108. Limitations on exclusive rights: Reproduction of works in
>   archival collections
>   Nothwithstanding the provisions of section 106, it is not an
> infringement of copyright for a nonprofit institution, having archival
> custody over collections of manuscripts, documents, or other unpub-
> lished works of value to scholarly research, to reproduce, without
> any purpose of direct or indirect commercial advantage, any such
> work in its collections in facsimile copies or phonorecords for
> purposes of preservation and security, or for deposit for research
> use in any other such institution.

The discussion of Section 108 in the Report explains the inclusion

of this section:

> SECTION 108. REPRODUCTION OF WORKS IN ARCHIVAL COLLECTIONS
>
>   Although the committee does not favor special fair use provisions
> dealing with the problems of library photocopying, it was impressed
> with the need for a specific exemption permitting reproduction of
> manuscript collections under certain conditions....
>   The committee has therefore adopted a new provision, section 108,
> under which a "non-profit institution, having archival custody over
> collections of manuscripts, documents, or other unpublished works of
> value to scholarly research," would be entitled to reproduce "any
> such work in its collections" under certain circumstances. Only unpub-
> lished works could be reproduced under this exemption, but the privilege

---

60/ Id. at 58

61/ Id. at 65. Cf. supra statements of Celebrezze, Willcox, and Burkhardt
at A-31.

would extend to any type of work, including photographs, motion pictures, and sound recordings.

The archival reproduction privilege accorded by section 108 would be available only where there was no "purpose of direct or indirect commercial advantage," and where the copies or phonorecords are reproduced in "facsimile." Under the exemption, for example, a repository could make photocopies of manuscripts by microfilm or electrostatic process, but could not reproduce the work in "machine-readable" language for storage in an information system.

The purposes of the reproduction must either be "preservation and security" or "deposit for research use in any other such institution." Thus, no facsimile copies or phonorecords made under this section can be distributed to scholars or the public; if they leave the institution that reproduced them, they must be deposited for research purposes in another "nonprofit institution" that has "archival custody over collections of manuscripts, documents, or other unpublished works of value to scholarly research."

This section is not intended to override any contractual arrangements under which the manuscript material was deposited in the institution. For example, if there is an express contractual prohibition against reproduction for any purpose, section 108 could not be construed as justifying a violation of the contract. 62/ [Emphasis added.]

This version of the bill also added an "innocent infringer" clause

in Section 504(c)(2) which would apply in the following instance:

In a case where an instructor in a nonprofit educational institution, who infringed by reproducing a copyrighted work in copies or phonorecords for use in the course of face-to-face treaching activities in a classroom or similar place normally devoted to instruction, sustains the burden of proving that he believed and had reasonable grounds for believing that the reproduction was a fair use under section 107, the court in its discretion may remit statutory damages in whole or in part.

Congress adjourned before taking any action on this bill.

THE NINETIETH CONGRESS

In the First Session of the 90th Congress Rep. Celler reintroduced

the revision bill as H. R. 2512 on January 17, 1967; S. 597 followed on

January 23. On March 8, the House Committee on the Judiciary reported

63/
H.R. 2512.   The Sectional Analysis and Discussions for Sections 107 and

64/
108   are virtually identical to those found in H.R. Rep. 89-2237. The

House of Representatives passed the bill, with several amendments, on

April 11, 1967.

62/ Id. at 66.

63/ H. R. Rep. No. 83, 90th Cong., 1st Sess. (1967).

64/ Id. at 29.

Meanwhile, the Subcommittee on Patents, Trademarks, and Copyrights

of the Senate Judiciary Committee held hearings on S. 597 in March and April

of 1967.

The transcripts of these hearings, issued in four parts, [65/] contain

numerous references to statements on photocopying:

Cable television emerged as a serious and long-lasting problem; thus,

no action was taken on the Copyright Revision Bill in the 90th Congress.

THE NATIONAL COMMISSION ON NEW TECHNOLOGICAL USES OF COPYRIGHTED WORKS

By the summer of 1967 it had become apparent that the Revision Bill

then before Congress did not deal with a number of copyright problems in

computer-related fields. On August 2 Senator McClellan introduced

a bill (S. 2216) to create a National Commission on New Technological Uses of

Copyrighted Works. Further discussion of this bill is found in the portion

of this Appendix dealing with computer-related works.

S. 2216 was passed by the Senate on October 12 but the House

of Representatives took no corresponding action during the 90th Congress.

65/ Copyright Law Revision; Hearings before the Subcomm. on Patents, Trademarks, and Copyrights of the Senate Comm. on the Judiciary, on S. 597, 90th Cong., 1st Sess. (1967).

THE NINETY-FIRST CONGRESS

On January 22 (legislative day of January 10), 1969, Senator

McClellan once again introduced the revision bill in the Senate as S. 543.

This bill combined most of the provisions of S. 597 and S. 2216 from

the 90th Congress. When the Senate Judiciary Subcommittee referred the

bill to the full Committee on December 10, 1969, Section 108 specified

the type of library which would be eligible for "isolated and unrelated

reproduction or distribution" exemptions and the conditions under which

copies could be made for patrons.

§ 108. Limitations on exclusive rights: Reproduction by libraries
and archives
(a) Notwithstanding the provisions of section 106, it is not
an infringement of copyright for a library or archives, or any of
its employees acting within the scope of their employment, to
reproduce no more than one copy or phonorecord of a work, or
distribute such copy or phonorecord, under the conditions specified
by this section and if:
(1) The reproduction or distribution is made without any
purpose of direct or indirect commercial advantage; and
(2) The collections of the library or archives are (i) open
to the public, or (ii) available not only to researchers affiliated
with the library or archives or with the institution of which it is
a part, but also to other persons doing research in a specialized
field.
(b) The rights of reproduction and distribution under this section
apply to a copy or phonorecord of an unpublished work duplicated in
facsimile form solely for purposes of preservation and security or for
deposit for research use in another library or archives of the type
described by clause (2) of subsection (a), if the copy or phonorecord reproduced is currently in the collections of the library
or archives.
(c) The right of reproduction under this section applies to a
copy or phonorecord of a published work duplicated in facsimile
form solely for the purpose of replacement of a copy or phonorecord that is damaged, deteriorating, lost, or stolen, if the
library or archives has, after a reasonable effort, determined
that an unused replacement cannot be obtained at a normal price
from commonly-known trade sources in the United States, including
authorized reproducing services.
(d) The rights of reproduction and distribution under this
section, apply to a copy of a work, other than a musical work,
a pictorial, graphic or sculptural work, or a motion picture
or other audio-visual work, made at the request of a user of
the collections of the library or archives, including a user
who makes his request through another library or archives, if:
(1) The user has established to the satisfaction of the
library or archives that an unused copy cannot be obtained
at a normal price from commonly known trade sources in the
United States, including authorized reproducing services;
(2) The copy becomes the property of the user, and the
library or archives has had no notice that the copy would
be used for any purpose other than private study, scholarship, or research; and

(3) The library or archives displays prominently, at the place where orders are accepted, and includes on its order form, a warning of copyrights in accordance with requirements that the Register of Copyrights shall prescribe by regulation.

(e) Nothing in this section--

(1) shall be construed to impose liability for copyright infringement upon a library or archives or its employees for the unsupervised use of reproducing equipment located on its premises; provided that such equipment displays a notice that the making of a copy may be subject to the copyright law.

(2) excuses a person who uses such reproducing equipment or who requests a copy under subsection (d) from liability for copyright infringement for any such act, or for any later use of such copy, if it exceeds fair use as provided by section 107;

(3) in any way affects the right of fair use as provided by section 107, or any contractual obligations assumed by the library or archives when it obtained a copy or phonorecord of the work for its collections.

(f) The rights of reproducing or distributing "no more than one copy or phonorecord" in accordance with this section extend to the isolated and unrelated reproduction or distribution of a single copy or phonorecord of the same work on separate occasions, but do not extend to cases where the library or archives, or its employees, is aware or has substantial reason to believe that it is engaging in the related or concerted reproduction or distribution of multiple copies or phonorecords of the same work, whether on one occasion or over a period of time, and whether intended for aggregate use by one individual or for separate use by the individual members of a group.

Section 504(c)(2) extended the "innocent infringer" status to librarians and archivists as well as to instructors in educational institutions. Disagreement on issues related to cable television again forestalled further Congressional action.

THE NINETY-SECOND CONGRESS

Senator McClellan introduced a bill (S. 644) which was, apart from minor amendments, virtually identical to that reported by the Senate Judiciary Subcommittee in the 91st Congress on February 18, 1971. As the Federal Communications Commission was engaged in formulating rules for cable television, the Senate took no action on S. 644. Public Law 92-140, for limited copyright in sound recordings, was enacted during this Congress.

THE NINETY-THIRD CONGRESS

The 93d Congress saw the introduction of a Copyright Revision Bill with the same provisions as that of the previous Congress' S. 644. S. 1361 was introduced on March 26, 1973, and more copyright hearings were held on

July 31 and August 1.

Testimony on photocopying was presented at these hearings [66/]

by the following individuals:

The Subcommittee invited interested parties to submit written state-

ments which were included in the record of the Hearings. The following

individuals and organizations responded to this invitation:

66/ Copyright Law Revision; Hearings before the Subcomm. on Patents, Trade-
Marks, and Copyrights of the Senate Comm. on the Judiciary, on S. 1361,
93d Cong., 1st Sess. (1973).

A number of those who testified at the hearings and submitted

written statements urged that the proposed National Commission undertake the

study of photocopying issues related to both educational uses of copyrighted

works and library reproduction and distribution of copyrighted works.

The Senate Judiciary Subcommittee reported S. 1361 on April 9, 1974.

The Subcommittee had made substantial changes in the wording of Section 108,

adding subsection (a)(3) which required a notice of copyright to be placed on

the copies made, and putting the phrase "at a fair price" in subsection (c)

in place of an earlier phrase requiring the library to check "commonly-known

trade sources in the United States, including authorized reproduction services."

Section 108 also distingushes between copies made for users of portions of

works [subsection (d)] and of whole works which are otherwise unavailable

[subsection (e)].   The Subcommittee added subsection (h) to specify those

works which might not be reproduced except for "preservation or security"

or because they are "damaged," etc.:

§ 108.   Limitations on exclusive rights: Reproduction by libraries
and archives
(a) Notwithstanding the provisions of section 106, it is not
an infringement of copyright for a library or archives, or any of
its employees acting within the scope of their employment, to
reproduce no more than one copy or phonorecord of a work, or distribute such copy or phonorecord, under the conditions specified by
this section, if:
(1) The reproduction or distribution is made without any
purpose of direct or indirect commercial advantage; and
(2) The collections of the library or archives are (i) open
to the public, or (ii) available not only to researchers
affiliated with the library or archives or with the institution
of which it is a part, but also to other persons doing research
in a specialized field,
(3) the reproduction or distribution of the work includes a
notice of copyright.
(b) The rights of reproduction and distribution under
this section apply to a copy or phonorecord of an unpublished
work duplicated in facsimile form solely for purposes of

preservation and security or for deposit for research use in another library or archives of the type described by clause (2) of subsection (a), if the copy or phonorecord reproduced is currently in the collections of the library or archives.

(c) The right of reproduction under this section applies to a copy or phonorecord of a published work duplicated in facsimile form solely for the purpose of replacement of a copy or phonorecord that is damaged, deteriorating, lost, or stolen, if the library or archives has, after a reasonable effort, determined that an unused replacement cannot be obtained at a fair price.

(d) The rights of reproduction and distribution under this section apply to a copy, made from the collection of a library or archives where the user makes his request or from that of another library or archives, of no more than one article or other contribution to a copyrighted collection or periodical issue, or to a copy or phonorecord of a small part of any other copyrighted work, if:

(1) The copy becomes the property of the user, and the library or archives has had no notice that the copy would be used for any purpose other than private study, scholarship, or research; and

(2) The library or archives displays prominently, at the place where orders are accepted, and includes on its order form, a warning of copyright in accordance with requirements that the Register of Copyrights shall prescribe by regulation.

(e) The rights of reproduction and distribution under this section apply to the entire work, or to a substantial part of it, made from the collection of a library or archives where the user makes his request or from that of another library or archives, if the library or archives had first determined, on the basis of a reasonable investigation that a copy or phonorecord of the copyrighted work cannot be obtained at a fair price, if:

(1) The copy becomes the property of the user, and the library or archives has had no notice that the copy would be used for any purpose other than private study, scholarship, or research; and

(2) The library or archives displays prominently, at the place where orders are accepted, and includes on its order form, a warning of copyright in accordance with requirements that the Register of Copyrights shall prescribe by regulation.

(f) Nothing in this section--

(1) shall be construed to impose liability for copyright infringement upon a library or archives or its employees for the unsupervised use of reproducing equipment located on its premises, provided that such equipment displays a notice that the making of a copy may be subject to the copyright law;

(2) excuses a person who uses such reproducing equipment or who requests a copy under subsection (d) from liability for copyright infringement for any such act, or for any later use of such copy, if it exceeds fair use as provided by section 107;

(3) in any way affects the right of fair use as provided by section 107, or any contractual obligation assumed at any time by the library or archives when it obtained a copy or phonorecord of a work in its collections.

(g) The rights of reproduction and distribution under this section extend to the isolated and unrelated reproduction or

distribution of a single copy or phonorecord of the same material
on separate occasions, but do not extend to cases where the
library or archives, or its employee:

(1) is aware or has substantial reason to believe that
it is engaging in the related or concerted reproduction
or distribution of multiple copies or phonorecords of
the same material, whether made on one occasion or over
a period of time, and whether intended for aggregate use
by one or more individuals or for separate use by the
individual members of a group; or

(2) engages in the systematic reproduction or
distribution of single or multiple copies or phonorecords
of material described in subsection (d).

(h) The rights of reproduction and distribution under this
section do not apply to a musical work, a pictorial, graphic
or sculptural work, or a motion picture or other audio-visual
work, except that no such limitation shall apply with respect
to rights granted by subsections (b) and (c).

The full Judiciary Committee of the Senate reported the bill

on July 3, 1974. There is considerable discussion of Section 108 in the

Senate Report. The legislators had found it difficult to define "systematic

reproduction or distribution," although they gave three examples of library

practice prohibited by Section 108(g)(1) and (2). 67/ The Report goes on

to state the following:

> The committee believes that section 108 provides an appro-
> priate statutory balancing of the rights of creators, and the
> needs of users. However, neither a statute nor legislative
> history can specify precisely which library photocopying practices
> constitute the making of "single copies" as distinguished from
> "systematic reproduction." Isolated single spontaneous requests
> must be distinguished from "systematic reproduction."
>
> The photocopying needs of such operations as multi-county
> regional systems, must be met. The committee therefore
> recommends that representatives of authors, book, and
> periodical publishers and other owners of copyrighted ma-
> terial meet with the library community to formulate photo-
> copying guidelines to assist library patrons and employees.
> Concerning library photocopying practices not authorized
> by this legislation, the committee recommends that workable
> clearance and licensing procedures be developed.
>
> In adopting these provisions on library photocopying, the
> committee is aware that through such programs as those of the
> National Commission on Libraries and Information Science there
> will be a significant evolution in the functioning and services
> of libraries. To consider the possible need for changes in
> copyright law and procedures as a result of new technology,
> title II of this legislation establishes a National Commission
> on New Technological Uses of Copyrighted Works. It is the desire
> of the committee that the Commission give priority to those
> aspects of the library-copyright interface which require
> further study and clarification. 68/

67/   S. Rep. No. 983, 93d Cong., 2d Sess. 122 (1974).

68/   Id.

S. 1361 was then referred to the Senate Commerce Committee on July 9. The Commerce Committee amended several sections and reported the bill July 29, 1974.

The Senate passed S. 1361 with several amendments on September 9.

The end of the 93d Congress was approaching and it did not seem likely that there would be time for S. 1361 to be considered in the House of Representatives. On the same day that S. 1361 passed the Senate, Senator McClellan introduced S. 3976, an interim bill which, among other provisions, would establish the National Commission on New Technological Uses of Copyrighted Works. The Senate considered and passed the bill within the one day, September 9, 1974.

The House Subcommittee held a hearing on S. 3974 on November 26. The Register of Copyrights testified at the hearing in support of the establishmer of the Commission.[69] The bill was amended to include "at least one member selected from among experts in consumer protection affairs" on the Commission. The House Judiciary Committee reported the bill on December 12, 1974, with a dissenting view by Representative Robert F. Drinan opposing the establishment of the Commission.[70] The House of Representatives considered and passed the bill on December 19, 1974. It was then signed by President Gerald Ford on on December 31, and became Public Law 93-573.

THE NINETY-FOURTH CONGRESS

Early in the 94th Congress a copyright revsion bill was introduced by Senator McClellan as S. 22 on January 15, 1975 and by Representative Kastenmeier as H.R. 2223 on January 28. The bill was substantially the the same as S. 1361 which had been passed by the Senate in the 93d Congress. The Senate Judiciary Committee reported S. 22 on November 20, 1975.[71]

69/ Copyright Miscellany; Hearing before the Subcomm. on Courts, Civil Liberties, and the Administration of Justice of the House Comm. on the Judiciary on S. 3976, 93d Cong., 2d Sess. 6 (1974).

70/ H.R. Rep. No. 1581, 93d Cong., 2d Sess. 17 (1974).

71/ S. Rep. No. 473, 94th Cong., 1st Sess. (1975).

In its disscussion of Section 108(g) the Committee repeated
its recommendation that

> representatives of authors, book and periodical publishers and
> other owners of copyrighted material meet with the library community
> to formulate photocopying guidelines to assist library patrons
> and employees. Concerning library photocopying practices not
> authorized by this legislation, the committee recommends that
> workable clearance and licensing procedures be developed.72/

The discussion went on to state that

> It is still uncertain how far a library may go under the
> Copyright Act of 1909 in supplying a photocopy of copyrighted
> material in its collection. The recent case of The Williams and
> Wilkins Company v. The United States failed to significantly
> illuminate the application of the fair use doctrine to library
> photocopying practices. Indeed, the opinion of the Court of
> Claims said the Court was engaged in "a 'holding operation' in
> the interim period before Congress enacted its preferred solution."
> While the several opinions in the Wilkins case have given the
> Congress little guidance as to the current state of the law on
> fair use, these opinions provide additional support for the
> balanced resolution of the photocopying issue adopted by the
> Senate last year in S. 1361 and preserved in section 108 of this
> legislation. As the Court of Claims opinion succinctly stated
> "there is much to be said on all sides."
> In adopting these provisions on library photocopying, the
> committee is aware that through such programs as those of the
> National Commission on Libraries and Information Science there will
> be a significant evolution in the functioning and services of
> libraries. To consider the possible need for changes in copyright
> law and procedures as a result of new technology, a National
> Commission on New Technological Uses of Copyrighted Works has been
> established (Public Law 93-573). 73/

Subsection 108(f)(4) was added to the bill

> [B]y the adoption of an amendment proposed by Senator [Howard]
> Baker [of Tennessee]. It is intended to permit libraries
> and archives, subject to the general conditions of this
> section, to make off-the-air videotape recordings of television
> news programs. Despite the importance of preserving television
> news, the United States currently has no institution performing
> this function on a systematic basis.
> The purpose of the clause is to prevent the copyright law from
> precluding such operations as the Vanderbilt University Television
> News Archive 74/

The text of the new subsection is as follows:

> § 108 (f) Nothing in this section—
> ....
> (4) shall be construed to limit the reproduction and distri-
> bution of a limited number of copies and excerpts by a

72/ Id. at 71.

73/ Id.

74/ Id. at 69.

library or archives of an audiovisual news program
subject to clauses (1), (2), or (3) of subsection (a).

Subsection 108(h) was changed in this version to read

§ 108(h) The rights of reproduction under this section do not
apply to a musical work, a pictorial, graphic or sculptural work,
or a motion picture or other audiovisual work other than an audiovisual work dealing with news, except that no such limitation shall
apply with respect to rights granted by subsections (b) and (c).

The Senate approved S. 22 unanimously on February 19, 1976.

The House Judiciary Subcommittee on Courts, Civil Liberties, and
the Administration of Justice held 18 days of hearings on H.R. 2223 in 1975. 75/

The Register of Copyrights testified at several hearings and presented material
from the Second Supplementary Report of the Register of Copyrights. 76/

During testimony received at these hearings, representatives of the
six national library associations, 77/ and author and publisher associations

discussed, among other topics, the definition of "systematic reproduction"

and a proposed copyright clearinghouse.

Testimony or statements from the following appear in the record:

Page

75/ Copyright Law Revision; Hearings before the Subcomm. on Courts, Civil
Liberties, and the Administration of Justice of the House Comm. on the
Judiciary on H.R. 2223. 94th Cong., 1st Sess. (1975).

76/ The Report has not yet been published. Copies of the Draft are available
from the Copyright Office.

77/ American Library Association, Association of Research Libraries, Medical
Library Association, Music Library Association, Special Libraries Association.

During the October hearings the Register of Copyrights in a discussion

of the Second Supplementary Report outlined the history of Section 108, defined

some of the continued problems in the interpretation of the section, and

called for "a much clearer statement in the report concerning the interrelation-

ship between sections 107 and 108, and a careful look at the wording and

content of subsections (g) and (h)."[78]

> She went on to say that
>   A line must be drawn between legitimate interlibrary loans
> using photocopies instead of bound books, and prearranged
> understandings that result in a particular library agreeing to
> become the source of an indeterminate number of photocopies. To
> find that line and draw it clearly is one of the most difficult
> legislative tasks remaining in the revision program.
>   . . . .
>   I also indicate that I think CONTU, the new National
> Commission on New Technological Uses of Copyrighted Works,
> should not be forgotten here. There are legitimate things
> it can do. But, at the meeting yesterday, at one point,
> there was a suggestion made that they shouldn't try to
> reinvent the wheel and that the Congress has a long his-
> tory behind this provision. And I think that proposals
> are coming to you, and maybe already have, that you should
> delay action on, or you should make interim action, pending
> what CONTU does. And I don't argue with that, as long as
> you lay a groundwork for what it does. I do feel the
> interrelationship between 108 and the Commission should
> be addressed in your report. I think it is important that
> you get out of the Commission what you want. You created it
> and it should do what you want it to do, in relation to this
> problem. [79]

The Register also stated that the phrase "without any purpose of

direct or indirect commerical advantage" was a problem with respect to

special libraries and needed clarification.[80]

78/ Hearings on H.R. 2223, supra note 72, at 1801.

79/ Id. at 1801-1802.

80/ Id. at 1804.

Appendix 2 of the hearings volumes contains a series of eighteen "Briefing Papers on Current Issues Raised by H.R. 2223" prepared by the staff of the Copyright Office, one portion of which covers Section 108. [81/] Appendix 3 is the "Report of Working Group of Conference on Resolution of Copyright Issues (Dealing with Library Photocopying)." [82/]

After these extensive hearings and the public markup sessions which followed, the House Subcommittee reported the bill on August 3, 1976. The full Judiciary Committee of the House reported the bill without further amendment on September 3. The Subcommittee had made two changes in Section 108 which the Judiciary Committee accepted and explained in this way:

Multiple copies and systematic reproduction

Subsection (g) provides that the rights granted by this section extend only to the "isolated and unrelated reproduction of a single copy or phonorecord of the same material on separate occasions." However, this section does not authorize the related or concerted reproduction of multiple copies or phonorecords of the same materials, whether made on one occasion or over a period of time, and whether intended for aggregate use by one individual or for separate use by the individual members of a group.

With respect to material described in subsection (d) -- articles or other contributions to periodicals or collections, and small parts of other copyrighted works -- subsection (g)(2) provides that the exemptions of section 108 do not apply if the library or archive [sic] engages in "systematic reproduction or distribution of single or multiple copies or phonorecords." This provision in S. 22 provoked a storm of controversy, centering around the extent to which the restrictions on "systematic" activities would prevent the continuation and development of interlibrary networks and other arrangements involving the exchange of photocopies. After thorough consideration, the Committee amended section 108(g)(2) to add the following proviso:

Provided, that nothing in this clause prevents a library or archives from participating in interlibrary arrangements that do not have, as their purpose or effect, that the library or archives receiving such copies or phonorecords for distribution does so in such aggregate quantities as to substitute for a subscription to or purchase of such work.

In addition, the Committee added a new subsection (i) to section 108, requiring the Register of Copyrights, five years from the effective date of the new Act and at five-year intervals thereafter, to report to Congress upon "the extent to which this section has achieved the intended statutory balancing of the rights of creators and the needs of users," and to make appropriate legislative or other recommendations. As noted in connection with section 107, the Committee also amended section 504(c) in a way that would insulate librarians from unwarranted liability for copyright infringement; this amendment is discussed below.

81/ Id. at 2057.

82/ Id. at 2092.

The key phrases in the Committee's amendment of section 108 (g)(2) are "aggregate quantities" and "substitute for a subscription to or purchase of" a work. To be implemented effectively in practice, these provisions will require the development and implementation of more-or-less specific guidelines establishing criteria to govern various situations.

The National Commission on New Technological Uses of Copyrighted Works (CONTU) offered to provide good offices in helping to develop these guidelines. This offer was accepted and, although the final text of guidelines has not yet been achieved, the Committee has reason to hope that, within the next month, some agreement can be reached on an initial set of guidelines covering practices under section 108(g)(2). 83/

The House Committee also addressed the issue of "indirect commercial advantage" in Section 108(a)(1) which the Register of Copyrights had pointed out as an area needing clarification in the hearings on H.R. 2223:

> The reference to "indirect commercial advantage" has raised questions as to the status of photocopying done by or for libraries or archival collections within industrial, profit-making, or proprietary institutions (such as the research and development departments of chemical, pharmaceutical, automobile, and oil corporations, the library of a proprietary hospital, the collections owned by a law or medical partnership, etc.).
>
> There is a direct interrelationship between this problem and the prohibitions against "multiple" and "systematic" photo-copying in section 108(g)(1) and (2). Under section 108, a library in a profit-making organization would not be authorized to:
>
> (a) use a single subscription or copy to supply its employees with multiple copies of material relevant to their work; or
>
> (b) use a single subscription or copy to supply its employees, on request, with single copies of material relevant to their work, where the arrangement is "systematic" in the sense of deliberately substituting photocopying for subscription or purchase; or
>
> (c) use "interlibrary loan" arrangements for obtaining photocopies in such aggregate quantities as to substitute for subscriptions or purchase of material needed by employees in their work.
>
> Moreover, a library in a profit-making organization could not evade these obligations by installing reproducing equipment on its premises for unsupervised use by the organization's staff.
>
> Isolated, spontaneous making of single photocopies by a library in a for-profit organization, without any systematic effort to substitute photocopying for subscriptions or purchases, would be covered by section 108, even though the copies are furnished to the employees of the organization for use in their work. Similarly, for-profit libraries could participate in interlibrary arrangements for exchange of photocopies as long as the production or distribution was not "systematic." These activities, by themselves, would ordinarily not be considered "for direct or indirect commercial advantages," since the "advantage" referred to in this clause must attach to the immediate commercial motivation behind the reproduction or distribution itself, rather than to the ultimate profit-making

---

83/ H.R. Rep. No. 1476, 94th Cong., 2d Sess. 77 (1976). Corrections appeared in 122 Cong. Rec. H10727 (daily edition, Sept. 21, 1976).

motivation behind the enterprise in which the library is
located. On the other hand, section 108 would not excuse
reproduction or distribution if there were a commercial motive
behind the actual making or distributing of the copies, if multiple
copies were made or distributed, or if the photocopying activities
were "systematic" in the sense that their aim was to substitute
for subscriptions or purchases. 84/

The Report contains, in addition, the Guidelines for Classroom
Copying in Not-for-Profit Educational Institutions 85/ and Guidelines for
Educational Use of Music. 86/

                              THE CONTU GUIDELINES 87/

On April 2, 1976, the National Commission on New Technological Uses

of Copyrighted Works (CONTU) adopted the following resolution:

> BE IT RESOLVED, that the National Commission on New Technological
> Uses of Copyrighted Works shall offer its assistance to the Subcommittee
> on Courts, Civil Liberties and the Administration of Justice of the
> House Committee on the Judiciary in helping to develop language and
> guidelines relating to library photocopying in the Senate Bill 22.

The House Subcommittee accepted the Commission's offer, as did the

Chairman of the Senate Judiciary Subcommittee, Senator McClellan.

The Commission requested written statements from parties who had expressed

interest in the library photocopying issue throughout the legislative

proceedings. The following submitted comments:

    American Association of Law Libraries
    American Institute of Physics
    American Library Association
    American Society for Testing and Materials
    Association of American Publishers
    Association of Research Libraries
    Authors League of America, Inc.
    Ben H. Weil
    Harcourt Brace Jovanovich, Inc.
    Macmillan Publishing Company, Inc.
    Medical Library Association
    Music Library Association
    National Commission on Libraries and Information Science
    National Library of Medicine
    Special Libraries Association
    Williams and Wilkins Company.

84/ Id. at 74.

85/ Id. at 68.

86/ Id. at 70.

87/ For a fuller discussion, see pp. 134-137, supra.

At its meeting on June 9-10, 1976, [88] the Commission discussed the comments received and began to draft guidelines. These draft guidelines were submitted to the interested parties, further comments were received, and a revised draft was drawn up. Representatives of the principal library, author, and publisher organizations accepted the revised guidelines, which were then submitted to the Chairman of the Conference Committee on September 22, 1976. The text of the guidelines may be found on pp. 136-137 of this Report.

THE CONFERENCE REPORT

S. 22, as reported by the House Judiciary Committee, was approved by the House of Representatives on September 22, 1976. A Conference Committee was appointed to reconcile the differences in the two versions of the bill; as noted above, the Senate had approved S. 22 some seven months previously. The Conference Committee accepted the House version of Section 108 along with the CONTU Guidelines, which were included in the Conference Report. [89]

The Committee also gave a further clarification of "indirect commercial advantage" as used in section 108(a)(1) in relation to proprietary libraries. [90]

Both Houses of Congress accepted the Conference Committee version of S. 22 on September 30, 1976, and President Ford signed the bill on October 19. [91]

PUBLIC LAW 93-573

TITLE II -- NATIONAL COMMISION ON NEW TECHNOLOGICAL USES OF COPYRIGHTED WORKS

ESTABLISHMENT AND PURPOSE OF COMMISSION

SEC. 201. (a) There is hereby created in the Library of Congress a National Commission on New Technological Uses of Copyrighted Works (hereafter called the Commission).

(b) The purpose of the Commission is to study and compile data on:

(1) the reproduction and use of copyrighted works of authorship --

---

[88] Transcript, CONTU Meeting No. 7 4 (1976). PB 254 766.

[89] H.R. Rep. No. 1733, 94th Cong., 2d Sess. 72 (1976).

[90] Id. at 73.

[91] Pub. L. No. 94-553 (1976).

(A) in conjunction with automatic systems capable of storing, processing, retrieving, and transferring information, and

(B) by various forms of machine reproduction, not including reproduction by or at the request of instructors for use in face-to-face teaching activities; and

(2) the creation of new works by the application or intervention of such automatic systems or machine reproduction.

(c) The Commission shall make recommendations as to such changes in copyright law or procedures that may be necessary to assure for such purposes access to copyrighted works, and to provide recognition of the rights of copyright owners.

MEMBERSHIP OF THE COMMISSION

SEC. 202. (a) The Commission shall be compsed of thirteen voting members, appointed as follows:

(1) Four members, to be appointed by the President, selected from authors and other copyright owners;

(2) Four members, to be appointed by the President, selected from users of copyright works;

(3) Four nongovernmental members to be appointed by the President, selected from the public generally, with at least one member selected from among experts in consumer protection affairs;

(4) The Librarian of Congress.

(b) The President shall appoint a Chairman, and a Vice Chairman who shall act as Chairman in the absence or disability of the Chairman or in the event of a vacancy in that office, from among the four members selected from the public generally, as provided by clause (3) of subsection (a). The Register of Copyrights shall serve ex officio as a nonvoting member of the Commission.

(c) Seven voting members of the Commission shall constitute a quorum.

(d) Any vacancy in the Commission shall not affect its powers and shall be filled in the same manner as the original appointment was made.

COMPENSATION OF MEMBERS OF COMMISSION

SEC. 203. (a) Members of the Commission, other than officers or employees of the Federal Government, shall receive compensation at the rate of $100 per day while engaged in the actual performance of Commission duties, plus reimbursement for travel, subsistence, and other necessary expenses in connection with such duties.

(b) Any members of the Commission who are officers or employees of the Federal Government shall serve on the Commission without compensation, but such members shall be reimbursed for travel, subsistence, and other necessary expenses in connection with the performance of their duties.

STAFF

SEC. 204. (a) To assist in its studies, the Commission may appoint a staff which shall be an administrative part of the Library of Congress. The staff shall be headed by an Executive Director, who shall be responsible to the Commission for the Administration of the duties entrusted to the staff.

(b) The Commission may procure temporary and intermittent services to the same extent as is authorized by section 3109 of title 5, United States Code, but at rates not to exceed $100 per day.

EXPENSES OF THE COMMISSION

SEC. 205.   There are hereby authorized to be appropriated such sums as may be necessary to carry out the provisions of this title until June 30, 1976.

REPORTS

SEC. 206.   (a) Within one year after the first meeting of the Commission it shall submit to the President and the Congress a preliminary report on its activities.

(b) Within three years after the enactment of this Act the Commission shall submit to the President and the Congress a final report on its study and investigation which shall include its recommendations and such proposals for legislation and administrative action as may be necessary to carry out its recommendations.

(c)   In addition to the preliminary report and final report required by this section, the Commission may publish such interim reports as it may determine, including but not limited to consustant's reports, transcripts of testimony, seminar reports, and other Commission findings.

POWERS OF THE COMMISSION

SEC. 207.   (a)   The Commission or, with the authorization of the Commission, any three or more of its members, may, for the purpose of carrying out the provisions of this title, hold hearings, administer oaths, and require, by subpoena or otherwise, the attendance and testimony of witnesses and the production of documentary material.

(b)   With the consent of the Commission, any of its members may hold any meetings, seminars, or conferences considered appropriate to provide a forum for discussion of the problems with which it is dealing.

TERMINATION

SEC. 208.   On the sixtieth day after the date of the submission of its final report, the Commission shall terminate and all offices and employment under it shall expire.

PUBLIC LAW 95-146

An Act to extend by seven months the term of the National Commission on

New Technological Uses of Copyrighted Works

Be it enacted by the Senate and House of Representatives of the United States of America in Congress assembled, That section 206(b) of Public Law 93-573 is amended to read as follows:

"(b)   On or before July 31, 1978 the Commission shall submit to the President and the Congress a final report on its study and investigation

which shall include its recommendations and such proposals for legislation and administrative action as may be necessary to carry out its
recommendations."

THE COMMISSIONERS

Stanley H. Fuld: Judge Fuld, Chairman of CONTU, served as
Chairman   Associate Judge of the New York Court of
                           Appeals from 1946 until 1966, and as Chief
                           Judge of the State of New York and the New
                           York Court of Appeals of New York, from 1967
                           through 1973. He is currently Special Counsel
                           to the law firm of Kaye, Scholer, Fierman,
                           Hays and Handler. He received his LL.B. from
                           Columbia University Law School in 1926, and
                           honorary LL.D. degrees from a number of
                           colleges and universities. He has served
                           on several occasions as a judge in the
                           Nathan Burkan Memorial Competition sponsored
                           by the American Society of Composers, Authors
                           and Publishers.

Melville B. Nimmer: Professor Nimmer teaches Copyright Law,
Vice-Chairman   Constitutional Law and Contracts at the
                           University of California, Los Angeles. He is
                           the author of the treatise Nimmer on Copyright
                           and of the casebook entitled Copyright and Other
                           Aspects of Law Pertaining to Literary, Musical
                           and Artistic Works. He has also written
                           numerous articles dealing with both freedom of
                           speech and copyright. He has been active in
                           international copyright meetings and has
                           served at various times as consultant to both
                           the Berne Convention Secretariat and UNESCO's
                           Copyright Division.

George D. Cary: Retired Register of Copyrights, Mr. Cary began
                           his career with the Copyright Office in 1947 after
                           serving in the Navy during World War II as
                           Lieutenant Commander. In the Copyright Office,
                           Mr. Cary served successively as Attorney,
                           Assistant Chief - Examining Division, Principal
                           Legal Advisor, General Counsel, Deputy Register,
                           and then Register. Commissioner Cary has been
                           a lecturer at The George Washington Law Center
                           and the Practising Law Institute. He is also
                           a trustee of the Copyright Society of the
                           United States.

William S. Dix: Dr. Dix was, at the time of his death on
                           February 22, 1978, Librarian Emeritus of
                           Princeton University. He retired in 1975 after
                           completing twenty-two years as Librarian of
                           Princeton University and had been before that
                           an Associate Professor and Librarian at the
                           Rice Institute, Houston, Texas. He received

a Ph.D. in English from the University of Chicago. He has been Chairman of the Association of Research Libraries, President of the American Library Association and served as Chairman of both the Intellectual Freedom and the International Relations Committees of A.L.A. Dr. Dix was also active in international library and cultural activities and served as Chairman of the United States National Commission for UNESCO.

John Hersey:

Mr. Hersey, a novelist and journalist, is the author of eighteen books and a winner of the Pulitzer Prize for fiction. He is President of the Authors League of America and Secretary of the American Academy of Arts and Letters. He served for five years as Master of Pierson College, Yale University, has been Writer-in-Residence at the American Academy in Rome, and has been Visiting Professor at the Massachusetts Institute of Technology and at Yale, where he presently teaches.

Rhoda H. Karpatkin:

Ms. Karpatkin is Executive Director of Consumers Union, the non-profit product-testing and consumer-advisory organization that publishes Consumer Reports. Before joining Consumers Union in 1974, Ms. Karpatkin had been engaged in the private practice of law, and had served as Consumer Union's legal counsel for sixteen years. Ms. Karpatkin chairs the Special Committee on Consumer Affairs of the Association of the Bar of the City of New York, and is a member of the Consumer Advisory Council of the City of New York. She is also a member of the American Bar Association Commission on Law and the Economy.

Dan M. Lacy:

Mr. Lacy is Senior Vice-President and Executive Assistant to the President, McGraw-Hill, Inc. From 1953 until 1966, Mr. Lacy was Managing Director of the American Book Publishers Council, with responsibility for representing book industry points of view on copyright. He later served for several years as a member and chairman of the industry's Copyright Committee. Commissioner Lacy has attended international copyright conferences both for the International Publishers Association and the United States delegation. He has been a member of the American Library Association and served for a number of years as an officer of the Library of Congress.

Arthur R. Miller:

Professor of Law at Harvard Law School since 1972, Professor Miller was Chairman of the Massachusetts Security and Privacy Council and also directed the Association of American Law Schools Project on Computer-Assisted Instruction. While Professor of Law at the University of Michigan Law School from 1965 to

1972, Mr. Miller served as Advisor to the
Special Committee on Computer Research for the
State Bar of Michigan. Computer technology
and aspects of copyright are among the many
topics on which he has testified, lectured,
and written.

E. Gabriel Perle:

Vice President-Law for Time, Inc., Mr. Perle
has long been active in the Copyright Society
of the United States. He has been President,
Vice President and a member of the Board of
Trustees of that organization. In 1972 and
1973 he was Vice President of the United
States Trademark Association and served as a
Director from 1969 through 1972 and from
1974 until the present. Also active in
copyright divisions of the American Bar
Association and the Association of the Bar
of the City of New York, he has been Chairman
of the Copyright Division of the Patent,
Trademark and Copyright Section of the ABA.

Hershel B. Sarbin:

Mr. Sarbin is Executive Vice President and a
Member of the Board of the Ziff Corporation.
He was formerly President of the company's
magazine publishing subsidiary. Mr. Sarbin
maintains an active interest in education,
writing and lecturing. He is co-author of
Photography and the Law and has written numerous articles and spoken frequently on marketing, travel, leisure activity and law-related
topics. He has taught at City College of New
York and Tufts University and in 1971 was
a visiting fellow at the Center for Advanced
Studies in the Behavioral Sciences at Stanford
University.

Robert Wedgeworth:

Executive Director of the American Library
Association since 1972, Mr. Wedgeworth is the former
editor of Library Resources and Technical Services,
the official journal of the American Library
Association Resources and Technical Services
Division. He is a member of the National Library
of Medicine Biomedical Library Review Committee,
the Chicago Quality of Life Committee and the
Chicago American Issues Forum Committee.

Alice E. Wilcox:

Ms. Wilcox currently is Director of MINITEX
(Minnesota Interlibrary Telecommunications Exchange)
a program of the Minnesota Higher Education
Coordinating Board. MINITEX administers a network
for the academic libraries in the state and major
public and state agency libraries. She has served
on the National Commission of Libraries and
Information Science's Committee on Periodical
Systems, the Midwest Library Network, and the
Executive Board of the Minnesota Library
Association. In 1974 she was named Minnesota
Librarian of the Year.

Daniel J. Boorstin:

Before being named Librarian of Congress in November 1975, Dr. Boorstin taught at the University of Chicago for twenty-five years and served as Senior Historian of the Museum of History and Technology, Smithsonian Institution. Both historian and lawyer, as well as the author of numerous books, he was awarded the Pulitzer Prize for History in 1974 for The Democratic Experience, the third volume of The Americans, a U. S. history.

Barbara A. Ringer:

Register of Copyrights in the Library of Congress since 1973, Ms. Ringer has been with the Copyright Office since 1949 when she began as an examiner. She left the Copyright Office briefly in 1972 to serve as the Director of the Copyright Division of UNESCO in Paris. Ms. Ringer has lectured on copyright throughout the world and has written many articles, monographs, and other documents on the subject which have been published both here and abroad.

THE STAFF

Arthur J. Levine
Executive Director

Mr. Levine was appointed by the Librarian of Congress in March 1975 as special consultant on planning for the new Commission and in October 1975 was named its Executive Director. Mr. Levine has lectured on copyright law and publishing at the Practicing Law Institute, and is an adjunct professor of law at Georgetown Law Center. He is a past trustee of the Copyright Society of the U.S.A. and is chairman of the Copyright Committee of the District of Columbia Bar Association and the American Bar Association's committee on Copyright and New Technology. He has been chairman of the American Bar Association's Committees on Copyright Office Affairs and on Copyright Law Revision. He was a contributing editor for the American Society for Information Science's Omnibus Copyright Revision in 1973.

Robert W. Frase
Assistant Executive
Director and Economist

Mr. Frase has served in economic and administrative positions in several Federal and international agencies. From 1950 to 1972 he was vice president and economist of the Association of American Publishers and its predecessor organizations. He has written widely on economic and public policy issues relating to publishing, libraries, and copyright. Most recently, he was a consulting economist in private practice.

Michael S. Keplinger
Assistant Executive
Director and Senior
 Attorney

Mr. Keplinger has a background in the computer
and information sciences having been a programmer
and system analyst at the National Bureau of
Standards. While at NBS he advised the Institute
for Computer Sciences on legal problems arising
from computer applications. He is a Vice President
and Director of the Computer Law Association and
has served as Chairman of the American Bar
Association's committees on Copyright and New
Technology and Government Relations to Copyright.
Mr. Keplinger has written and lectured extensively
on legal problems arising from computer use.

Jeffrey L. Squires
Staff Attorney

Mr. Squires received his B.A. from Washington
University in St. Louis in 1968 and his J.D.
from the University of Wisconsin in 1973. Prior
to his appointment to the Commission staff in
January 1976, he was associated with a law
firm in the District of Columbia. He has
lectured in copyright law at the Washington
College of Law at the American University.

Christopher A. Meyer
Staff Attorney

Mr. Meyer served as a judicial clerk for the
Maryland Court of Special Appeals. He is a
graduate of the George Washington University
and Rutgers Law School. His professional
activities have included membership on the Board
of Governors of the Maryland Civil Liberties
Union, lecturing on the Uniform Commercial Code,
and membership in the Maryland Bar Association's
section on legal education and admission to
the bar.

Patricia T. Barber
Librarian/Analyst

Mrs. Barber has received degrees from Rice
University and Simmons College. She has been
employed as a Librarian by the Peabody Museum
of Natural History, Yale University and the
Brown University Library.

David Y. Peyton
Policy Analyst

Mr. Peyton received a B.A. in government and
foreign affairs from the University of Virginia
in 1974 and a master's degree in public policy
from the University of California, Berkeley in
1976. He has worked both for the Department
of Health, Education and Welfare and on an
outside study of HEW reporting requirements
regarding Title XX of the Social Security Act.

Dolores K. Dougherty
Administrative Officer

Mrs. Dougherty has been employed by the Federal
Government for almost thirty years, in positions
ranging from secretary to supervising research.
She held the position of Research Assistant with
the House Banking and Currency Committee for nine

years. From 1956-1959, Mrs. Dougherty was a member
of the Research Project for Revision of the Copyright Law in the Copyright Office.

Secretarial and Administrative Staff:

Vicki A. Burke

Carol A. Orr

Jean C. Yancoskie

Jeffrey S. Winter

LISTS OF WITNESSES

Copyright and Computer-Related Issues

Fifth Meeting, April 1-2, 1976, New York City

. Ira Herrenstein, Standard and Poors'
. William Eustis, Senior Attorney, New York Times
. Joseph Taphorn, Copyright Attorney, International Business
  Machines Corporation
. Paul G. Zurkowski, President, Information Industry Association
. John Rothman, New York Times Information Bank

Sixth Meeting, May 6-7, 1976, Arlington, Virginia

. Peter F. McCloskey, President, and Oliver Smoot, Vice-President,
  Computer and Business Equipment Manufacturers' Association
. Philip Nyborg, Director, Washington Office, American Federation
  of Information Processing Societies
     with
  Herbert Bright, representing Association for Computing Machinery
  William Moser, representing Data Processing Management Association
  Herbert Koller, representing Computer Society of the Institute
  for Electrical and Electronic Engineers
. Joseph Wyatt, President, Interuniversity Communications Council
  (EDUCOM)
. A. G. W. Biddle, President, Computer Industry Association
     with
  Carol Cohen, General Counsel, Applied Data Research
  Theodore Lorah, Vice-President, INFORMATICS
  Terry Mahn, General Counsel, Computer Industry Association
. Paul G. Zurkowski, President, Information Industry Association
     with
  Joseph Taphorn, Proprietary Rights Committee, Information Industry
  Association

Seventh Meeting, June 9-10, 1976, Arlington, Virginia

. Nicholas Henry, Director, Center for Public Affairs, Arizona State
  University
. Susan H. Nycum, Esq.
. Theodore Puckorius, Commissioner, General Services Administration
     with
  George Dodson, Assistant Commissioner for Automated Data Management
  Services, GSA

Isaac McKinney, Chief, Procurement Policy Branch, Automated Data
Management Services, GSA
Robert Coyer, Director, Office of Management Policy and Planning, GSA
Allie B. Latimer, Assistant General Counsel, GSA

- August Steinhilber and Anna L. Hyer, Ad Hoc Committee on Copyright Law
- Quincy Rogers, Executive Director, Domestic Council on the Right to
  Privacy

Eighth Meeting, September 16-17, 1976, Los Angeles, California

- Herbert R. J. Grosch, President, Association for Computing Machinery
- M. Thomas Risner, Director, National Information Center (NICEM)
- Patricia Ferguson and Donna Chamberlain, Documentation Associates
  Information Services, Inc.
- Peter E. Weiner, Head, Information Science Department, Rand Corporation

Tenth Meeting, November 18, 1976, New York City

- Daniel McCracken, Consultant

Thirteenth Meeting, March 31-April 1, 1977, New York City

- Allen R. Ferguson, President, Public Interest Economics Center

Fifteenth Meeting, July 11-12, 1977, Washington, D. C.

- William J. Baumol, Professor of Economics, Princeton and New York
  Universities
     with
  Yale Braunstein, New York University
- Roy G. Saltman, Program Manager for Technology Tranfer, Institute
  for Computer Sciences and Technology, National Bureau of Standards

Sixteenth Meeting, September 15-16, 1977, Chicago, Illinois

- Daniel McCracken, Vice-President, Susan Nycum, Chairman, Legal
  Issues Committee, and Philip Dorn, Member, Legal Issues Committee,
  Association of Computing Machinery
- Martin Goetz, Senior Vice-President, Applied Data Research
- Frank H. Cullen and Joseph Genovese, Proprietary Rights Committee,
  Computing and Business Equipment Manufacturers' Association
- Paul G. Zurkowski, President, Joseph Taphorn, Chairman, Software
  Committee, and George C. Baron, Legal Advisor, Software Committee,
  Information Industry Association

Eighteenth Meeting, November 17-18, 1977, Cambridge, Massachusetts

- Richard I. Miller, Vice-President, Harbridge House, Inc.

Nineteenth Meeting, January 11-12, 1978, Los Angeles, California

- Roger Borovoy, Vice-President, General Counsel and Secretary,
  Intel Corporation

Twentieth Meeting, February 16-17, 1978, New York City

- Theodor H. Nelson, Author

Copyright and Photocopy Issues

Third Meeting, December 18-19, 1975, New York City

. David Catterns, Legal Research Officer, Australian Copyright Council

Fifth Meeting, April 1-2, 1976, New York City

. Samuel Freedman, Research Publications
. John Rothman, New York Times Information Bank

Eighth Meeting, September 16-17, 1976, Los Angeles, California

. Patricia Ferguson and Donna Chamberlain, Documentation Associates
  Information Services, Inc.

Ninth Meeting, October 21-22, 1976, Arlington, Virginia

. Vernon E. Palmour, Public Research Institute, Center for Naval Analyses
. Donald King, King Research, Inc.
. Melvin S. Day, Deputy Director, and H. Schoolman, Assistant Deputy
  Director, National Library of Medicine
. Gordon Williams, Director, Center for Research Libraries
. Thomas D. Gillies, Director, Linda Hall Library
. Maurice B. Line, Director, British Library Lending Division

Eleventh Meeting, January 13-14, 1977, Arlington, Virginia

. Richard A. Farley, Director, and Wallace Olsen, Deputy Director of
  Library Services, National Agricultural Library
. Gerald Sophar, former Executive Director, Committee to Investigate
  Copyright Problems Affecting Communication in Science and Education,
  Inc.
. Edward C. McIrvine, Manager, Technical Assessment, Xerox Corp.
. Ben H. Weil, Exxon Research and Engineering Company
. Peter F. Urbach, Deputy Director, National Technical Information
  Service
. Charles Lieb, Copyright Counsel, Association of American Publishers
. Paul G. Zurkowski, President, Information Industry Association
. Irwin Karp, Authors League of America

Thirteenth Meeting, March 31-April 1, 1977, New York City

. Charles Lieb, Copyright Counsel, Association of American Publishers
      with
  Michael Harris and Ben H. Weil for the Association of American
  Publishers
. H. William Koch, Director, American Institute of Physics
. Ed Brown, President, Newsletter Association of America
. Allen R. Ferguson, President, Public Interest Economics Center

Fifteenth Meeting, July 11-12, 1977, Washington, D. C.

. Fritz Machlup, Professor of Economics, Princeton and New York
  Universities
. Vernon E. Palmour, Public Research Institute, Center for Naval Analyses
. Allen R. Ferguson, President, Public Interest Economics Center and Bert
  Cowlan, Co-Director, Public Interest Satellite Association
      with
  Larry Haverkamp, Public Interest Economics Center

Sixteenth Meeting, September 15-16, 1977, Chicago, Illinois

. Donald King, President, King Research, Inc.
. Stevens Rice, Vice-President, University Microfilms

Seventeenth Meeting, October 21, 1977, Washington, D. C.

. Frank E. McKenna, Chairman
    with
  Julius L. Marke, Edward G. Holley, John G. Lorenz, Nina Matheson, and
  Susan Sommer, Members of the Committee on Copyright Law Practice and
  Implementation, Council of National Library Associations
. Eugene Garfield, President, Institute for Scientific Information, Inc.
. Irwin Karp, Esq., Authors League of America
. Charles Lieb, Copyright Counsel, and Michael Harris, Association
  of American Publishers
. Ben H. Weil, Vice-President and Secretary,
    with
  David P. Waite, President, and Michael Harris, Chairman of the Board,
  Copyright Clearance Center, Inc.

Twentieth Meeting, February 16-17, New York City

. Michael Harris, Chairman of the Board, Copyright Clearance Center, Inc.

Twenty-first Meeting, April 20, 1978, Washington, D. C.

. Douglas Price, Deputy Director, National Commission on Libraries
  and Information Science
. William Frawley, Pharmaceutical Manufacturers Association
. Paul G. Zurkowski, President, Information Industry Association
. Frank E. McKenna, Chairman, Committee on Copyright Law and Implementation,
  Council of National Library Associations
    with
  Ellen Mahar, John Lorenz, Naomi Broering and Eileen Cooke, Members
. Charles Lieb, Association of American Publishers

Witnesses Supplying Background Information

Second Meeting, November 19, 1975, Washington, D. C.

. Michael S. Keplinger, Institute for Computer Sciences and Technology,
  National Bureau of Standards
. Alphonse Trezza, Executive Director, National Commission on Libraries
  and Information Science
. Bernard M. Fry, Dean, Graduate Library School, Indiana University

Third Meeting, December 18-19, 1975, New York City

. Joseph Taphorn, Copyright Attorney, International Business Machines
. R. R. Stanley, IBM
. Ralph Gommery, Vice-President and Director of Research, International
  Business Machines
. Jack Garland, IBM
. Joshua Smith, Executive Director, American Society for Information
  Science

Fourth Meeting, February 11-13, 1976, Bethesda, Maryland

. Martha Williams, Director, Information Retrieval Research Laboratory,
  University of Illinois, Champaign-Urbana
. Lee Burchinal, Head, Office of Science Information Service, National
  Science Foundation
. Martin M. Cummings, Director, and Melvin S. Day, Deputy Librarian,
  National Library of Medicine
. Jerome Rubin, President, Mead Data Control
. Arnold O. Ginnow, West Publishing Company
. Lawrence Berul, Vice-President, Aspen Systems
. Donald King, Director, Center for Quantitative Sciences, Market Facts,
  Inc.
. Seldon W. Terrant, Head, R and D. Books and Journals, American Chemical
  Society
. Charles B. Warden, Vice-President, Data Resources, Inc.

Fifth Meeting, April 1-2, 1976, New York City

. Norman Nisenoff, Forecasting International
. Joel Goldhar, Program Director of User Requirements, Division of
  Science Information, National Science Foundation

Eighth Meeting, September 16-17, 1976, Los Angeles, California

. Donn Parker, Information Science Laboratory, Stanford Research Institute

Thirteenth Meeting, March 31-April 1, 1977, New York City

. Bernard Korman, General Counsel, American Society of Composers,
  Authors and Publishers (ASCAP)
. Edward Cramer, President, Broadcast Music, Inc. (BMI)

Eighteenth Meeting, November 17-18, 1977, Cambridge Massachusetts

. Lee Burchinal, Director, Division of Science Information, National
  Science Foundation
. Barbara Arkeny, Acquisitions Editor, MIT Press
. William J. Baumol, Professor of Economics, Princeton and New York
  Universities
. Charles M. Goldstein, Chief, Computer Technology Branch, Lister Hill
  Center for Biomedical Communications, National Library of Medicine
. J. C. R. Licklider, Professor of Electrical Engineering, MIT
. Stuart Mathison, Vice-President, TELENET Corporation
. John Shoch, Xerox Palo Alto Research Center
. Joseph Weizenbaum, Professor of Computer Science and Engineering, MIT

ALPHABETICAL LISTING OF PERSONS APPEARING BEFORE THE COMMISSION

Name and Organization	Meeting
Barbara Ankeny, MIT Press	Eighteenth
George C. Baron, Information Industry Association	Sixteenth
William J. Baumol, Princeton and New York Universities	Fifteenth Eighteenth

Lawrence Berul, Aspen Systems Corporation	Fourth
A. G. W. Biddle, Computer Industry Association	Sixth
Yale Braunstein, New York University	Fifteenth
Roger Borovoy, Intel Corporation	Nineteenth
Herbert Bright, Association for Computing Machinery	Sixth
Naomi Broering, Council of National Library Associations	Twenty-first
Ed Brown, Newsletter Association of America	Thirteenth
Lee G. Burchinal, National Science Foundation	Fourth Eighteenth
David Catterns, Australian Copyright Council	Third
Donna Chamberlain, Documentation Associates Information Services, Inc.	Sixteenth
Carol Cohen, Applied Data Research	Sixth
Eileen Cooke, Council of National Library Associations	Twenty-first
Bert Cowlan, Public Interest Satellite Association	Thirteenth
Robert Coyer, General Services Administration	Seventh
Edward Cramer, Broadcast Music, Inc.	Thirteenth
Frank H. Cullen, Computing and Business Equipment Manufacturers Association	Sixteenth
Martin Cummings, National Library of Medicine	Fourth
Melvin S. Day, National Library of Medicine	Fourth Ninth
George Dodson, General Services Administration	Seventh
Philip Dorn, Association for Computing Machinery	Sixteenth
Truman W. Eustis, New York Times	Fifth
Paul Fagan, American Society of Composers, Authors and Publishers	Thirteenth
Richard A. Farley, National Agricultural Library	Eleventh
Allen R. Ferguson, Public Interest Economics Center	Thirteenth Fifteenth
Patricia Ferguson, Documentation Associates Information Services, Inc.	Eighth
William Frawley, Pharmaceutical Manufacturers Assn.	Twenty-first
Samuel Freedman, Research Publications, Inc.	Fifth
Bernard M. Fry, Indiana University	Second
Eugene Garfield, Institute for Scientific Information	Seventeenth

Jack Garland, IBM	Third
Joseph Genovese, Computing and Business Equipment Manufacturers Association	Fifteenth
Thomas D. Gillies, Linda Hall Library	Ninth
Arnold O. Ginnow, West Publishing Company	Fourth
Martin Goetz, Applied Data Research	Sixteenth
Joel D. Goldhar, National Science Foundation	Fifth
Charles M. Goldstein, National Library of Medicine	Eighteenth
Ralph Gommery, IBM	Third
Herbert R. J. Grosch, Association for Computing Machinery	Third
Michael Harris, Copyright Clearance Center, Inc.	Thirteenth Seventeenth Twentieth
Larry Haverkamp, Public Interest Economics Center	Fifteenth
Nicholas L. Henry, Arizona State University	Seventh
Ira Herrenstein, Standard and Poors	Thirteenth
Anna L. Heyer, Ad Hoc Committee on Copyright Law	Seventh
Edward G. Holley, Council of National Library Associations	Seventeenth
Irwin Karp, Authors League of America, Inc.	Eleventh Seventeenth
Michael S. Keplinger, National Bureau of Standards	Second
Donald W. King, Market Facts, Inc., and King Research, Inc.	Third Ninth Sixteenth
H. William Koch, American Institute of Physics	Thirteenth
Herbert R. Koller, Institute for Electrical and Electronic Engineers	Sixth
Bernard Korman, American Society of Composers, Authors, and Publishers	Thirteenth
Allie B. Latimer, General Services Administration	Seventh
J.C.R. Licklider, MIT	Eighteenth
Charles Lieb, Association of American Publishers	Fourth Thirteenth Seventeenth Twenty-first
Maruice B. Line, British Library Lending Division	Ninth
Theodore Lorah, Computer Industry Association	Sixth

John Lorenz, Council of National Library Associations	Seventeenth Twenty-first
Peter McCloskey, Computer and Business Equipment Manufacturers Association	Sixth
Daniel McCracken, Association for Computing Machines	Tenth Sixteenth
Fritz Machlup, Princeton and New York Universities	Fifteenth
Edward C. McIrvine, Xerox Corporation	Eleventh
Frank E. McKenna, Council of National Library Associations	Seventeenth Twenty-first
Isaac McKinney, General Services Administration	Seventh
Ellen Mahar, Council of National Library Associations	Twenty-first
Terry Mahn, Computer Industry Association	Sixth
Julius L. Marke, Council of National Library Associations	Seventeenth
Nina Matheson, Council of National Library Associations	Seventeenth
Stuart Mathison, TELENET Corporation	Eighteenth
Richard I. Miller, Harbridge House, Inc.	Eighteenth
William J. Moser, Data Processing Management Association	Sixth
Theodor H. Nelson, Author	Twentieth
Norman Nisenoff, Forecasting International	Fifth
Philip S. Nyborg, American Federation of Information Processing Societies	Sixth
Susan H. Nycum, Association for Computing Machinery	Seventh Sixteenth
Vernon E. Palmour, Public Research Institute	Ninth Fifteenth
Donn Parker, Stanford Research Institute	Eighth
Douglas Price, National Commission on Libraries and Information Science	Twenty-first
Theodore Puckorius, General Services Administration	Seventh
Stevens Rice, University Microfilms	Fifteenth
M. Thomas Risner, National Information Center for Educational Media	Eighth
Quincy Rogers, Domestic Council on Right to Privacy	Seventh
John Rothman, New York Times	Fifth
Jerome Rubin, Mead Data Central	Fourth
Roy G. Saltman, National Bureau of Standards	Fifteenth

John Shoch, Xerox Palo Alto Research Laboratory	Eighteenth
Joshua Smith, American Society for Information Science	Third
Susan Sommer, Council of National Library Associations	Seventeenth
Gerald Sophar, Committee to Investigate Copyright Problems...	Eleventh
R. R. Stanley, IBM	Third
August Steinhilber, Ad Hoc Committee on Copyright Law	Seventh
Joseph Taphorn, IBM	Third Fifth Sixth Sixteenth
Seldon W. Terrant, American Chemical Society	Fourth
Alphonse F. Trezza, National Commission on Libraries and Information Science	Second
Peter F. Urbach, National Technical Information Service	Eleventh
David P. Waite, Copyright Clearance Center, Inc.	Seventeenth
Charles B. Warden, Data Resources, Inc.	Fourth
Ben H. Weil, Exxon Corporation and Copyright Clearance Center, Inc.	Eleventh Thirteenth Seventeenth
Peter Weiner, Rand Corporation	Eighth
Joseph Weizenbaum, MIT	Eighteenth
Gordon Williams, Center for Research Libraries	Ninth
Martha Williams, University of Illinois	Fourth
Joe Wyatt, Interuniversity Communications Council	Sixth
Paul G. Zurkowski, Information Industries Association	Fifth Sixth Eleventh Sixteenth Twenty-first

TRANSCRIPTS OF COMMISSION MEETINGS[1]

Meetings 1 through 5. 1975. PB 253 757.

Summaries of the first five meetings of CONTU, held on October 17, November 19, December 18-19, 1975, February 11-13, and April 1-2, 1976. The first meeting was organizational; the second concerned photocopying, computers and data bases, and

---

[1] Transcripts of Commission meetings are available from the National Technical Information Service, Springfield, VA 22161, in either paper or microform copies.

related topics; the third, computers, the Australian copyright
case, and the economics of the publishing industry; the fourth,
information systems, the operations of the National Library of
Medicine, and the economics of computerized information storage
and retrieval systems; and the fifth, presentations by the
Information Industry Association, the New York Times Information
Bank and the results of a study on future alternatives to
present-day scientific and technical journals.

Transcript, CONTU Meeting No. 6. May 6-7, 1976. Arlington, Virginia.
PB 254 765.

     The major subject of the meeting was protection of computer
software, with presentations by Computer and Business Equipment
Manufacturers Association (Peter F. McCloskey); American Federa-
tion of Information Processing Societies (Philip Nyborg); Associa-
tion for Computing Machinery (Herbert Bright); Data Processing
Management Association (William Moser); Computer Society of the
IEEE (Herbert Koller); EDUCOM (Joseph Wyatt); Computer Industry
Association (A.G.W. Biddle, Carol Cohen, Theodore Lorah, Terry
Mahn); Information Industry Association (Paul G. Zurkowski and
Joseph Taphorn).

Transcript, CONTU Meeting No. 7, June 9-10, 1976. Arlington, Virginia.
PB 254 766.

     Verbatim transcript of hearings on protection of computer
software and a discussion of photocopying guidelines. Presentations by Nicholas Henry, Arizona State University; Susan A. Nycum,
Esq.; Theodore Puckorius, and others, General Services Administration; Anna L. Hyer, National Education Association; August
Steinhilber, National School Boards Association; Quincy Rogers,
Domestic Council on the Right to Privacy.

Transcript, CONTU Meeting No. 8. September 16-17, 1976, Los Angeles,
California. PB 259 749.

The meeting addressed copyright protection for data bases, with
testimony given by Herbert R. J. Grosch, Association for
Computing Machinery; M. Thomas Risner, National Information
Center for Educational Media (NICEM); Patricia Ferguson and
Donna Chamberlain, Documentation Associates Information Services,
Inc.; Peter Weiner, Rand Corporation; and Donn Parker, Stanford
Research Institute.

Transcript, CONTU Meeting No. 9. October 21-22, 1976, Arlington,
Virginia. PB 261 947.

     Transcript of hearings on photocopying, interlibrary loans,
and library practices, with presentations by Barbara Ringer,
Register of Copyrights, on the new law; Vernon Palmour on an
NCLIS study of a national periodical bank; Donald King on an
NCLIS photocopying study; H. Schoolman and Melville Day on the
National Library of Medicine; Gordon Williams on the Center for
Research Libraries; Thomas D. Gillies on the Linda Hall Library;
and Maurice Line on the British Library Lending Division.

Transcript, CONTU Meeting no. 10. November 18-19, 1976, New York City.
PB 261 946.

     Testimony on the copyrightability of computer software was
presented by Daniel McCracken, Association for Computing

Machinery. The Commission considered the reports of the
Subcommittees on Photocopying, Software, New Works, and Data
Bases.

Transcript, CONTU Meeting No. 11. January 13-14, 1977, Arlington,
    Virginia. PB 263 160.

  At a meeting on photocopying the Commission heard testimony
which included a description of current photocopying practices
at the National Agricultural Library (Richard A. Farley and Gerald
Sophar) and Exxon (Ben H. Weil); the technological capabilities
of copying equipment (Edward C. McIrvine); an NTIS proposal for
supplying authorized photocopies of journal articles (Peter F.
Urbach). Other witness testifying on photocopying were the
following: Charles Lieb, Association of American Publishers; Paul
Zurkowski, Information Industry Association; and Irwin Karp,
Authors League of America.

Transcript, CONTU Meeting No. 12. February 24-25, 1977, New York City.
    PB 265 765.

  Matters under consideration were copyright protection for
computer software and automated data bases, and possible
approaches to check unauthorized photocopying of copyrighted
materials. There was no testimony presented before the
Commission at this meeting.

Transcript, CONTU Meeting No. 13. March 31 and April 1, 1977, New York
    City. PB 266 277.

  Testimony included the following subjects: the Association
of American Publishers' proposal for a copy payment center
(Charles Lieb, Ben H. Weil, Michael Harris); the publishing and
reprint sales activities of the American Institute of Physics
(H. William Koch); the sampling, licensing and payment system
of the American Society of Composers, Authors and Publishers
(Paul Fagan and Bernard Korman); the licensing, sampling and
payment system of Broadcast Music, Inc. (Edward Cramer); the
problems of newsletter publishers vis-a-vis unauthorized photocopying (Ed Brown, Newsletter Association of America) and an
analysis of computer and photocopying issues from the point of
view of the general public (Allen R. Ferguson, Public Interest
Economics Center).

Transcript, CONTU Meeting No. 14. May 5, 1977, Arlington, Virginia.
    PB 267 332.

  The Commission discussed the CONTU Subcommittee reports
on copyright protection for computer software and automated
data bases, made recommendations for amendments to the reports
and agreed to circulate them with dissenting and concurring
opinions. The Photocopy Subcommittee discussed a request for
additional guidelines to interpret further terms in Section 108
of the Copyright Act and the Commission agreed to offer its good
offices to this end.

Transcript, CONTU Meeting No. 15. July 11-12, 1977. Washington, D.C.
    PB 271 326.

  Testimony included the following subjects: the economics
of property rights as applied to computer software and data bases
(William J. Baumol, Princeton and New York Universities); the

economics of property rights (Fritz Machlup, New York University);
an analysis of computer and photocopying copyright issues from the
point of view of the general public and ultimate consumer (Allen
Ferguson, Public Interest Economics Center, and Bert Cowlan,
Public Interest Satellite Association); a survey of publisher
practices and present attitudes on authorized journal article
copying and licensing (Bernard M. Fry, Graduate Library School,
Indiana University); the costs of owning, borrowing, and
disposing of periodical publications (Vernon Palmour, Public
Research Institute); and testimony on copyright for computer
software and data bases (Roy Saltman, National Bureau of
Standards).

Transcript, CONTU Meeting No. 16. September 15-16, 1977, Chicago, Illinois.
PB 273 594.

   Testimony on the Commission Subcommittee Reports on Computer
Software and Data Bases with Additional Comments was presented
by the following representatives of the computer industry: Susan
Nycum, Daniel McCracken, and Philip Dorn (Association for Computing
Machinery); Martin Goetz (Applied Data Research); Frank Cullen
and Joseph Genovese (Computer and Business Equipment Manufacturers'
Association); Paul G. Zurkowski, George C. Baron, and Joseph
Taphorn (Information Industry Association). The Commission also
a report on a study on library photocopying in the United States
and its implications for the deveopment of a copyright royalty
payment mechanism by Donald King (King Research, Inc.) and a
description of the licensed photocopying activities of University
Microfilms by Stevens Rice (Xerox University Microfilms).

Transcript, CONTU Meeting No. 17. October 21, 1977, Washington, D.C.
PB 275 786.

   Testimony on photocopying was presented by representatives
of the Council of National Library Associations' Committee on
Copyright Law and Implementation (Frank E. McKenna, Julius L.
Marke, Edward G. Holley, John G. Lorenz, Nina W. Matheson, Susan
Sommer); Eugene Garfield, Institute for Scientific Information;
Irwin Karp, Authors League of America; Charles Lieb and Michael
Harris, Association of American Publishers; and Ben H. Weil,
David P. Waite, and Michael Harris, Copyright Clearance Center.
Statements by Peter F. Urbach, National Technical Information
Service, and Susan K. Martin, editor of the Journal of Library
Automation, were read into the record.

Transacript, CONTU Meeting No. 18. November 17-18, 1977, Cambridge,
Massachusetts. PB 278 329.

   The first day was a round table discussion on the technologies which affect the present and future development of
the collection, retention, organization, and delivery of infor-
mation. Panel members were Dr. Lee Burchinal (National Science
Foundation), Moderator; Ms. Barbara Ankeny (MIT Press); Professor
William Baumol (Princeton and New York Universities); Professors
J.C.R. Licklider and Joseph Weizenbaum (MIT); Mr. John Shoch
(Xerox Palo Alto Research Center); Mr. Stuart Mathison (TELENET);
and Mr. Charles M. Goldstein (National Library of Medicine).
The second day Mr. Richard I. Miller, Vice-President of Harbridge
House, Inc., summarized a study sponsored by CONTU: Legal
Protection of Computer Software; An Industrial Survey.

Transcript, CONTU Meeting No. 19.   January 12-13, 1978, Los Angeles,
      California.   PB 280 052.

      Mr. Roger Borovoy, Vice President General Counsel and
Secretary, Intel Corporation, testified on copyright protection
for computer software; the Commissioners heard summaries of current
progress on Subcommittee Reports from members of the Staff.
      Material on photocopying for corporate, special, and medical
librarians has been included in the transcript at the request of
the Association of American Publishers, the Special Libraries
Association, and the Medical Library Association, respectively.

Transcript, CONTU Meeting No. 20.   February 16-17, 1978, New York City.
      PB number not available.

      Witnesses were Mr. Theodor H. Nelson, developer of Xanadu
and the Hypertext Network, speaking on copyright protection for
computer software, and Mr. Michael Harris, Chairman of the Board
of the Copyright Clearance Center, Inc., who gave a progress
report on the first six weeks' operation of the Center.
      The Commission also adopted the report of the Data Base
Subcommittee, discussed the report of the Software Subcommittee,
and discussed a draft report of the Photocopy Subcommittee.

Transcript, CONTU Meeting No. 21.   April 20-21, 1978, Washington, D.C.
      PB 281 710.

      The following witnesses presented testimony on the Draft
Report of the Photocopy Subcommittee: Douglas S. Price (National
Commission on Libraries and Information Science); Paul G.
Zurkowski (Information Industry Association); Frank E. McKenna
and others (Council of National Library Associations); and Charles
Lieb (Association of American Publishers). The Commission also
discussed the Reports of the New Works and Software Subcommittees.
The majority of the Commissioners voted to accept the Report
of the Software Committee.

SUMMARIES OF COMMISSION-SPONSORED STUDIES

REPORT TITLE: Economics of Property Rights as Applied to Computer
                    Software and Data Bases

CONTRACTOR: New York University Economics Department

AUTHORS: Yale M. Braunstein, Dietrich M. Fischer, Janusz A.
                    Ordover and William J. Baumol

NTIS ORDER NO.   PB 268 787

BACKGROUND

      For the past several years, the New York University Economics

Department has conducted a basic investigation of the economics of

information. This work, sponsored by the National Science Foundation,

has delineated the difference between the peculiar characteristics of information as an economic commodity and the characteristics of ordinary goods and services and has explained why a private market for information products may not function properly. A special area of study has been the transfer of information, in particular through scientific and technical journals. In this report the authors apply their basic research on the economics of information to the production of computer programs.

CONCLUSIONS

1. The discipline of economics offers a basis for making analytical statements regarding the pertinence of intellectual property rights in general, and copyrights in particular, to the production of computer software.

2. As the American economy relies increasingly on information products and electronic data processing, the importance of software will grow. Examples suggest that private production in response to incentives may not entirely meet the nation's needs and that some public subsidy may be justified. A failure to develop an adequate policy towards computer software could conceivably have an inhibiting effect on the overall growth of the economy.

3. With proper specifications, and under certain conditions, copyright can provide an erffective incentive for the production of computer software. The authors prefer a system of copyright protection to the currently prevailing reliance on trade secrecy on a variety of counts. Trade secrecy, which works better for intermediate than final products, restricts the range of direct users in a way that copyright would not. Trade secrets necessarily restrict the flow of information about computer programs, thus making it more likely that separate efforts will result in wasteful duplication, making it more difficult for buyers to search out suitable products, and possibly making it more difficult for new firms to go into the programming business. One can also expect trade secrecy to result in the bundling of programs with other services

or products as part of an overall package, to the detriment of customers or consumers. Finally, the need to maintain secrecy leads to building certain undesirable qualities into software, such as obscure codes and unnecessary complexity. Copyright is claimed to have superior characteristics in all of the above interests.

4. In general, the New York University economists support broad specification of property rights through the copyright mechanism, so as to allow the copyright owner to exploit as many markets as possible. In this vein, the practice of charging some customers a higher price than others, which sometimes involves an antitrust violation, can have merit if it permits an otherwise unprofitable enterprise to make money and hence be undertaken. The exemption of certain users of copyrighted works, whether through fair use or library or educational provisions, results in an implicit subsidy for those favored users, a subsidy whose burden is felt partly by other users who are fully subject to the provisions of the copyright law. Economists generally prefer open subsidies borne by the general public through taxes as both more efficient and more equitable.

5. This report specifies a model to estimate the best length of copyright protection in order to provide maximum benefits for the public but taking into account the need to provide adequate incentives to producers. The length of protection should be greater than the time needed for a producer to recover costs and make a profit, but less than a work's useful lifespan, so that some software will be in the public domain while still useful. The variables employed in the calculations included the average useful lifetime of programs, the possibility of economies of scale in production, the responsiveness of demand to changes in price, the rate of decay of what customers will pay for a given program over time, and the social interest rate. Since the values of these variables were not known definitely, the best length of protection was estimated as falling in the range between two and fourteen years.

6. Any legislature has only two basic considerations in
designing a copyright law to provide incentives: the breadth or scope
of protection, and its length. Increasing either one increases the opportunity for profit but also imposes a greater cost on the public.
There exists a tradeoff between these two dimensions: the more there
is of one, the less there needs to be of the other. The Copyright Act
of 1976 stands at one extreme, with a very long period of protection
but filled with multiple exemptions. However, a quite different
system might work for computer software: very short but very tight
protection.

REPORT TITLE: Legal Protection of Computer Software: An
                 Industrial Survey

CONTRACTOR: Harbridge House Inc.

AUTHORS: Richard I Miller, Clarence O'N. Brown, Francis J. Kelley,
                 Deborah C. Notman, and Michael A. Walker

NTIS ORDER NO.

BACKGROUND

In 1973, Harbridge House conducted a small-scale survey of
the computer software industry as part of a more comprehensive project
on law and technological innovation sponsored by the National Science
Foundation. The survey showed that software firms relied primarily
on trade secret licenses and confidential disclosure clauses in order
to secure proprietary products. The respondents saw protection as most
significant for general business and financial programs but, as a rule,
knew of no instances in which fear of inadequate legal protection had
led a company to forego developing an innovative program The survey
sponsored by CONTU updates and expands the work done in 1973.

THE SURVEY

The survey aimed first at obtaining descriptions of firms in the
software industry with respect to kinds of products and services offered.

size, age, ownership, and amount of investment in research and development.
The next set of questions inquired about what sort of legal methods had
been used to protect proprietary products, which particular products
had been felt most in need of protection, how satisfactory the legal
methods employed had proved, and in what ways marketing practices might
change due to legal revisions.

As in 1973, the Association of Data Processing Service
Organizations (ADAPSO) offered its help in the distribution of questionnaires. Over 300 companies belonging to ADAPSO received questionnaires, of which more than 100 responded. In addition, ten other
companies responded to a shortened form of the questionnaire published
in Computerworld, a weekly trade newspaper.

FINDINGS

Character of Firms

The typical responding software firm was independently owned,
young, and small. Founded within the last ten years, it employed fewer
than 100 people, had annual sales under $5 million, and spent about
$100,000 a year on research and development. The most common lines
of business included consulting, contract programming, developing software
packages, and managing data center operations. These firms showed a
certain tendency toward specialization in one sort of product or service.
A typical firm developed internally ten to twenty-five computer programs
a year and a similar number for specific customers.

Legal Protection

The Harbridge House survey, as tabulated, showed that many of
the firms surveyed were not greatly concerned with legal protection
of software; many chose not to answer the question on preferred mode
of legal protection. Those who did answer showed a strong preference
for contractual restraint through trade secrecy over either patent
or copyright. There was a clearly discernible difference, however,

in respondents' attitudes with respect to the distinction between general

business or financial programs and engineering, scientific or systems

programs. The former were felt to be in some need of protection, the

latter not.

Only a small minority (4%) of respondents reported having abandoned

the development of a program for lack of protection. The 15% who indicated

that their marketing practices might change if legal protection improved

tended to be larger companies. On the other hand, 76% said that the Copy-

right Act of 1976 would have no effect on their current scheme of marketing.

A mere 1% called for further legal protection.

To a certain degree, then, the 1977 results agree with the 1973

results, particularly in the predominant use of trade secrecy. Many of

the respondents in the second survey, however, seemed willing to rely

largely on their technological resourcefulness or the uniqueness of their

products to maintain their competitive position.

REPORT TITLE: Costs of Owning, Borrowing, and Disposing of
                 Periodical Publications

CONTRACTOR: Public Research Institute, Center for Naval Analyses

AUTHORS: Vernon E. Palmour, Marcia C. Bellassai, and
                 Robert R. V. Wiederkehr

NTIS ORDER NO.: PB 274 821

BACKGROUND

A library has two ways of satisfying its user's requirements for

periodical literature: it can either subscribe and keep issues on the shelf,

or it can borrow from another library. At low levels of usage, it is cheaper

for the library to fulfill patron requirements through borrowing; at higher

levels of usage, subscribing is cheaper. This study specifies a mathematical

model which states exactly the conditions under which each course of action

is preferable from the library's own point of view. The work done for CONTU

represents an updating of the model originally developed by the same authors

for the Association of Research Libraries in 1968.

SPECIFICATIONS OF THE MODEL

1. <u>Library Cost Components Included</u>: Data were collected from three different libraries in order to estimate the magnitude of the following library costs which vary depending on subscription decisions:

  a) Initial costs of acquiring and cataloguing a new title,

  b) Annual recurring costs of maintaining and servicing journal materials,

  c) The internal costs of circulation, reshelving, and lending to others, and

  d) The internal cost of processing an interlibrary loan transaction.

The model explicitly does not take into account the loss of browsing capacity due to dropping a subscription or the cost in terms of delay to the patron due to borrowing.

Since the fee, if any, a lending library may charge for the use of its materials, or external borrowing cost, can vary widely from case to case, the model takes this as a variable. The levels of journal use at which libraries should either drop or add subscriptions, called the crossover points, are given for different specified external lending fees. Since lending fees often do not exist or do not cover the lending library's costs, interlibrary loan can be unrealistically cheap from the borrower's point of view, and the crossover points of journal usage from a social point of view would therefore be higher.

2. <u>Journal Usage Over Time and Length of Holdings</u>: Use of journal literature decays rather rapidly. Almost 80% of usage occurs within five years after publication and almost 95% within fifteen years. Based on studies at two large libraries, the model includes two schedules, one for science and technology and one for the social and life sciences, to take this pattern of usage into account.

The number of years of back holdings that a library has on the shelves will vary from journal to journal. However, five requests or uses for a journal with five years of back files does not have the same meaning as five requests for a fifteen-year old title holding. To account

for this, the mathematical model includes a "normalization" factor. Since
the crossover points are specified for journals with ten years of back
holdings, one needs to adjust for the length of a particular journal's
back files before applying the add/drop decision criterion supplied by the
crossover point.

    3. <u>Subscription Prices</u> also vary widely. Accordingly, the model
specifies crossover points according to different subscription price levels.

    4. <u>Planning Period</u>: The model uses a 25-year planning period; that
is, the library deciding whether to subscribe or borrow is assumed to take
into account all costs and user requests up to twenty-five years away but to
ignore any years farther in the future.

CONCLUSIONS

    1. The crossover points are very similar for the decision to add
a journal title and the decision to drop one. The only difference lies in
the library's one-time cost of acquiring a new title.

    2. A typical crossover point for the add/drop decision is four
or five uses per journal title per year. This is the result, for example,
with a subscription price of $40 and external lending fees of $8.

    3. It is unlikely, then, that libraries will be engaging in much
interlibrary lending activity that falls outside the limits specified by
the CONTU guidelines (see pp. 136 of this report), which permit each
requesting library up to five copies of articles from the most recent
five years of each journal title to which it does not subscribe. This is
especially true given libraries' current tendency to maintain subscriptions even at very low levels of usage.

REPORT TITLE: An Analysis of Computer and Photocopying Issues from the
                          Point of View of the General Public and the Ultimate
                          Consumer

CONTRACTOR: The Public Interest Economics Center

AUTHORS: Marc Breslow, Allen R. Ferguson, and Larry Haverkamp

NTIS ORDER NO: PB

BACKGROUND

Although numerous studies on the subject of copyright had been done before CONTU came into existence, apparently none of them had focused on the particular question of how changes in the copyright law would affect members of the general public considered as retail consumers. Previous efforts, such as the series of thirty-four studies done under the supervision of the Register of Copyrights, had largely taken a legal point of view and had not considered broad economic questions concerning the general public. However, the Commission came to feel that the new technologies whose effect on copyright it was charged to examine might have altered the relationship of the general public to copyright. The ubiquity of the photocopier meant that ordinary citizens could be engaging in potentially infringing acts. Likewise, the latest developments in microcircuitry make it appear that widespread use of computers in the home is not too many years away.

In such circumstances it seemed necessary to examine copyright questions from a consumer point of view. The Commission contracted with the Public Interest Economics Center (PIE-C) to provide background and briefing material for two conferences of representatives of nonprofit, public interest-oriented groups, convened by the Public Interest Satellite Association (PISA), a co-contractor. Such conferences seemed the most practical way to find out how proposed or actual changes in the copyright law would affect members of the general public.

CONCLUSIONS

Computers

PIE-C concluded that small, independent computer software firms needed strong legal support for the production of software. Accordingly, they recommended that such firms be able to assert both trade secret and copyright interests in their products depending on the sort of usage and amount of distribution. On the other hand, they

feared that copyright protection for software produced by large manufacturers of computer hardware might serve to reinforce the dominant
position of those companies. Besides, large manufacturers already
had reason to produce software as a complement to their machinery and
did not especially need legal protection. PIE-C thus concluded that
only small firms, and not large computer hardware manufacturers, should
be able to assert copyright in software, without discussing the legal
aspect of its proposal.

PIE-C also saw data bases in computerized form as needing
protection. PIE-C saw no reason why copyright liability should not
attach at both the input and output phases of computerized data base
use. Such data bases promised to provide important general stores
of information, and no consumer interest would be disserved by the
dual copyright liability. Similarly, PIE-C decided that no consumer
interest would be adversely affected by the provision of copyright
protection for works in whose composition or preparation a computer
was used as an aid. None of the representatives of the public interest-
oriented groups at the PISA conferences voiced serious objections to
these conclusions on computer issues.

Photocopying

PIE-C's basic conclusion was that no one making photocopies
of copyright material should have to pay the publisher a copying
fee unless the photocopies were resold. These economists found that
the overall publishing industry had adequate returns and were unable
to find that photocopying specifically had a deleterious effect on
publishing. Hence, they saw no reason why students, teachers, researchers,
and librarians should not be able to make essentially unlimited numbers
of photocopies for their own noncommercial use. Specifically, PIE-C
recommended that any organization that qualified for tax exemptions
under section 501(c)(3) of the Internal Revenue Code be able to do

such copyright-exempt internal photocopying as long as the copies were not resold. All of the organizations represented at the PISA conferences would have qualified for this exemption, and the attending representatives expressed strong support for this particular proposal.

General

There was some disagreement between the PIE-C economists and the PISA conference representatives about how best to define the public interest. PIE-C chose to define the public interest in terms of members of the general public in their roles as retail consumers, while the representatives felt that the sorts of nonprofit organizations for which they worked provided a more concrete embodiment of the public interest. Other unresolved issues concerned the importance of competition in copyright industries and the permissibility of transfer of copyright ownership away from the original owner, the author. However, conference representatives felt, and PIE-C eventually came to accept, that small copyright owners faced a relative disadvantage in protecting their copyrights and might need help from the government in this regard, but no specific suggestions were made as to the nature of such help.

THE PISA CONFERENCES

The conferences of representatives from nonprofit organizations in the public interest community were held on May 2 and June 13, 1977. Mr. Bert Cowlan of PISA chaired both sessions, assisted by Mr. Andy Horowitz. The authors of the PIE-C report and members of the Commission staff also attended each time. Commissioner Karpatkin and Janusz Ordover, one of the authors of the New York University report, were able to attend the second meeting. The list of representatives follows:

Dr. Donna Allen
Media Report to Women
Washington, D. C.

Ms. Gertrude Barnstone
Texas Civil Liberty Foundation
Houston, Texas

Dr. Charles E. Bryant
Louis A. Martinet Legal Society
Baton Rouge, Louisiana

Dr. Carl Clark
Monsour Medical Foundation
   Field Office
Catonsville, Maryland

Ms. Phyllis Cole
Peoples Computer Company
Menlo Park, California

Mr. Louis Hausman
National Council on the Aging
Washington, D. C.

Mr. Wayne Horiuchi
Japanese-American Citizens League
Washington, D. C.

Ms. Marion Hayes Hull
Cable Communications Resource Center
Washington, D. C.

Ms. Katherine Montague
Southwest Research & Information
   Center
Albuquerque, New Mexico

Ms. Irene Kessel
Consumer Federation of America
Washington, D. C.

Ms. Annie King Phillips
National Association of Neighborhood
   Health Centers
Washington, D. C.

Mr. Martin Rogol
National Public Interest
   Research Groups
Washington, D. C.

Mr. Mark Silbergeld
Consumers Union
Washington, D. C.

Dr. David Horton Smith
Boston College
Chestnut Hill, Massachusetts

Mr. Tom Thomas
National Federation of
   Community Broadcasters
Washington, D. C.

Ms. Deborah Sanchez Wunderbaum
Commission on Spanish
   Speaking Affairs
Lansing, Michigan

Ms. Jan Zimmerman
National Women's Agenda
Santa Monica, California

REPORT TITLE: Survey of Publisher Practices and Current
                Attitudes on Authorized Journal Article
                Copying and Licensing

CONTRACTOR: Research Center for Library and Information Science,
                Graduate Library School, Indiana University at
                Bloomington

AUTHORS: Bernard M. Fry, Herbert S. White, and Elizabeth L. Johnson

NTIS ORDER NO: PB 271 003

BACKGROUND

In 1975, the Indiana Graduate Library School completed a large-
scale study, sponsored by the National Science Foundation (NSF), on the
acquisition of materials by libraries and the economic status of scholarly,
scientific, and technical journals, which depend heavily on libraries

as a market.[1/] The study involved the analysis of questionnaires filled

out by libraries and journal publishers. The libraries surveyed showed

a marked shift in their materials budgets from books to periodicals in

the period from 1969 to 1973. Fry and White have delivered a follow-up

survey of libraries to NSF, which shows a continuance in 1974-76 of the

earlier trend.[2/] As for publishers, subscription levels showed a generally

upward trend, but not all publishers were in sound financial condition.

While commercial publishers had adequate returns, society publishers had

small but positive margins, and many university presses were operating

at increasing deficits. It was this part of the original Indiana Uni-

versity study on which the survey by CONTU builds.

THE SURVEY

The survey had a two-fold purpose. First, it aimed to discover

the extent to which publishers of U. S. scholarly, scientific, and technical

journals currently provide copies of back articles or issues, or else make

provision for authorized reproduction, either directly or by means of an

agent. Second, the survey attempted to gauge the willingness of publishers

to participate in some sort of national clearinghouse mechanism for the

authorizing of reproduction and the collection and distribution of fees.

A subject of particular interest was the amount of payment that publishers

would expect to receive for authorization to make copies.

The Indiana University Researchers updated the master list of

publishers and journals used in the earlier survey. The final list included

almost 1,700 publishers of about 2,500 journals. Over 500 publishers filled

out questionnaires covering almost 1,000 journals. The overwhelming majority

of these publishers are small: 450 of them put out only one journal. Further-

more, most of the journals are small: over half have fewer than 3,000 sub-

---

1/ See note 215, at 127 supra.

2/ Id.

scriptions. While 90% of the responding journals had registered for copyright, only 60% of the journals which did not respond had registered. The
questionnaires were mailed out in February, 1977, and the cutoff date for
replies was in May; thus, the new law was not yet in effect, and plans for
the Copyright Clearance Center were still only in the formulative stage
and not widely known. These considerations affect the interpretation of
some of the responses.

FINDINGS

Journals and Fees

At the time of the survey, more than half of the responding journals sold reprints directly and about a third through an agent; the two dominant agents used are Xerox University Microfilms and Information Unlimited.
A typical charge for a reprint of a ten-page article was $5. Journals which
did not then sell reprints said they hypothetically would be willing to
settle for a lesser fee. Two-thirds of the journals generated less than six
reprint orders a week: at the other extreme, 13% generated 150 or more each
week. About half of the journals said they filled orders within five days.

Half of the copyrighted journals expected no royalty payments from
any participation in a national clearinghouse. A majority of the remainder
would have accepted a 50-cent payment, but a small minority held out for $5
or more. As for microform editions, journals preferred to sell them through
an agent, rather than directly; in addition, they were largely unwilling to
permit unrestricted copying from microforms, either of current or back
issues. Willingness to permit copying from paper issues was also low,
except for copying of back issues by nonprofit organizations. Most publishers not then supplying reprints or photocopies expressed an unwillingness to do so in the future.

Publishers and Services

One may also state the results of the survey by characterizing
publishers rather than journals. Publishers preferred to license

reproduction and supply reprints directly as opposed to delegating those functions to a clearinghouse. A large majority of publishers was willing to accept telephone orders, but few publishers saw merit in other modes of telecommunication. Similarly, publishers preferred payment with each order and disliked open or deposit accounts.

The time at which this survey was conducted needs to be considered in assessing the results. Since the plans for the Copyright Clearance Center were only in the formulation stage and not widely known, the hypothetical questions about participation in a clearinghouse had an abstract character, and the responses may not necessarily indicate the level of willingness to participate in the CCC or other actual body. In addition, one should remember that the bulk of the respondents publish only one journal and do not have a sophisticated knowledge of the workings of copyright. This helps to account for the lack of expectation of revenues from copying fees and fear of organizational encumbrance from a clearinghouse; it may also explain the unreasonably high fees expected by some. Those high expectations could also be interpreted as restating an unwillingness to participate or as reflecting a desire to maintain circulation by making copying very expensive.

REPORT TITLE: Library Photocopying in the United States: With Implications for the Development of a Royalty Payment Mechanism

CONTRACTOR: King Research, Inc.

AUTHORS: Donald W. King and others

NTIS ORDER NO.:   PB 278 300 (Also available from the Superintendent of Documents, Government Printing Office, No. 052-003-00443-7)

BACKGROUND

This study was funded and sponsored by three organizations: the National Commission on Libraries and Information Science (NCLIS), the National Science Foundation (NSF), and CONTU. The need for it became apparent when the Working Group of the Conference on Resolution of

Copyright Issues (CORCI) found itself unable to agree on the actual
volume of library photocopying. The conference, which had been organized
in 1974 by the Register of Copyrights and the Chairman of NCLIS, agreed
in 1975 to participate in drawing up a Request for Proposals. NCLIS
was joined by the National Science Foundation, and in 1976 the contract
was let to Market Facts, Inc. (later King Research). Soon thereafter,
CONTU added funds to enable a detailed analysis of the transactions
of the Minnesota Interlibrary Telecommunications Exchange (MINITEX).

THE SURVEY

The contractor secured from the National Center for Educational
Statistics (NCES) and other sources a master list or sample frame of
over 21,000 libraries in the United States, a list believed to include
most libraries of any consequence except for public and private elementary
and secondary school libraries, which are considerably more numerous.
Libraries were divided into four kinds or types: academic, public, federal,
and special (the latter frequently but not always serving for-profit organizations). A sample of 360 libraries was drawn so as to fully represent each
type. While most of the sample was chosen randomly, a number of the largest
libraries were deliberately chosen because of the scale of their photocopying
activities. Responding libraries reported only on photocopying done on
machines operated or supervised by staff members; unsupervised (including
coin-operated) machines were excluded. The libraries in the sample frame
had over 35,000 photocopying machines, of which 20,000 were used exclusively
by staff.

The numbers found throughout the King Study generally constitute
estimates based on projections against the nationwide sample frame, rather
than actual data or observations, from which the estimates are extrapolated.
The estimates are subject to varying amounts of uncertainty, depending
on the number of observations or the length of time in which they were
made. Estimates about photocopying in one kind of library are therefore
often subject to a greater amount of uncertainty than estimates about

all libraries. One of the reasons for adding the MINITEX part of the
study was to provide a basis for checking the results of the national
library survey, and the results agree quite well.

FINDINGS

The following tables present some of the basic results for the
calendar year 1976. Some totals may not add exactly due to rounding.
Materials of indeterminate copyright status are not included in the stated
totals of numbers of copies made from copyrighted works. The unit of count
is a complete document, whether one page or twenty pages long.

HALF OF COPYING COMES FROM COPYRIGHTED WORKS[1]

Type of Library	1 No. of Libraries (x 1,000)	2 Av. No. of copies (x 1,000)	3 Tot. No. of copies (= 1 x 2) (x 1,000,000)	4 % copy-righted	5 No. copyrighted copies (= 3 x 4) (x 1,000,000)
Public	8.3	7.7	64	37%	24
Special	8.5	3.1	26	69%	18
Academic	3.0	5.5	17	48%	8
Federal	1.4	4.9	7	58%	4
U.S. Totals	21.3	5.4	114	47%	54

[1] See text, pp. 3-4.

The above table shows that, for all kinds of materials about
half of copies made came from copyright-protected works. The 114 million
copies amounted to about 1 billion pages; copyright status could not
be determined in 17 million copies. The next table shows that, for all
kinds of libraries throughout the United States, serial publications
accounted for most copying of copyrighted works:

Due to the unclear interpretation of some of the definitions in Section 108 of the new law, and without prejudice to their resolution, King Research felt it necessary to break down copying into three kinds of services: copying for ordinary local users, including employees of organizations served by the library, copying for users at another branch within an overall library system, and copying for interlibrary loan. As the next table shows, for all kinds of libraries and materials, copying for local uses was the dominant activity.

MOST COPYING IS FOR LOCAL USERS [1]

Kind of Service	1 No. copies (x 1,000,000)	2 % copy- righted	3 No. copyrighted copies (= 1 x 2) (x 1,000,000)
Local Use	76	41%	31
Intrasystem	27	47%	17
Interlibrary Loan	11	50%	6

[1] Cf. King Study, pp. 45, 47, 49. The table on p. 47 has two typographical errors in the "All Libraries" row in the sixth and tenth columns.

An area of particular interest was that of copying from copyrighted serials for interlibrary loan. The King Study revealed that the CONTU Guidelines (see pp. 136 of this report), in combination with provisions of the Copyright Law itself, greatly reduced the number of such copies needing authorization. There were 3.8 million such copies made in 1976, a number reduced to 2.4 million if one excludes copies made from serials over five years old. The exemptions for replacement of damaged or missing items and for classroom use further reduce the number to 2.0 million. After applying the CONTU Guidelines, which permit up to five copies per serial title for each requesting library in a given year, there remain 500,000 remaining copies needing authorization. The status of material over five years old remains unclear, however, making this estimate a lower limit.

The distribution of copying, by size of library, was quite uneven. Large libraries dominated: in particular, 20% of all libraries accounted for almost 80% of copies made for local users and almost 75% of those made for interlibrary loan. Indeed, since the number of supervised machines in the libraries surveyed was smaller than the number of libraries themselves, some must have had no supervised machines at all.

The distribution of copying was also uneven with respect to source materials, especially serials. Although copying from journals seemed to bear little or no relation to circulation levels, 20% of them accounted for almost 70% of copies made for local use and over 85% made for interlibrary loan. If all the exemptions for interlibrary loans were applied, 90% of serial titles would have 50 or less copies made needing authorization from them throughout the country. Very few, if any, would have 100 or more such copies.

In addition to counting photocopies and estimating totals, the King Study also asked libraries about their preferences regarding the design of a mechanism to collect and distribute royalties for photocopies needing authorization under the copyright law. Describing the choice to be made between a system of complete reporting of copying activity at one end, and a system of minimum reporting at the other, the report noted that greater accuracy in collection and distribution of payments would require a more complex and costly system. Librarians seemed to prefer a simpler system which, although less exact in its payments, would be easier to administer.

BIBLIOGRAPHY

Selected List of Works on Computers and Copyright

Ad Hoc Task Group on Legal Aspects Involved in National Information Systems. The copyright law as it relates to information systems and national programs; final report. Washington, D. C.: Committee on Scientific and Technical Information, Federal Council for Science and Technology, 1967.

Adequate legal protection for computer programs. Utah Law Review, No. 3
    (September 1968), pp. 369-394.

Advisory group of non-governmental experts on the protection of computer
    programs (Geneva, May 17 to 20, 1976). Copyright, Vol. 12, no. 7-8,
    (July-August 1976), pp. 163-164.

American Bar Association--Special Committee on Electronic Data Retrieval.
    Computers and the Law; An Introductory Handbook. New York: Commerce
    Clearing House, 1966.

Banzhaf, John F. Copyright law revision: a recent amendment favors
    information storage and retrieval--a report to the data processing
    community. Computers and Automation, Vol. 15, no. 12 (December 1966),
    pp. 10-11.

----------. Copyright protection for computer programs. Copyright Law
    Symposium, No. 14 (1966), pp. 119-179.

----------. Copyrighted computer programs: some questions and answers.
    Computers and Automation (July 1965), pp. 22-25.

----------. Legal protection of computer programs. Data Processing
    (July 1964), pp. 8-12.

---------. When a computer needs a lawyer. New York Law Journal, Vol. 158,
    no. 5 (July 10, 1967), p. 1 ff.; Vol. 158, No. 6 (July 11, 1967) p. 1 ff.

Beard, Joseph. The copyright issue. In Annual Review of Information Science
    and Technology, Vol. 9 (1974), pp. 381-411.

Bender, David. Computer programs: shall they be patentable? Columbia Law
    Review, Vol. 68, No. 2 (February 1968), pp. 241-259.

----------. Trade secret protection of software. George Washington
    University Law Review, Vol. 38, no. 5 (1970), pp. 909-957.

----------. Trade secret software protection. APLA Quarterly Journal,
    Vol. 5, no. 1 (1977), pp. 49-70.

Benjamin, Curtis G. Computers and copyrights: restrictions on computer
    use of copyrighted material would protect authors, publishers, and even
    users. Science, Vol. 152, no. 3719 (April 8, 1966), pp. 181-184.

----------. Computers, Copyrights and Educators. An address . . . delivered
    at the 75th Annual Meeting. American Society for Engineering Education,
    Michigan State University, June 19-22, 1967. New York, 1967.

Bigelow, Robert P. Attorney for the computer user. American Bar Association
    Journal. Vol. 63 (July 1977), pp. 954-958.

----------. The computer as a copyright infringer. Law and Computer
    Technology, Vol. 1, no. 5 (May 1968), pp. 2-5.

----------. Computer Law Service. Chicago: Callaghan, 1972-

----------. Your Computer and the Law. Englewood Cliffs, N.J.: Prentice
    Hall, 1975.

Breyer, Stephen. The uneasy case for copyright: A study of copyright
    in books, photocopies, and computer programming. Harvard Law Review,
    Vol. 84, no. 2 (December 1970), pp. 281-351.

Buckman, T. Protection of proprietary interest in computer programs. Journal of the Patent Office Society, Vol. 51, no. 3 (March 1969), pp. 135-151.

Bush, George P. Technology and Copyright: Annotated Bibliography and Source Materials. Mt. Airy, Md.: Lomond, 1972.

Cambridge Research Institute. Omnibus Copyright Revision: Comparative Analysis of the Issues. Washington, D.C.: American Society for Information Science, 1973.

Cary, George D. Copyright registration and computer programs. Bulletin of the Copyright Society of the U.S.A., Vol. 11, no. 6 (August 1964), pp. 362-368.

Cohen, Eric. Comprehensive copyright legislative proposal backfires-- omnibus or blunderbuss? Jurimetrics Journal, Vol. 15 (1974), pp. 32 ff.

----------. Patentability of computer programs. University of Miami Law Review, Vol. 27, nos. 3-4 (Spring-Summer 1973), pp. 494-504.

Computer program classification: A limitation in program patentability as a process. Oregon Law Review, Vol. 53, no. 4 (1974), pp. 501-531.

Computer programs and proposed revisions of the patent and copyright laws. Harvard Law Review, Vol. 81, no. 7 (May 1968), pp. 1541-1557.

Computer programs and subject matter patentability. Rutgers Journal of Computers and the Law, Vol. 6 (1977), pp. 1-25.

Computer software: Beyond the limits of existing proprietary protection. Brooklyn Law Review, Vol. 40 (1973), pp. 116-146.

Computers, Communications, and the Public Interest, M. Greenberger, ed. Baltimore: Johns Hopkins University Press, 1971.

Copyright implications in the new science of data storage and retrieval. Publishers Weekly, Vol. 186, no. 22 (November 30, 1964), pp. 20-23.

Copyright law revision: its impact on classroom copying and information storage and retrieval systems. Iowa Law Review, Vol. 52, no. 6 (June 1967), pp. 1141-1169.

Copyright protection for computer programs. Columbia Law Review, Vol. 64 (1964), pp. 1274 ff.

Coraskic, M. J., and B. C. Brockway. Protection of computer-based information. Albany Law Review. Vol. 40 (1975), pp. 113-153.

Cunningham, Dewey J. Information retrieval and the copyright law. Bulletin of the Copyright Society of the U.S.A., Vol. 14, no. 1 (October 1966), pp. 22-27.

Duggan, Michael A. Law, logic, and the computer; bibliography with assorted background material. Computing Reviews, Vol. 7, no. 1 (January-February 1966), pp. 95-117. Supplement in Computing Reviews, Vol. 8, no. 2 (March-April 1967), pp. 171-188.

Etienne, Alexander I. Patent and copyright implications of electronic data processing. Idea, Vol. 8 (1964 Conference Volume), pp. 176-182.

Felsman, Robert A. and others. Computer program protection. Texas Bar Journal, Vol. 34, no. 1 (January 22, 1971), pp. 33-40, 53-61.

Fletcher, Richard L. and Stephen P. Smith. Computers, the copyright law and its revision. University of Florida Law Review, Vol. 20, no. 3 (Winter 1968), pp. 386-410.

Freed, Roy N. Computers and the Law: A Reference Work, 5th ed. Boston, 1976.

Galbi, Elmer. Proposal for new legislation to protect computer programming. Bulletin of the Copyright Society of the U.S.A., Vol. 17, no. 4 (1970), pp. 280-296.

George Washington University, Washington, D.C.--Computers-in-Law Institute. The law of software; 1968 proceedings. Washington, D.C., 1968.

----------. The law of software; 1969 proceedings. Washington, D.C., 1969.

George Washington University, Washington, D.C.--Patent, Trademark and Copyright Institute. Proceedings of the Eighth Annual Public Conference. Washington, D.C., 1964.

Gipe, George A. Nearer to the Dust: Copyright and the Machine. Baltimore: Williams and Wilkins, 1967.

Goldberg, Morton David. Patent and copyright implications of electronic data processing. Idea, Vol. 8, Conference Number (1964), pp. 183-190.

Gonda, Edward C. Patents, copyrights, unfair competition and confidentiality of information. In Course of Study Transcript: Law and Computers in the Mid-60's. Philadelphia: Joint Committee on Continuing Legal Education of the American Law Institute and the American Bar Association, 1966, pp. 213-247.

Gotlieb, A., C. Dalfen and K. Katz. Transborder transfer of information by communications and computer systems: Issues and approaches to guiding principles. American Journal of International Law, Vol. 68 (1974), pp. 227-257.

Gottschalk v. Benson (93 Sup Ct 253): A bright light with a dim future. Baylor Law Review, Vol. 28 (1976), pp. 187-196.

Gottschalk v. Benson (93 Sup Ct 253)--The Supreme Court takes a hard line on software. St. John's Law Review, Vol. 47 (May 1973), pp. 635-671.

Gotzen, Frank. Copyright and the computer. Copyright, vol. 13, no. 1 (January 1977), pp. 15-21.

Greenbaum, Arthur J. Computers, copyrights, and the law prior to revision. Bulletin of the Copyright Society of the U.S.A., Vol. 15, no. 3 (February 1968), pp. 164-173.

Gunning, W. J. Computer programs. CIPA, Vol. 5, no. 5 (1976), pp. 150-154.

Hamann, H. Frederick. Commments on the copyright aspects of automatic information storage and retrieval systems. Bulletin of the Copyright Society of the U.S.A., Vol. 15, no. 3 (February 1968), pp. 164-173.

Henderson, Madeline M. Copyright impacts of future technology. Journal of Chemical Information and Computer Sciences, Vol. 16, no. 2 (1976), pp. 72-74.

Henry, Nicholas. Copyright: Its adequacy in technological societies. Science, Vol. 186, no. 4168 (December 13, 1974), pp. 993-1004.

----------. Copyright, public policy, and information technology. Science, Vol. 183, no. 4123 (Feb. 1, 1974), pp. 384-391.

Hill, James. Scope of protection for computer programs under the Copyright Act. De Paul Law Review, Vol. 14, no. 2 (Spring-Summer 1965), pp. 360-370.

Horty, John F. Computers and copyright: A third area. Bulletin of the Copyright Society of the U.S.A., Vol. 15, no. 1 (October 1967), pp. 19-23.

Impacts of copyright developments on chemical information transmission and use. Journal of Chemical Information and Computer Sciences, Vol. 16, no. 2 (May 1976), pp. 63-75.

In re Johnston (502 F 2d 765): New output by the CCPA on the patentability of computer software. University of Pittsburgh Law Review, Vol. 36, (1975), pp. 739-755.

In re Johnston (502 F 2d 765): Patentability of computer software--the battle rages on. Ohio Northern Law Review, Vol. 2 (1975), pp. 782-787.

Irwin, Manley R. The computer utility: Competition or regulation? Yale Law Journal, Vol. 76, no. 7 (June 1967), pp. 1299-1320.

Iskrant, John. The impact of the multiple forms of computer programs on their adequate protection by copyright. Copyright Law Symposium, No. 18 (1970), pp. 92-134.

Jacobs, Morton C. Computer technology (Hardware and software): Some legal implications for antitrust, copyrights, and patents. Rutgers Journal of Computers and the Law (1970), pp. 50-69.

----------. Patent protection of computer programs. Journal of the Patent Office Society, Vol. 47, no. 1 (January 1965), pp. 6-14.

----------. Patents, copyrights and trade secrets. In American Bar Association.... Computers and the Law, cited above, pp. 90-93.

Jovanovich, William. To vouchsafe identity. Bulletin of the Copyright Society of the U.S.A., Vol. 14, no. 5 (June 1967), pp. 355-366.

Kastenmeier, Robert W. The information explosion and copyright law revision. Bulletin of the Copyright Society of the U.S.A., Vol. 14, no. 3 (February 1967), pp. 195-204.

Katona, Gabriel P. Legal protection of computer programs. Journal of the Patent Office Society, Vol. 47, no. 12 (December 1965), pp. 955-979.

Kolle, Gert. Computer software protection -- present situation and future prospects. Copyright, Vol. 13, no. 3 (March 1976) pp. 70-79

Koller, Herbert. Computer software protection. Idea, Vol. 13 (1969), pp. 351-372.

---------- and Jack Moshman. Patent protection for computer software. Idea, Vol. 12, no. 4 (1968/69), pp. 1109-1127.

Lawlor, Reed C. Applications of computers to law; a progress report. In Data Processing Yearbook, 1963-1964. Detroit, 1963, pp. 199-206.

----------. Bibliography re patent and copyright law in relation to computer technology. Modern Uses of Logic in Law, (June 1965), pp. 53-55.

----------. Copyright aspects of computer usage. Bulletin of the Copyright Society of the U.S.A., Vol. 11, no. 6 (August 1964), pp. 380-403.

---------- Information Technology and the Law. New York: Academic Press, 1962.

Licklider, J. C. R. Libraries of the Future. Cambridge, Massachusetts: MIT Press, 1965.

Lieb, Charles. The computer and copyright: The next five years. Bulletin of the Copyright Society of the U.S.A., Vol. 15, no. 1 (October 1967), pp. 13-18.

Linden, Bella L. Copyright, photocopying, and computer usage. Bulletin of the American Society for Information Science, Vol. 11 (May 1975), pp. 12-14.

----------. The law of copyright and unfair competition: The impact of new technology on the dissemination of information. Modern Uses of Logic in Law, (June 1965), pp. 44-52.

Lorr, Richard. Copyright computers and compulsory licensing. Rutgers Journal of Computers and the Law, Vol. 5, no. 1 (1975), pp. 149-169.

McFarlane, Gavin. Legal protection of computer programs. Journal of Business Law, Vol. 1970 (July 1970), pp. 204-208.

McTiernan, Charles E. The Protection of Programs through Copyright and Other Methods. Abington, Pennsylvania: Association of Data Processing Service Organizations, 1964.

Marke, Julius J. Copyright and Intellectual Property. New York: Fund for the Advancement of Education, 1967.

Milde, Karl F. Can a computer be an "author" or an "inventor"? Journal of the Patent Office Society, Vol. 51, no. 6 (June 1969), pp. 378-405.

Miller, Arthur R. Computers and copyright law. Michigan State Bar Journal, Vol. 46 (1967), p. 11-18.

Miller, James G. EDUCOM: Interuniversity Communications Council. Science, Vol. 154, no. 3748 (October 28, 1966), pp. 483-488.

Model provisions on the protection of computer software, prepared by the International Bureau of the World Intellectual Property Organization. Industrial Property, Vol. 16, no. 12 (December 1977), pp. 259-275 and Law and Computer Technology, Vol. 11, no. 1 (1978), pp. 2-27.

Mooers, Calvin N. Computer software and copyright. Computing Surveys, Vol. 7 (March 1975), pp. 46 ff.

----------. Copyright seen as best program protection, covers unauthorized use, translations. Computerworld, Vol. 5, no. 41 (Oct. 13, 1971), p. 28.

----------. Preventing software piracy. Computer (March 1977), p. 30.

National Academy of Sciences--Panel on the Application of Copyright on Computer Usage. Report on the Application of Copyright on Computer Usage. Washington, D.C., 1967.

Nawrocki, Boleslaw. Electronic machines and intellectual creation; some legal problems arising in connection with the use of electronic machines in the creation and dissemination of intellectual works. Copyright, Vol. 5, no. 2 (February 1969), pp. 29-37.

Nelson, Greg J. The copyrightability of computer programs. Arizona Law Review, Vol. 7, no. 2 (Spring 1966), pp. 204-218.

Note: Protection of computer programs: Resurrection of the standard. Notre Dame Lawyer, Vol. 50 (1974), pp. 333-345.

Nycum, P. Law and computers: overview update 1975. Law Library Journal, Vol. 68, (August 1975), pp. 234-253.

Oberman, Michael S. Copyright protection for computer-produced directories. Copyright Law Symposium, No. 22 (1977), pp. 1-52.

Ogden, Mark H. Protection of computer software--a hard problem. Drake Law Review, Vol. 26, no. 1 (1976-77), pp. 180-198.

Oler, Harriet. Statutory copyright protection for electronic digital computer programs: Administrative considerations. Law and Computer Technology, vol. 7, no. 4 (July/August 1974), pp. 96-116 and no. 5 (September/October 1974), pp. 118-122.

Pagenberg, B.A. Patentability of computer programs on the national and international level. International Review of Industrial Property and Copyright Law, Vol. 5 (1974), pp. 1-43.

Pataki, Louis Peter. Copyright protection for computer programs under the 1976 copyright act. Indiana Law Journal, vol. 52, no. 2 (Winter 1977), pp. 503-16.

Patentability: piecing together the computer software patent puzzle. St. Louis University Law Journal, Vol. 19 (Spring 1975), pp. 351-74.

Patentability of computer software: the nonobviousness issue. Indiana Law Review, Vol. 62 (1976), pp. 615-35.

Perle, E. Gabriel. Copyright and new technology. Bulletin of the Copyright Society of the U.S.A., Vol. 25 (February 1978), pp. 250-254.

Petre, David C. Statutory copyright protection for books and magazines against machine copying. Notre Dame Lawyer, Vol. 39, no. 2 (February 1964), pp. 161-184.

Popper, H. R. Technology and programming--is it a problem in definitions? APLA Quarterly Journal, Vol. 5, no. 1 (1977), pp. 13-29.

Prasinos, N. Worldwide protection of computer programs by copyright. Rutgers Journal of Computers and the Law, Vol. 4 (1974), pp. 42-85.

Protecting proprietary rights of computer programs: The need for legislative action. Catholic University Law Review, Vol. 21 (1971) pp. 181-200.

Protection of computer software--a hard problem. Drake Law Review, Vol. 26, (1976-77), pp. 180-198.

Puckett, Allen W. The limits of copyright and patent protection for computer programs. Copyright Law Symposium, No. 16 (1968), pp. 81-142.

Rackman, Michael I. The patentability of computer programs. New York University Law Review, Vol. 38, no. 5 (November 1963), pp. 891-916.

----------. Re: Legal protection of computer programs. Journal of the Patent Office Society, Vol. 48, no. 4 (April 1966), pp. 275-277.

Saltman, Roy G. Copyright in Computer-Readable Works. (National Bureau of Standards special publication 500-17). Washington, D.C.: Government Printing Office (1977), Stock No. 003-003-01843-1.

Scaffetta, J. Computer software and unfair methods of competition. John Marshall Journal, Vol. 10 (Spring 1977), pp. 447-64.

----------. Program technology as an infringement. APLA Quarterly Journal, Vol. 5, no. 1 (1977), pp. 35-48.

Schiffer, George. Computers and copyright law revision. Bulletin of the Copyright Society of the U.S.A., Vol. 11, no. 6 (August 1964), pp. 404-407.

Schulman, John. The copyright law--is it a roadblock to information retrieval? Bulletin of the Copyright Society of the U.S.A., Vol. 11, no. 6 (August 1964), pp. 369-379.

Schuyler, William E. Protecting property in computer software. U.S. Department of Commerce News (October 8, 1969).

Seidel, Arthur H. Antitrust, patent, and copyright law implications of computer technology. Journal of the Patent Office Society, Vol. 44, no. 2 (February 1962), pp. 116-125.

Stedman, John C. Copyright developments in the United States. American Association of University Presses Bulletin, Vol. 62, no. 3 (October 1976), pp. 308-19.

Stork, Philip. Legal protection for computer programs: A practicing attorney's approach. Copyright Law Symposium, No. 20 (1972), pp. 112-139.

Teaching machines: The impact of new devices on educational publishing. Publishers Weekly, Vol. 189, no. 10 (March 7, 1966), pp. 103 ff.

Telex v. IBM 367 F. Supp. 258): implications for the businessman and the computer manufacturer. Virginia Law Review, Vol. 60 (May 1974), pp. 884-909.

Ulmer, Eugen. Automatic and in particular, computerized information and documentation systems and the copyright law. Copyright, Vol. 11, no. 12 (December 1975), pp. 239-246.

----------. Copyright problems arising from the use of copyright materials in automatic information and documentation systems. Copyright, Vol. 14, no. 2 (February 1978), pp. 66-70.

Veaner, Allen B. Developments in copying methods and graphic communication, 1965. Library Resources and Technical Services, Vol. 10, no. 2 (Spring 1966), pp. 199-209.

Wessel, M. R. Legal protection of computer programs. Harvard Business Review, Vol. 43 (1965), pp. 97-106.

----------. Telex v. IBM (367 F. Supp. 258): another viewpoint. Rutgers Journal of Computers and the Law. Vol. 5 (1975), pp. 1-13.

Weil, Ben H. Symposium on the impacts of copyright developments on chemical-information transmission and use: Introduction. Journal of Chemical Information and Computer Sciences, Vol. 16, no. 2 (1976), pp. 63-67.

----------. Where do we go from here on copyright impacts and solutions? Journal of Chemical Information and Computer Sciences, Vol. 16, no. 2 (1976), p. 75.

Wild, Robert W. Computer porgram protection: The need to legislate a solution. Cornell Law Review, Vol. 54, no. 4 (April 1969), pp. 586-609.

Wolfle, Dael. Copyright and computers. Science, Vol. 156, no. 3773 (April 21, 1967), p. 319.

Selected List of Documents Relating to Photocopying and the

1976 Copyright Act

Part I. Interpretations and guides issued by organizations

Copyright: New Law and New Directions. Association for Educational Communications and Technology and National Audiovisual Association, 1977.

Copyright and Educational Media: A Guide to Fair Use and Permission Procedures. Prepared by the Association for Educational Communications and Technology and the Association of Media Producers. Washington, D.C.: AECT and AMP, 1977.

The Copyright Law and the Health Sciences Librarian. Chicago: Medical Library Association, 1978.

Explaining the New Copyright Law: A guide to Legitimate Photocopying of Copyrighted Materials. [Washington, D.C.]: Association of American Publishers, 1977.

Guidelines for Seeking or Making a Copy of an Entire Copyrighted Work for a Library, Archives, or User. Prepared by the Implementation of the Copyright Revision Act Committee, Resources and Technical Services Division, American Library Association. Chicago: ALA, 1977. [Included in Librarian's Copyright Kit.]

Librarian's Copyright Kit: What You Must Know Now. Chicago: American Library Association, 1978. [11 items, various pag.]

Librarian's Guide to the New Copyright Law. Chicago: American Library Association, 1977. [Reprinted from ALA Washington Newsletter, Vol. 28, no. 18 (November 15, 1976). Included in Librarian s Copyright Kit.]

Library Photocopying and the U.S. Copyright Law of 1976: An Overview for Librarians and Their Counsel. New York: Special Libraries Association, 1977.

The New Copyright Law: Questions Teachers and Librarians Ask. A joint project of the American Library Association, the National Council of Teachers of English, and the National Education Association. Washington, D.C.: NEA, 1977. [Included in Librarians s Copyright Kit.]

North, William D. An Interim Look at the Copyright Revision Act of 1976. Chicago: American Library Association, 1977. [Included in Librarian s Copyright Kit.]

Photocopying by Academic, Public, and Nonprofit Research Libraries.
     Prepared by the Association of American Publishers, Inc. and by the
     Authors League of America, Inc. [Washington, D.C.: AAP], 1978.

Photocopying by Corporate Libraries. Prepared by the Association of
     American Publisher, Inc. and the Authors League, Inc. [Washington,
     D.C.: AAP], 1978.

The United States Copyright Law: A Guide for Music Educators. Music
     Educators National Conference and others. [Washington, D.C.?],
     1977.

Part II. Articles on Sections 107, 108, and the CONTU Guidelines

After 67 years--a new U.S. copyright law. National Music Publishers
     Association Bulletin, No. 5602 (November 1976), pp. 2-12.

Butler, Meredith. Copyright and reserve books--what libraries are doing.
     College and Research Libraries News, No. 5 (May 1978), pp. 125-129.

Broering, Naomi C. Capitol Notes: Royalty payments and P.H.S. grant
     publications. MLA News, No. 101 (April 1978), pp. 3-4.

Cardozo, Michael H. To copy or not to copy for teaching and scholarship:
     What shall I tell my client? Journal of College and University Law,
     Vol. 4, (Winter 1976-1977), pp. 59-83.

Carroll, Hardy. Primary resources for understanding the new copyright law.
     College and Research Library News, No. 1 (January 1977), pp. 1-2.

CNLA on photocopying. MLA News, No. 101 (April 1978), p. 1.

Computer program warns of copyright violation. Library Journal, Vol. 103,
     no. 3 (February 1, 1978), p. 311.

Cooke, Eileen, and Carol C. Henderson. Preparing for the new copyright law.
     Wilson Library Bulletin, Vol. 51, no. 5 (January 1977), p. 446.

----------. Watch out for reproduction right offers. Wilson Library
     Bulletin, Vol. 51, no. 6 (February 1977), p. 542.

Copyright and reserve shelf: more on library liability. Library Journal,
     Vol. 103, no. 4 (February 15, 1978), pp. 416-417.

Copyright fair use accounting system. MLA News, No. 100 (March 1978), p. 9.

Copyright law prompts new ILL form. American Libraries, Vol. 8, no. 9
     (October 1977), pp. 492B-492C.

Coughlin, E. K. Are limits on copying unconstitutional? Law Dean L. R.
     Patterson questions 1976 copyright revisions. Chronicle of Higher
     Education, Vol. 14, no. 17 (July 5, 1977), p. 10.

De Gennaro, Richard. Copyright, resource sharing, and hard times: A view
     from the field. American Libraries, Vol. 8, no. 8 (September 1977),
     pp. 430-435.

Doherty, Austin. Library photocopying: Recent surveys indicate its nature
     and scale. New York Law Journal, (March 27, 1978), pp. 24-25.

Dugan, P. Double bind: The environmental impact of the 1976 Copyright Revision Law. Journal of Academic Librarianship, Vol. 3, no. (July 1977), pp. 146-148.

Education and the copyright law: Still an open issue. Fordham Law Review, Vol. 46, no. 1 (October 1977), pp. 91-138.

Flacks, Lewis I. Living in the gap of ambiguity; an attorney's advice to librarians on the copyright law. American Libraries, Vol. 8, no. 5, (May 1977), pp. 252-257. [Included in Librarian's Copyright Kit.]

Fried, Stephen. Fair use and the new Act. New York Law School Law Review, Vol. 22, no. 3 (1977), pp. 497-519.

Guidelines: Records of interlibrary photocpying requests. American Libraries, Vol. 8, no. 11 (December 1977), p. 624. [Included in Librarian's Copyright Kit.]

Holley, Edward G. A librarian looks at the new copyright law. American Libraries, Vol. 8, no. 5 (May 1977), pp. 247-251. [Included in Librarian's Copyright Kit.]

Jensen, J. E. The new copyright law and faculty library services. Maryland State Medical Journal, Vol. 26, no. 12 (December 1977), p. 12.

Librarians puzzled by limits of new copyright act. Times Higher Education Supplement, Vol. 325, no. 3 (January 27, 1978), p. 1.

Library copying in the new copyright law. EPIE gram: Materials, Vol. 16 (December 1977), p. 3.

Just a reminder. Special Libraries, Vol. 69, no. 3 (March 1978), p. 127.

Lieb, Charles. New Copyright Law: Overview. New York: Association of American Publishers, 1976.

----------. An overview of the new Copyright Law. In Bowker Annual 1977. New York: R.R. Bowker & Sons, 1977, pp. 164-171.

Magarrell, Jack. Copyright law excuses unknowing violators. Chronicle of Higher Education, Vol. 15, no. 19 (January 23, 1978), pp. 1, 10.

Marke, Julius J. Copyright revision and issues of concern to the librarian. In Bowker Annual 1977. New York: R. R. Bowker & Sons, 1977, pp. 159-163.

----------. New copyright law; Authors and librarians resume "fair use" debate. New York Law Journal (March 27, 1978), pp. 23, 26-27.

----------. United States copyright revision and its legislative history. Law Library Journal, Vol. 70, no. 2 (May 1977), pp. 121-152.

Marshall, Nancy H., and Ronald P. Naylor. Interlibrary loan issues. RQ, Vol. 16, no. 4 (Summer 1977), pp. 330-331.

----------. Interlibrary loan issues. RQ, Vol. 17, no. 1 (Fall 1977), pp. 59-64.

----------. Interlibrary loan issues. RQ, Vol. 17, no. 2 (Winter 1977), pp. 178-180.

Martell, Charles. Copyright law and reserve operations--an interpretation. College and Research Libraries News, No. 1 (January 1978), pp. 1-6.

Meyer, Ellen T. Government update: The new copyright law and micrographics.
Micrographics Today, Vol. 12, no. 5 (January 1978), pp. 60-61.

Meyers, Ernest S. Sound recordings and the new Copyright Act. New York
Law School Law Review, Vol. 22, no. 3 (January 1977), pp. 573-588.

Middleton, Dale R. Predicting the impact of copyright specifications on
interlibrary borrowing. Medical Library Association Bulletin, Vol. 65,
no. 4 (October 1977), pp. 449-451.

More copyright information. American Libraries, Vol. 8, no. 11 (December
1977),
pp. 624-625. [Included in Librarian's Copyright Kit.]

The new copyright law; Copyright and reserve shelf: Library liability.
Library Journal, Vol. 103, no. 3 (February 1, 1978), pp. 310-311.

New rules on photocopy limits and classroom use set forth in full text of
copyright addenda. American Libraries, Vol. 7, no. 10 (November 1976),
pp. 610-611.

Ringer, Barbara. Finding your way around in the new copyright law.
Publishers Weekly, Vol. 210, no. 24 (December 13, 1976), pp. 38-41.

-----------. First thoughts on the Copyright Act of 1976. New York Law
School Law Review, Vol. 22, no. 3 (January 1977), pp. 477-495.

Robinson, D. B. Copyright legislation: Guidelines for libraries, educators,
and students. Contemporary Education, Vol. 48 (Summer 1977), pp. 228-229.

Robinson, Donald W. Copyright and photocopying. Phi Delta Kappan, Vol. 58,
no. 5 (February 1977), pp. 495-497.

Smith, Lester K. Copying for reserve reading--a different viewpoint.
College and Research Libraries News, No. 5 (May 1978), pp. 129-130.

Stedman, John C. Academic library reserves, photocopying, and the copyright
law. Special issue of ALA Washington Newsletter, Vol. 30, no. 7
(July 14, 1978).

----------. The new copyright law: Photocopying for educational use.
AAUP Bulletin, Vol. 63, no. 1 (February 1977), pp. 5-16.

Swinton, Cordelia W. A personal view from Penn State. College and Research
Libraries News, No. 5, (May 1978), pp. 129-130

Thatcher, Sanford G. A publisher's guide to the new U.S. copyright law.
Scholarly Publishing, Vol. 8, no. 4 (July 1977), pp. 315-333.

Treece, James M. Library photocopying. UCLA Law Review, Vol. 24, nos. 5
and 6 (June-August 1977), pp. 1025-1069.

Wagner, Susan. Copying and the copyright bill; where the new revision stands
on fair use. Publishers Weekly, Vol. 210, no. 16 (October 18, 1976),
pp. 28-30.

----------. New copyright law primer. Part 1: The basics. Publishers
Weekly, Vol. 212, no. 25 (December 26, 1977), pp. 37-42.

----------. New copyright law primer. Part 2: The formalities. Publishers
Weekly, Vol. 213, no. 5 (January 30, 1978), pp. 65-70.

Part III. Documents relating to copyright clearance mechanisms

Handbook for Libraries and Other Organizational Users Which Copy from Serials
   and Separates: Procedures for Using the Programs of the Copyright
   Clearance Center, Inc. New York: Copyright Clearance Center, Inc., 1977.

Permissions to Photo-Copy: Publisher's Fee List. Serials Articles Issue.
   New York: Copyright Clearance Center, Inc., 1978.

Proposed Copyright Clearance Procedures for Photocopying: Information for
   Librarians. Prepared by the Council of National Library Association's
   Committee on Copyright Practice and Implementation. Special issue of
   ALA Washington Newsletter, Vol. 29, no. 15 (October 28, 1977).
   [Also published in American Libraries, Vol. 8, no. 11 (December 1977),
   pp. 624-625 and included in the Librarian s Copyright Kit.]

Part IV. Documents and articles relating to sources of authorized fee-paid
   copies of copyrighted materials

A. Institute for Scientific Information, Inc.

OATS (Original Article Tear Sheet) Service. [Information on this service
   of the Institute for Scientific Information, Inc. is included in each
   issue of Current Contents publications, as well as other publications
   of I.S.I.]

B. National Technical Information Service

JACS Directory: NTIS Journal Article Copy Service. Springfield, Va.:
   National Technical Information Service, 1978. NTIS/JACS-78/01.

Rosenfield, H. E. Article-copying service by NTIS takes off. Wilson Library
   Bulletin, Vol. 52, no. 12 (December 1977), p. 284.

C. University Microfilms International

A New Article Copy Service in Education from University Microfilms
   International. Ann Arbor, Michigan: University Microfilms
   International, 1977.

Reprints Catalog: Periodical Articles and Issues. Ann Arbor, Michigan:
   University Microfilms International, 1976.

D. General

Wood, James L. Document access in the United States. Interlending Review,
   Vol. 6, no. 1 (January 1978), pp. 6-9.

Articles Written by the Commission Staff

Frase, Robert W. Legislation affecting publishing in 1974. In Bowker Annual 1975. New York: R.R. Bowker & Co., 1975, pp. 109-119.

----------. Legislation affecting publishing in 1975. In Bowker Annual 1976, pp. 127-136.

----------. Legislation affecting publishing in 1976. In Bowker Annual 1977, pp. 107-115.

----------. Legislation affecting publishing in 1977. In Bowker Annual 1978, pp. 119-126.

Keplinger, Michael S. Automation and the individual: Constitutional, legal, and regulatory aspects. In Automation Opportunities in the Service Sector, Report to the Federal Council on Science and Technology, May 1975.

----------. Computer intellectual property claims: Computer software and data base protection. Washington University Law Quarterly, Vol. 1977 no. 3 (Summer 1977), pp. 461-467.

----------. Copyright and personal computing. AFIPS Personal Computing Digest, 1978, pp. 37-42.

----------. Copyright law, higher education, and technological change. EDUCOM Bulletin, Vol. 12, no. 4 (Winter 1977), pp. 2-7.

----------. Implications of the new copyright law for libraries and computer users. International Technical Communications Conference Proceedings, 1978, pp. 203-209.

----------. Input of copyrighted works to computer systems as copyright infringement. In Computer Law Service, R.P. Bigelow, ed., October 1973.

---------- and Robert W. Frase. The role of CONTU in computers and photo-copying. IEEE Transactions on Professional Communication, Vol. PC-20, no. 3 (November 1977), pp. 167-170.

Levine, Arthur J. Copyrighted Works, National Commission on New Technological Uses of (CONTU). In ALA Yearbook 1976 ed. Chicago: American Library Association, 1976, pp. 146-147.

----------. CONTU. In ALA Yearbook 1977 ed., pp. 97-98.

----------. National Commission on New Technological Uses of Copyrighted Works. In Bowker Annual 1976, pp. 122-125.

----------. National Commission on New Technological Uses of Copyrighted Works (CONTU). In Bowker Annual 1977, pp. 31-34.

----------. National Commission on New Technological Uses of Copyrighted Works. In Bowker Annual 1978, pp. 51-54.

---------- and Christopher A. Meyer. Unfinished business--copyright issues unresolved by the Act of 1976. APLA Quarterly Journal, Vol. 6, no. 1 (1978), pp. 61-73.

---------- and Jeffrey L. Squires. Notice, deposit and registration:

The importance of being formal. UCLA Law Review, Nol. 24, nos. 5 and 6 (June-August 1977), pp. 1232-1264.

Risher, Carol.[1] The National Commission on New Technological Uses of Copyrighted Works (CONTU). The Serials Librarian, Vol. 2, no. 2 (Winter 1977), pp. 129-137.

Squires, Jeffrey L. Copyright and compilations in the computer era: Old wine in new bottles. Bulletin of the Copyright Society of the U.S.A., Vol. 24, no. 1 (October 1976), pp. 18-46.

SELECTED PROVISIONS OF THE COPYRIGHT ACT OF 1976 AND

COPYRIGHT OFFICE REGULATIONS

§ 101. Definitions

* * *

A "collective work" is a work, such as a periodical issue, anthology, or encyclopedia, in which a number of contributions, constituting separate and independent works in themselves, are assembled into a collective whole.

A "compilation" is a work formed by the collection and assembling of preexisting materials or of data that are selected, coordinated, or arranged in such a way that the resulting work as a whole constitutes an original work of authorship. The term "compilation" includes collective works.

"Copies" are material objects, other than phonorecords, in which a work is fixed by any method now known or later developed, and from which the work can be perceived, reproduced, or otherwise communicated, either directly or with the aid of a machine or device. The term "copies" includes the material object, other than a phonorecord, in which the work is first fixed.

* * *

A work is "created" when it is fixed in a copy or phonorecord for the first time; where a work is prepared over a period of time, the portion of it that has been fixed at any particular time constitutes the work as of that time, and where the work has been prepared in different versions, each version constitutes a separate work.

A "derivative work" is a work based upon one or more preexisting works, such as a translation, musical arrangement, dramatization, fictionalization, motion picture version, sound recording, art reproduction, abridgment, condensation, or any other form in which a work may be recast, transformed, or adapted. A work consisting of editorial revisions, annotations, elaborations, or other modifications which, as a whole, represent an original work of authorship, is a "derivative work."

A "device", "machine", or "process" is one now known or later developed.

To "display" a work means to show a copy of it, either directly or by means of a film, slide, television image, or any other

---

[1] Ms. Risher was formerly Information Officer, National Commission on New Technological Uses of Copyrighted Works.

device or process or, in the case of a motion picture or other
audiovisual work, to show individual images nonsequentially.

A work is "fixed" in a tangible medium of expression when its
embodiment in a copy or phonorecord, by or under the authority
of the author, is sufficiently permanent or stable to permit it
to be perceived, reproduced, or otherwise communicated for a
period of more than transitory duration. A work consisting
of sounds, images, or both, that are being transmitted, is
"fixed" for purposes of this title if a fixation of the work
is being made simultaneously with its transmission.

* * *

"Literary works" are works, other than audiovisual works,
expressed in words, numbers, or other verbal or numerical symbols
or indicia, regardless of the nature of the material objects, such
as books, periodicals, manuscripts, phonorecords, film, tapes,
disks, or cards, in which they are embodied.

* * *

A "pseudonymous work" is a work on the copies or phonorecords
of which the author is identified under a fictitious name.

"Publication" is the distribution of copies or phonorecords
of a work to the public by sale or other transfer of ownership,
or by rental, lease, or lending. The offering to distribute
copies or phonorecords to a group of persons for purposes of
further distribution, public performance, or public display,
constitutes publication. A public performance or display of
a work does not of itself constitute publication.

To perform or display a work "publicly" means –

(1) to perform or display it at a place open to the
public or at any place where a substantial number of
persons outside of a normal circle of a family and
its social acquaintances is gathered; or

(2) to transmit or otherwise communicate a performance or display of the work to a place specified by
clause (1) or to the public, by means of any device
or process, whether the members of the public capable
of receiving the performance or display receive it
in the same place or in separate places and at the
same time or at different times.

* * *

A "work made for hire" is –

(1) a work prepared by an employee within the scope of
his or her employment; or

(2) a work specially ordered or commissioned for use
as a contribution to a collective work, as a part of
a motion picture or other audiovisual work, as a translation, as a supplementary work, as a compilation, as
an instructional text, as a test, as answer material
for a test, or as an atlas, if the parties expressly
agree in a written instrument signed by them that the
work shall be considered a work made for hire.

* * *

§ 102. Subject matter of copyright: In general

(a) Copyright protection subsists, in accordance with this
title, in original works of authorship fixed in any tangible
medium of expression, now known or later developed, from

which they can be perceived, reproduced, or otherwise
communicated, either directly or with the aid of a machine
or device. Works of authorship include the following categories:
    (1) literary works;
    (2) musical works, including any accompanying words;
    (3) dramatic works, inclding any accompanying music;
    (4) pantomimes and choreographic works;
    (5) pictorial, graphic, and sculptural works;
    (6) motion pictures and other audiovisual works; and
    (7) sound recordings.
  (b) In no case does copyright protection for an original
work of authorship extend to any idea, procedure, process,
system, method of operation, concept, principle, or discovery,
regardless of the form in which it is described, explained,
illustrated, or embodied in such work.

§ 103. Subject matter of copyright: Compilations and derivative
       works
  (a) The subject matter of copyright as specified by section
102 includes compilations and derivative works, but protection
for a work employing preexisting material in which copyright
subsists does not extend to any part of the work in which such
material has been used unlawfully.
  (b) The copyright in a compilation or derivative work extends
only to the material contributed by the author of such work, as
distinguished from the preexisting material employed in the
work, and does not imply any exclusive right in the preexisting
material. The copyright in such work is independent of, and
does not affect or enlarge the scope, duration, ownership,
or subsistence of, any copyright protection in the preexisting
material.

   * * *

§ 106. Exclusive rights in copyrighted works
  Subject to sections 107 through 118, the owner of copyright under this title has the exclusive rights to do and to
authorize any of the following:
    (1) to reproduce the copyrighted work in copies or
phonorecords;
    (2) to prepare derivative works based upon the
copyrighted work;
    (3) to distribute copies or phonorecords of the
copyrighted work to the public by sale or other transfer
of ownership, or by rental, lease, or lending;
    (4) in the case of literary, musical, dramatic, and
choreographic works, pantomimes, and motion pictures and
other audiovisual works, to perform the copyrighted work
publicly; and
    (5) in the case of literary, musical, dramatic, and
choreographic works, pantomimes, and pictorial, graphic,
or sculptural works, including the individual images of a
motion picture or other audiovisual work, to display the
copyrighted work publicly.

§ 107. Limitations on exclusive rights: Fair use
  Notwithstanding the provisions of section 106, the fair use
of a copyrighted work, including such use by reproduction in
copies or phonorecords or by any other means specified by that
section, for purposes such as criticism, comment, news reporting,
teaching (including multiple copies for classroom use), scholar-

ship, or research, is not an infringement of copyright. In
determining whether the use made of a work in any particular
case is a fair use the factors to be considered shall include
 (1) the purpose and character of the use, including
whether such use is of a commercial nature or is for
nonprofit educational purposes;
 (2) the nature of the copyrighted work;
 (3) the amount and substantiality of the portion used
in relation to the copyrighted work as a whole; and
 (4) the effect of the use upon the potential market
for or value of the copyrighted work.

§ 108. Limitations on exclusive rights: Reproduction by
   libraries and archives
 (a) Notwithstanding the provisions of section 106, it is
not an infringement of copyright for a library or archives,
or any of its employees acting within the scope of their
employment, to reproduce no more than one copy or phonorecord
of a work, or to distribute such copy or phonorecord, under
the conditions specified by this section, if --
 (1) the reproduction or distribution is made without
any purpose of direct or indirect commercial advantage;
 (2) the collections of the library or archives are
(i) open to the public, or (ii) available not only to
researchers affiliated with the library or archives
or with the institution of which it is a part, but also
to other persons doing research in a specialized field;
and
 (3) the reproduction or distribution of the work
includes a notice of copyright.
 (b) The rights of reproduction and distribution under
this section apply to a copy or phonorecord of an unpublished
work duplicated in facsimile form solely for purposes of
preservation and security or for deposit for research use in
another library or archives of the type described by clause
(2) if subsection (a), if the copy or phonorecord reproduced
is currently in the collections of the library or archives.
 (c) The right of reproduction under this section applies
to a copy or phonorecord of a published work duplicated in
facsimile form solely for the purpose of replacement of a
copy or phonorecord that is damaged, deteriorating, lost,
or stolen, if the library or archives has, after a reasonable
effort, determined that an unused replacement cannot be
obtained at a fair price.
 (d) The rights of reproduction and distribution under
this section apply to a copy, made from the collection of
a library or archives where the user makes his or her request
or from that of another library or archives, of no more than
one article or other contribution to a copyrighted collection
or periodical issue, or to a copy or phonorecord of a small
part of any other copyrighted work, if --
 (1) the copy or phonorecord becomes the property of
the user, and the library or archives has had no notice
that the copy or phonorecord would be used for any
purpose other than private study, scholarship, or
research; and
 (2) the library or archives displays prominently,
at the place where orders are accepted, and includes
on its order form, a warning of copyright in accordance
with requirements that the Register of Copyrights shall
prescribe by regulation.
 (e) The rights of reproduction and distribution under this

section apply to the entire work, or to a substantial part of
it, made from the collection of a library or archives where
the user makes his or her request or from that of another
library or archives, if the library or archives has first
determined, on the basis of a reasonable investigation,
that a copy or phonorecord of the copyrighted work cannot
be obtained at a fair price, if --

(1) the copy or phonorecord becomes the property of
the user, and the library or archives has had no notice
that the copy or phonorecord would be used for any
purpose other than private study, scholarship, or
research; and

(2) the library or archives displays prominently, at
the place where orders are accepted, and includes on
its order form, a warning of copyright in accordance
with requirements that the Register of Copyrights
shall prescribe by regulation.

(f) Nothing in this section --

(1) shall be construed to impose liability for copyright
infringement upon a library or archives or its employees
for the unsupervised use of reproducing equipment located
on its premises: Provided, That such equipment displays
a notice that the making of a copy may be subject to
the copyright law;

(2) excuses a person who uses such reproducing equipment or who requests a copy or phonorecord under subsection (d) from liability for copyright infringement
for any such act, or for any later use of such copy or
phonorecord, if it exceeds fair use as provided by
section 107;

(3) shall be construed to limit the reproduction and
distribution by lending of a limited number of copies
and excerpts by a library or archives of an audiovisual
news program, subject to clauses (1), (2), and (3) of
subsection (a); or

(4) in any way affects the right of fair use as
provided by section 107, or any contractual obligations
assumed at any time by the library or archives when it
obtained a copy or phonorecord of a work in its collections.

(g) The rights of reproduction and distribution under this
section extend to the isolated and unrelated reproduction or
distribution of a single copy or phonorecord of the same
material on separate occasions, but do not extend to cases
where the library or archives, or its employee --

(1) is aware or has substantial reason to believe that
it is engaging in the related or concerted reproduction
or distribution of multiple copies or phonorecords of
the same material, whether made on one occasion or
over a period of time, and whether intended for
aggregate use by one or more individuals or for
separate use by the individual members of a group; or

(2) engages in the systematic reproduction or
distribution of single or multiple copies or phonorecords of material described in subsection (d):
Provided, That nothing in this clause prevents a
library or archives from participating in interlibrary
arrangements that do not have, as their purpose or
effect, that the library or archives receiving such
copies or phonorecords for distribution does so in
such aggregate quantities as to substitute for a
subscription to or purchase of such work.

(h) The rights of reproduction and distribution under this
section do not apply to a musical work, a pictorial, graphic

or sculptural work, or a motion picture or other audiovisual
work other than an audiovisual work dealing with news,
except that no such limitation shall apply with respect
to rights granted by subsections (b) and (c), or with
respect to pictorial or graphic works published as illus-
trations, diagrams, or similar adjuncts to works of which
copies are reproduced or distributed in accordance with
subsections (d) and (e).

(i) Five years from the effective date of this Act, and
at five-year intervals thereafter, the Register of Copyrights,
after consulting with representatives of authors, book and
periodical publishers, and other owners of copyrighted
materials, and with representatives of library users and
librarians, shall submit to the Congress a report setting
forth the extent to which this section has achieved the
intended statutory balancing of the rights of creators,
and the needs of users. The report should also describe
any problems that may have arisen, and present legislative
or other recommendations, if warranted.

    * * *

§ 117. Scope of exclusive rights: Use in conjunction with
      computers and similar information systems
Notwithstanding the provisions of sections 106 through 116
and 118, this title does not afford to the owner of copyright
in a work any greater or lesser rights with respect to the
use of the work in conjunction with automatic systems capable
of storing, processing, retrieving, or tansferring information,
or in conjunction with any similar device, machine, or process,
than those afforded to works under the law, whether title 17
or the common law or statutes of a State, in effect on
December 31, 1977, as held applicable and construed by a
court in an action brought under this title.

    * * *

§ 301. Preemption with respect to other laws
(a) On and after January 1, 1978, all legal or equitable
rights that are equivalent to any of the exclusive rights
within the general scope of copyright as specified by section
106 in works of authorship that are fixed in a tangible
medium of expression and come within the subject matter of
copyright as specified by sections 102 and 103, whether
created before or after that date and whether published
or unpublished, are governed exclusively by this title.
Thereafter, no person is entitled to any such right or
equivalent right in any such work under the common law
or statutes of any State.

(b) Nothing in this title annuls or limits any rights
or remedies under the common law or statutes of any State
with respect to --
(1) subject matter that does not come within the
subject matter of copyright as specified by sections
102 and 103, including works of authorship not fixed
in any tangible medium of expression; or
(2) any cause of action arising from undertakings
commenced before January 1, 1978; or
(3) activities violating legal or equitable rights
that are not equivalent to any of the exclusive
rights within the general scope of copyright as
specified by section 106.

* * *

(d) Nothing in this title annuls or limits any rights or remedies under any other Federal statute.

§ 302. Duration of copyright: Works created on or after
      January 1, 1978
    (a) In General. -- Copyright in a work created on or after January 1, 1978, subsists from its creation and, except as provided by the following subsections, endures for a term consisting of the life of the author and fifty years after the author's death.
    (b) Joint Works. -- In the case of a joint work prepared by two or more authors who did not work for hire, the copyright endures for a term consisting of the life of the last surviving author and fifty years after such last surviving author's death.
    (c) Anonymous Works, Pseudonymous Works, and Works Made For Hire. -- In the case of an anonymous work, a pseudonymous work, or a work made for hire, the copyright endures for a term of seventy-five years from the year of its first publication, or a term of one hundred years from the year of its creation, whichever expires first.

* * *

§ 401. Notice of copyright: Visually perceptible copies
    (a) General Requirement. -- Whenever a work protected under this title is published in the United States or elsewhere by authority of the copyright owner, a notice of copyright as provided by this section shall be placed on all publicly distributed copies from which the work can be visually perceived, either directly or with the aid of a machine or device.
    (b) Form of Notice. -- The notice appearing on the copies shall consist of the following three elements:
        (1) the symbol © (the letter C in a circle), or the word "Copyright", or the abbreviation "Copr."; and
        (2) the year of first publication of the work; in the case of compilations or derivative works incorporating previously published material, the year date of first publication of the compilation or derivative work is sufficient. The year date may be omitted where a pictorial, graphic, or sculptural work, with accompanying text matter, if any, is reproduced in or on greeting cards, postcards, stationery, jewelry, dolls, toys, or any useful articles; and
        (3) the name of the owner of copyright in the work, or an abbreviation by which the name can be recognized, or a generally known alternative designation of the owner.
    (c) Position of Notice. -- The notice shall be affixed to the copies in such manner and location as to give reasonable notice of the claim of copyright. The Register of Copyrights shall prescribe by regulation, as examples, specific methods of affixation and positions of the notice on various types of works that will satisfy this requirement, but these specifications shall not be considered exhaustive.

* * *

§405. Notice of copyright: Omission of notice.
    (a) Effect of Omission on Copyright. -- The omission of

the copyright notice prescribed by sections 401 through 403
from copies or phonorecords publicly distributed by authority
of the copyright owner does not invalidate the copyright in
a work if --

    (1) the notice has been omitted from no more than
a relatively small number of copies or phonorecords
distributed to the public; or

    (2) registration for the work has been made before
or is made within five years after the publication
without notice, and a reasonable effort is made to
add notice to all copies or phonorecords that are
distributed to the public in the United States after
the omission has been discovered; or

    (3) the notice has been omitted in violation of an
express requirement in writing that, as a condition
of the copyright owner's authorization of the public
distribution of copies or phonorecords, they bear
the prescribed notice.

    (b) Effect of Omission on Innocent Infringers. -- Any
person who innocently infringes a copyright, in reliance
upon an authorized copy or phonorecord from which the
copyright notice has been omitted, incurs no liability
for actual or statutory damages under section 504 for any
infringing acts committed before receiving actual notice
that registration for the work has been made under section
408, if such person proves that he or she was misled
by the omission of notice. In a suit for infringement
in such a case the court may allow or disallow recovery
of any of the infringer's profits attributable to the
infringement, and may enjoin the continuation of the
infringing undertaking or may require, as a condition
of permitting the continuation of the infringing
undertaking, that the infringer pay the copyright
owner a reasonable license fee in an amount and on
terms fixed by the court.

    (c) Removal of Notice. -- Protection under this title
is not affected by the removal, destruction, or
obliteration of the notice, without the authorization
of the copyright owner, from any publicly distributed
copies or phonorecords.

    * * *

§ 407. Deposit of copies or phonorecords for Library
       of Congress

    (a) Except as provided by subsection (c), and subject
to the provisions of subsection (e), the owner of copyright
or of the exclusive right of publication in a work published
with notice of copyright in the United States shall deposit,
within three months after the date of such publication --

    (1) two complete copies of the best edition; or

    (2) if the work is a sound recording, two complete
phonorecords of the best edition, together with any
printed or other visually perceptible material published
with such phonorecords.

Neither the deposit requirements of this subsection nor the
acquisition provisions of subsection (e) are conditions of
copyright protection.

    (b) The required copies or phonorecords shall be deposited
in the Copyright Office for the use or disposition of the
Library of Congress. The Register of Copyrights shall, when
requested by the depositor and upon payment of the fee prescribed by section 708, issue a receipt for the deposit.

(c) The Register of Copyrights may by regulation exempt
any categories of material from the deposit requirements
of this section, or require deposit of only one copy or
phonorecord with respect to any categories. Such regulations
shall provide either for complete exemption from the deposit
requirements of this section, or for alternative forms of
deposit aimed at providing a satisfactory archival record
of forms of deposit aimed at providing a satisfactory
archival record of a work without imposing practical or
financial hardships on the depositor, where the individual
author is the owner of copyright in a pictorial, graphic,
or sculptural work and (i) less than five copies of the
work have been published, or (ii) the work has been
published in a limited edition consisting of numbered
copies, the monetary value of which would make the
mandatory deposit of two copies of the best edition of
the work burdensome, unfair, or unreasonable.

(d) At any time after publication of a work as provided
by subsection (a), the Register of Copyrights may make
written demand for the required deposit on any of the
persons obligated to make the deposit under subsection
(a). Unless deposit is made within three months after
the demand is received, the person or persons on whom
the demand was made are liable --

(1) to a fine of not more than $250 for each work; and

(2) to pay into a specially designated fund in the
Library of Congress the total retail price of the copies
or phonorecords demanded, or, if no retail price has
been fixed, the reasonable cost of the Library of
Congress of acquiring them; and

(3) to pay a fine of $2,500, in addition to any fine
or liability imposed under clauses (1) and (2), if
such person willfully or repeatedly fails or refuses
to comply with such a demand.

(e) With respect to transmission programs that have been
fixed and transmitted to the public in the United States
but have not been published, the Register of Copyrights
shall, after consulting with the Librarian of Congress and
other interested organizations and officials, establish
regulations governing the acquisition, through deposit or
otherwise, of copies or phonorecords of such programs for
the collections of the Library of Congress.

(1) The Librarian of Congress shall be permitted, under
the standards and conditions set forth in such regulations,
to make a fixation of a transmission program directly from
a transmission to the public, and to reproduce one copy
or phonorecord from such fixation for archival purposes.

(2) Such regulations shall also provide standards and
procedures by which the Register of Copyrights may make
written demand, upon the owner of the right of transmission
in the United States, for the deposit of a copy or phonorecord of a specific transmission program. Such deposit
may, at the option of the owner of the right of transmission in the United States, be accomplished by gift,
by loan for purposes of reproduction, or by sale at a
price not to exceed the cost of reproducing and supplying
the copy or phonorecord. The regulations established
under this clause shall provide reasonable periods of
not less than three months for compliance with a demand,
and shall allow for extensions of such periods and
adjustments in the scope of the demand or the methods
for fulfilling it, as reasonably warranted by the
circumstances. Willful failure or refusal to comply

with the conditions prescribed by such regulations
shall subject the owner of the right of transmission
in the United States to liability for an amount, not
to exceed the cost of reproducing and supplying the
copy or phonorecord in question, to be paid into a
specially designated fund in the Library of Congress.

(3) Nothing in this subsection shall be construed
to require the making or retention, for purposes
of deposit, of any copy or phonorecord of an unpublished transmission program, the transmission of
which occurs before the receipt of a specific
written demand as provided by clause (2).

(4) No activity undertaken in compliance with
regulations prescribed under clauses (1) or (2) of
subsection shall result in liability if intended
solely to assist in the acquisition of copies or
phonorecords under this subsection.

§ 408. Copyright registration in general

(a) Registration Permissive. -- At any time during the
subsistence of copyright in any published or unpublished
work, the owner of copyright or of any exclusive right
in the work may obtain registration of the copyright
claim by delivering to the Copyright Office the deposit
specified by this section, together with the application
and fee specified by sections 409 and 708. Subject to
the provisions of section 405(a), such registration is
not a condition of copyright protection.

(b) Deposit for Copyright Registration. -- Except as
provided by subsection (c), the material deposited for
registration shall include -

(1) in the case of an unpublished work, one complete
copy or phonorecord;

(2) in the case of a published work, two complete
copies or phonorecords of the best edition;

(3) in the case of a work first published outside
the United States, one complete copy or phonorecord
as so published;

(4) in the case of a contribution to a collective
work, one complete copy or phonorecord of the best
edition of the collective work.

Copies or phonorecords deposited for the Library of Congress
under section 407 may be used to satisfy the deposit provisions of this section, if they are accompanied by the
prescribed application and fee, and by any additional
identifying material that the Register may, by regulation,
require. The Register shall also prescribe regulations
establishing requirements under which copies or phonorecords acquired for the Library of Congress under
subsection (e) of section 407, otherwise than by deposit,
may be used to satisfy the deposit provisions of this
section.

(c) Administrative Classification and Optional Deposit. --

(1) The Register of Copyrights is authorized to
specify by regulation the administrative classes
into which works are to be placed for purposes of
deposit and registration, and the nature of the
copies or phonorecords to be deposited in the
various classes specified. The regulations may
require or permit, for particular classes, the
deposit of identifying material instead of copies
or phonorecords, the deposit of only one copy or

phonorecord where two would normally be required,
or a single registration for a group of related
works. This administrative classification of
works has no significance with respect to the
subject matter of copyright or the exclusive
rights provided by this title.

(2) Without prejudice to the general authority
provided under clause (1), the Register of Copyrights
shall establish regulations specifically permitting
a single registration for a group of works by the
same individual author, all first published as
contributions to periodicals, including newspapers,
within a twelve-month period, on the basis of a
single deposit application, and registration fee,
under all of the following conditions --

(A) if each of the works as first published
bore a separate copyright notice, and the name
of the owner of copyright in the work, or an
abbreviation by which the name can be recognized,
or a generally known alternative designation
of the owner was the same in each notice; and

(B) if the deposit consists of one copy of the
entire issue of the periodical, or of the entire
section in the case of a newspaper, in which each
contribution was first published; and

(C) if the application identifies each work
separately, including the periodical containing
it and its date of first publication.

(3) As an alternative to separate renewal registrations
under subsection (a) of section 304, a single renewal
registration may be made for a group of works by the same
individual author, all first published as contributions
to periodicals, including newspapers, upon the filing of
a single application and fee, under all of the following
conditions:

(A) the renewal claimant or claimants, and
the basis of claim or claims under section 304
(a), is the same for each of the works; and

(B) the works were all copyrighted upon their
first publication, either through separate copyright
notice and registration or by virtue of a general
copyright notice in the periodical issue as a whole;
and

(C) the renewal application and fee are received
not more than twenty-eight or less than twenty-
seven years after the thirty-first day of December
of the calendar year in which all of the works
were first pubished; and

(D) the renewal application identifies each
work separately, including the periodical
containing it and its date of first publication.

(d) Corrections and Amplifications. -- The Register may also
establish, by regulation, formal procedures for the filing
of an application for supplementary registration, to correct
an error in a copyright registration or to amplify the
information given in a registration. Such application shall
be accompanied by the fee provided by section 708, and shall
clearly identify the registration to be corrected or amplified.
The information contained in a supplementary registration
augments but does not supersede that contained in the
earlier registration.

(e) Published Edition of Previously Registered Work. --
Registration for the first published edition of a work

previously registered in unpublished form may be made even
though the work as published is substantially the same as
the unpublished version.

§ 412. Registration as prerequisite to certain remedies for
        infringement
    In any action under this title, other than an action
instituted under section 411(b), no award of statutory damages
or of attorney's fees, as provided by sections 504 and 505,
shall be made for --
    (1) any infringement of copyright in an unpublished
work commenced before the effective date of its registration;
or
    (2) any infringement of copyright commenced after first
publication of the work and before the effective date of
its registration, unless such registration is made within
three months after the first publication of the work.

§ 501. Infringement of copyright
    (a) Anyone who violates any of the exclusive rights of the
copyright owner as provided by sections 106 through 118, or who
imports copies or phonorecords into the United States in
violation of section 602, is an infringer of the copyright....

§ 502. Remedies for infringement: Injunctions
    (a) Any court having jurisdiction of a civil action arising
under this title may, subject to the provisions of section 1498
of title 28, grant temporary and final injunctions on such
terms as it may deem reasonable to prevent or restrain infringement of a copyright.
    (b) Any such injunction may be served anywhere in the United
States on the person enjoined; it shall be operative throughout
the United States and shall be enforceable, by proceedings in
contempt or otherwise, by any United States court having
jurisdiction of that person. The clerk of the court granting
the injunction shall, when requested by any other court in
which enforcement of the injunction is sought, transmit
promptly to the other court a certified copy of all the
papers in the case on file in such clerk's office.

    * * *

§ 505. Remedies for infringement: Costs and attorney's fees
    In any civil action under this title, the court in its
discretion may allow the recovery of full costs by or against
any party other than the United States or an officer thereof.
Except as otherwise provided by this title, the court may
also award a reasonable attorney's fee to the prevailing
party as part of the costs.

§ 506. Criminal offenses
    (a) Criminal Infringement. -- Any person who infringes a copy-
right willfully and for purposes of commercial advantage or
private financial gain shall be fined not more than $10,000
or imprisoned for not more than one year, or both: <u>Provided</u>,
<u>however</u>, That any person who infringes willfully and for purposes
of commercial advantage or private financial gain the copyright
in a sound recording afforded by subsections (1), (2), or (3)

of section 106 or the copyright in a motion picture afforded
by subsections (1), (3), or (4) of section 106 shall be fined
not more than $25,000 or imprisioned for not more than one year,
or both, for the first such offense and shall bé fined not more
than $50,000 or imprisioned for not more than two years, or both,
for any subsequent offense.

(b) Forfeiture and Destruction. -- When any person is convicted
of any violation of subsection (a), the court in its judgment of
conviction shall, in addition to the penalty therein prescribed,
order the forfeiture and destruction or other disposition of all
infringing copies or phonorecords and all implements, devices,
or equipment used in the manufacture of such infringing copies
or phonorecords.

(c) Fraudulent Copyright Notice. -- Any person who, with fraudulent intent, places on any article a notice of copyright or
words of the same purport that such person knows to be false, or
who, with fraudulent intent, publicly distributes or imports
for public distribution any article bearing such notice or
words that such person knows to be false, shall be fined not
more that $2,500.

(d) Fraudulent Removal of Copyright Notice. -- Any person who,
with fraudulent intent, removes or alters any notice of copyright appearing on a copy of a copyrighted work shall be fined
not more than $2,500.

(e) False Representation. -- Any person who knowingly makes
a false representation of a material fact in the application
for copyright registration provided for by section 409, or in
any written statement filed in connection with the application,
shall be fined not more than $2,500.

* * *

§ 602. Infringing importation of copies or phonorecords
(a) Importation into the United States, without the authority
of the owner of copyright under this title, of copies or phonorecords of a work that have been acquired outside the United
States is an infringement of the exclusive right to distribute
copies or phonorecords under section 106, actionable under
section 501. This subsection does not apply to -

* * *

(3) importation by or for an organization operated for
scholarly, educational, or religious purposes and not for
private gain, with respect to no more than one copy of
                                                 purposes,
and no more than five copies or phonorecords of any other
work for its library lending or archival purposes, unless
the importation of such copies or phonorecords is part an
activity consisting of systematic reproduction or distribution,
engaged in by such organization in violation of the
provisions of section 108(g)(2).

ANNOUNCEMENT FROM THE COPYRIGHT OFFICE ...

[1410-03]

LIBRARY OF CONGRESS

Copyright Office

[37 CFR Part 201]

[Docket RM 77-14]

METHODS OF AFFIXATION AND POSITIONS
OF THE COPYRIGHT NOTICE 1/

Proposed Rulemaking

AGENCY: Library of Congress, Copyright Office.

ACTION: Proposed rule.

SUMMARY: This notice of proposed rulemaking is issued to
inform the public that the Copyright Office of the Library
of Congress is considering adoption of a new regulation
implementing section 401(c) of the Act for General Revision of the Copyright Law. That section directs the
Register of Copyrights to "prescribe by regulation, as
examples, specific methods of affixation and positions
of the copyright notice on various types of works" that
will satisfy the requirement that the copyright notice
"be affixed to the copies in such manner and location as
to give reasonable notice of the claim of copyright."
The effect of the proposed regulation is to provide examples of methods of affixation and positions for the
guidance of persons seeking to affix the notice in a
manner and location that will comply with the statutory requirements.

* * *

§201.20 Methods of affixation and positions of the
    copyright notice on various types of works.

(a) General. (1) This section specifies examples of
methods of affixation and positions of the copyright
notice on various types of works that will satisfy the
notice requirement of section 401(c) of title 17 of
the United States Code, as amended by Pub. L. 94-553.
A notice considered "acceptable" under this regulation
shall be considered to satisfy the requirement of that
section that it be "affixed to the copies in such manner and location as to give reasonable notice of the
claim of copyright." As provided by that section,
the examples specified in this regulation shall not
be considered exhaustive of methods of affixation
and positions giving reasonable notice of the claim
of copyright.
    (2) The provisions of this section are only appli-
cable to works first published on or after the effective date of this section. The adequacy of a copy-

---

1/   42 Fed. Reg. 64374 (December 23, 1977).

right notice on works first published before such
date shall be determined by the law in effect at the
time of first publication.

* * *

(c) Manner of Affixation and Position Generally.
(1) In all cases dealt with in this section, the
acceptability of a notice depends upon its being
permanently legible to an ordinary user of the
work, and affixed to the copies in such manner and
position that it is not concealed from view upon
reasonable examination. (2) Where, in a particular case, a notice does not appear in one of the
precise locations prescribed in this section but
a person looking in one of those locations would
be reasonably certain to find a notice in another
somewhat different location, that notice will be
acceptable under this section.

* * *

(g) Works Reproduced in Machine-Readable Copies.
For works reproduced in machine-readable copies
(such as magnetic tapes or disks, punched cards, or
the like) from which the work cannot ordinarily be
visually perceived except with the aid of a machine
or device, the following constitute examples of
acceptable methods of affixation and position of
the notice:

(1) A notice embodied in the copies in machine-
readable form in such a manner that on visually
perceptible printouts it appears either with or
near the title, or at the end of the work;

(2) A notice that is displayed at the user's terminal
at sign on;

(3) A notice that is continuously on terminal display;

(4) A permanently legible notice reproduced on a
gummed or other label securely affixed to the copies or
to a box, reel, cartridge, cassette, or other container
used as a permanent receptacle for the copies.

[1410-03]

Title 37 -- Patents, Trademarks, and Copyrights

CHAPTER II -- COPYRIGHT OFFICE, LIBRARY OF CONGRESS

[Docket Rm 77-11]

PART 202 -- REGISTRATION OF CLAIMS TO COPYRIGHT DEPOSIT
REQUIREMENTS 2/

AGENCY: Library of Congress, Copyright Office.

ACTION: Final regulations.

2/ 43 Fed. Reg. 763 (January 4, 1968).

*Error; line should read: "§202.19 Deposit of published
copies or"

SUMMARY: This notice is issued to inform the public that
the Copyright Office of the Library of Congress is adopting new regulations implementing the deposit requirements
of sections 407 and 408 of the Act for General Revision
of the Copyright Law. These requirements involve the
mandatory deposit of copies or phonorecords of published
works for the collections of the Library of Congress, and
the deposit of material to accompany applications for
copyright registration of both unpublished and published
works. The effect of the proposed regulations is: (a) To
exempt certain categories of published works from mandatory
deposit for the Library of Congress under section 407;
(b) to establish requirements governing the nature of the
mandatory deposit to be made to all other cases under section 407; and (c) to establish the nature of the deposit
to be made as part of copyright registration.

§ 202.19 Deposit of published copies of* phonorecords
for the Library of Congress.

(a) General. This section prescribes rules pertaining
to the deposit of copies and phonorecords of published
works for the Library of Congress under section 407 of
title 17 of the United States Code, as amended by Pub.
L. 94-553. The provisions of this section are not applicable to the deposit of copies and phonorecords for purposes of copyright registration under section 408 of
title 17, except as expressly adopted in § 202.20 of
these regulations.

* * *

(c) Exemptions from deposit requirements. The following categories of material are exempt from the deposit
requirements of section 407(a) of title 17:

* * *

(5) Literary works, including computer programs and
automated data bases, published in the United States only
in the form of machine-readable copies (such as magnetic
tape or disks, punched cards, or the like) from which the
work cannot ordinarily be visually perceived except with
the aid of a machine or device. Works published in a
form requiring the use of a machine or device for purposes of optical enlargement (such as film, filmstrips,
slide films and works published in any variety of microform), and works published in visually perceivable form
but used in connection with optical scanning devices,
are not within this category and are subject to the
applicable deposit requirements.

* * *

§ 202.20 Deposit of copies and phonorecords
for copyright registration.

(a) General. This section prescribes rules pertaining
to the deposit of copies and phonorecords of published and
unpublished works for the purpose of copyright registration
under section 408 of title 17 of the United States Code, as
amended by Pub. L. 94-553. The provisions of this section
are not applicable to the deposit of copies and phonorecords

for the Library of Congress under section 407 of title 17,
except as expressly adopted in § 202.19 of these regulations.

* * *

  (c) <u>Nature of required deposit</u>. (1) Subject to the
provisions of paragraph (c)(2) of this section, the deposit
required to accompany an application for registration of
claim to copyright under section 408 of title 17 shall
consist of:

* * *

  (2) In the case of certain works, the special provisions
set forth in this clause shall apply. In any case where
this clause specifies that one copy or phonorecord may be
submitted, that copy or phonorecord shall represent the best
edition, or the work as first published, as set forth in
paragraph (c)(1) of this section.

* * *

  (vii) <u>Machine-readable works</u>. In cases where an unpublished literary work is fixed, or a published literary
work is published in the United States, only in the form
of machine-readable copies (such as magnetic tape or disks,
punched cards, or the like) from which the work cannot
ordinarily be perceived except with the aid of a machine
or device, the deposit shall consist of:

  (A) For published or unpublished computer programs,
one copy of identifying portions of the program, reproduced in a form visually perceptible without the aid of
a machine or device, either on paper or in microform.
For these purposes, "identifying portions" shall mean
either the first and last twenty-five pages or equivalent units of the program if reproduced on paper, or at
least the first and last twenty-five pages or equivalent
units of the program if reproduced in microform, together
with the page or equivalent unit containing the copyright
notice, if any.
  (B) For published and unpublished automated data bases,
compilations, statistical compendia, and other literary
works so fixed or published, one copy of identifying portions of the work, reproduced in a form visually perceptible without the aid of a machine or device, either on
paper or in microform. For these purposes: (1) "identifying portions" shall mean either the first and last
twenty-five pages or equivalent units of the work if
reproduced on paper, or at least the first and last
twenty-five pages or equivalent units of work if reproduced on microform, or, in the case of automated data
bases comprising separate and distinct data files,
representative portions of each separate data file
consisting of either 50 complete data records from
each file or the entire file, whichever is less; and
(2) "data file" and "file" mean a group of data records pertaining to a common subject matter, regardless of the physical size of the records or the number
of data items included in them. (In the case of revised versions of such data bases, the portions
deposited must contain representative data records
which have been added or modified.) In any case

where the deposit comprises representative portions
of each separate file of an automated data base as
indicated above, it shall be accompanied by a typed
or printed descriptive statement containing: The
title of the data base; the name and address of the
copyright claimant; the name and content of each
separate file within the data base, including the
subject matter involved, the origin(s) of the data,
and the approximate number of individual records
within the file; and a description of the exact
contents of any machine-readable copyright notice
employed in or with the work and the manner and
frequency with which it is displayed (e.g., at user's
terminal only at sign-on, or continuously on terminal
display, or on printouts, etc.).   If a visually-
perceptible copyright notice is placed on any copies
of the work (such as magnetic tape reels) or their
container, a sample of such notice must also accompany
the statement.

Index

Compiled by Susan Ruth Stein